Letts study aids

Revise English

A complete revision course for O level and CSE

Stephen Tunnicliffe MA

formerly Head of English Department, Newtown High School, Powys

Frances Glendenning BA

Head of English Department, Clayton High School, Newcastle-under-Lyme

Denys Thompson MA

formerly Headmaster of Yeovil School

Charles Letts & Co Ltd
London, Edinburgh & New York

First published 1979
by Charles Letts & Co Ltd
Diary House, Borough Road, London SE1 1DW

Revised 1981, 1983
Reprinted 1986

Design: Ben Sands

Illustrations: Ed Perera, Ben Sands and Peter Benoist

ISBN 0 85097 584 0

Printed and bound by
Charles Letts (Scotland) Ltd

Contents

	Page
Section I Introduction and guide to using this book	1
Aim	1
Content	1
Method	2
Getting down to it	2
Examination Boards' names and addresses	5
List of syllabus requirements	6

Section II (Core units 1 – 5)

Reading, understanding, writing — 18

1 Composition — 18

1.1 Types of essay question; **1.2** Fictional essays; **1.3** Discussion essays; **1.4** Descriptive essays; **1.5** Picture-based essays.

2 Comprehension — 47

2.1 What is comprehension? **2.2** Types of comprehension question; **2.3** Drawing inferences; **2.4** Cloze procedure tests; **2.5** Interpreting statistics; **2.6** Persuasive writing; **2.7** Objective or multiple choice tests; **2.8** Further practice; **2.9** Check-list of comprehension passages.

3 Summaries and notes — 77

3.1 How to summarise; **3.2** Understanding the question; **3.3** Making notes; **3.4** Further practice; **3.5** Check-list of summary passages.

4 Letters, reports, practical writing; books and poetry; oral English — 104

4.1 Writing letters; **4.2** Reports and practical writing; **4.3** Writing about books and poetry; **4.4** Speaking and listening.

5 Essential skills — 121

5.1 Spelling; **5.2** Punctuation; **5.3** Grammar and usage; **5.4** Using a dictionary; **5.5** Style.

Section III Self-test units	145
Tests check-list	158
Section IV General advice for candidates taking English examinations	159
Section V Practice in answering examination questions	164
GCE questions	164
SCE questions	173
CSE questions	175
Section VI Answers	184
– to Core unit exercises	184
– to Self-test units	202
Hints on answering examination questions	207
Glossary	217
Index	220

Acknowledgements

We are grateful to the following organisations for permitting
us to reproduce photographs for which they hold the copyright –
Keystone Press Agency Ltd: pp. 18, 37, 38, 103, 136;
Syndication International: pp. 28, 134, 141;
Sport and General: p. 30;
British Broadcasting Corporation: pp. 33, 41;
Press Association: p. 42;
Duckworth and Co. Ltd: p. 44;
London Newspaper Services (photograph by Ian Swift): p. 83;
Spectrum Colour Library: p. 91.

We should also like to thank the following Examination Boards
for their permission to reproduce questions from past papers:
Joint Matriculation Board, University of London University
Entrance and School Examinations Council, Oxford and Cambridge Schools
Examination Board, East Anglian Examinations Board, Scottish Certificate
of Education Examination Board.

Preface

This is not a textbook, but a *revision* guide for students preparing for GCE 'O'-level, SCE and CSE examinations in English. The revision material and information it contains relate directly to the requirements of all the various Examination Boards. We have included a complete syllabus summary and a selection of recent questions actually set.

Students, parents and teachers welcomed the first edition of *Revise English* in 1979 as a genuine, organised revision course, not a mere 'crammer'. This new edition incorporates syllabus changes which have occurred since the book first appeared; the syllabus summary has been brought up to date, and a wider range of questions included, with more guidance on how to tackle them. We have checked the text throughout, modified parts of the revision material, and added a glossary of useful terms and an index. A greatly expanded 'Answers' section appears in red type towards the end of the book. The book now includes for the first time questions and a syllabus summary for the Scottish Certificate of Education.

No book can promise to 'get you through' an examination; that depends on the effort and dedication the student is prepared to put into his or her preparation. We can say, categorically, that if this book is used fully, along the lines of the advice given in the opening pages, the student will gain skill and assurance in the control of English, and will be able to enter the examination room with confidence.

This is a book to be used frequently and continually. It embodies a new approach to revision, aimed directly at students, with a special section for self-testing and assessment. Because we believe that cheerfulness achieves more than gloom we have included material that is light-hearted and humorous. We hope it will therefore prove to be entertaining as well as instructive.

We aim to maintain the usefulness of this book as an up-to-date revision aid. Any changes in syllabus – such as may follow the present move towards a common examination system – will be included as they occur in future editions of *Revise English*.

Stephen Tunnicliffe 1983

Section I
Introduction and guide to using this book

Aim

This book is planned to help you find your way towards better English. It will help you to

— revise for an English examination,
— gain confidence if you need to re-take an examination, and to
— teach yourself, even if you are no longer getting regular help from an English teacher.

Has your English suffered because of changes of teacher, or some other break in continuity (illness, change of home)? Are you trying to pick up the threads after a period – perhaps years – without formal English teaching? Are you behind the others in your work or slower at completing English exercises? Or do you just want to feel fully prepared for examination day? You will find what you need in the pages that follow.

Content

You will find three kinds of material to help you:

Section II: Reading, understanding, writing
Here is the core material of the book. This section, which includes many practice exercises, deals with all the kinds of practical English you are likely to need – that is, with everything that English examinations are designed to test:

— composition
— comprehension
— grammar
— spelling
— punctuation
— summary
— note-making
— letters
— appreciation
— poetry
— speaking
— listening

Section III: Self-test units

These are nearly all self-testing (with answers in Section VI) so that you can check your own progress and learn from your mistakes. Each test deals with an important aspect of English.

Section V: Practice in answering examination questions

This section features actual examination questions taken from GCE, SCE and CSE English papers set by a range of Examination Boards. Hints are also given (in Section VI) on how to *answer* these questions.

METHOD

The way you use this book will depend on your own situation. Decide what you need most. General revision? Help with particular weaknesses (spelling, grammar, written expression, note-making for instance)? Practice to reinforce what you are being taught, or have been taught in school? Opportunities to test yourself in English, or to compare your standard with others, or to work with other students?

● You can read and work systematically through the book, following the practice suggestions as they occur, and building up your confidence by working the tests and examination questions.

● You can pick out the units you need most (using the index), and concentrate on them.

● You can use the book to support your English classwork. It will give you further information,

a fresh slant on particular skills like summarising, or setting out answers to comprehension questions, or getting in the right frame of mind for oral work (spoken English).

● You can dip into the book or use it as a reader. There is plenty of interesting reading for you, whether or not you choose to study the pieces more closely. The books from which the extracts come are worth reading too.

● If two or three of you working for the same examination have your own copies of the book, you can compare progress, check each other's work, mark each other's tests and exercises. This is one of the best ways to be sure you are making progress.

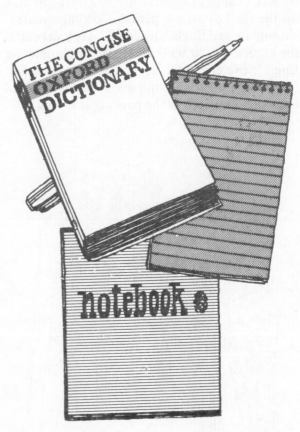

GETTING DOWN TO IT

Before you start, make sure you have:

● a good dictionary (see p. 137 for guidance),

● a notebook,

● paper for jottings, rough work etc.,

● information (see pp. 6-17 for guidance) on which Examination Board will set the English examination you are taking, what to expect when you read the examination paper, and the date of the examination.

Plan to set aside a definite amount of time each day, or each week, for English. Any time you spend reading for your own enjoyment will give you extra English practice if you choose your books well. If you haven't got the reading habit this is a good time to start. In the course of the book we have included short pieces of writing on many topics. If one interests you particularly ask in your school or local library for the book it comes from, or for others on the same topic.

All English examinations involve writing. Some consist entirely of questions requiring written answers. When it comes to *writing* a keen *reader* has a start over someone who hardly ever reads . . . Why?

● He discovers for himself how interesting stories can be – even those printed in an examination paper.

● He will be better informed, particularly about his own special interest or hobby, from the books he has read.

● He can visit the moon, climb Everest, explore the Polar ice-cap, plumb the Pacific, live with an African tribe, or become a millionaire . . . You name it, there's a book about it.

● He learns, without even trying to, about the way sentences work, how words are used and spelt, what good writing looks like.

Town libraries, village library vans and school libraries have one thing in common— **books** (all there for the asking). If you've never been to your local library, pay it a visit. Librarians are interested in people who are interested in books . . . books . . . books . . . on anything under the sun!

AMERICA	NEWTS
BOATING	ORNITHOLOGY
COOKING	PHILATELY
DANCING	QUEEN BEES
ELECTRONICS	ROWING
FLY FISHING	SHEEP
GARDENING	TRAINS
HISTORY	UNIVERSE
IRON-WORK	VARNISH
JAPAN	WHITE MICE
KARATE	X-RAYS
LOOMS	YORKSHIRE
MOUNTAINEERING	ZOOS

(See pp. 111-112 for more ideas on choosing books.)

4

You want that certificate?   It's a deal!

The examiners hand over what you want when you hand over what they want. What they want is

● to know that you can express yourself clearly and vigorously;
● to enjoy what you have written for them because it is genuine, interesting and lively;
● to be convinced by what you write or say that you know what you are talking about.

| If your handwriting is untidy or hard to read **they get annoyed!** | If spelling and punctuation are careless **they get more annoyed!** | If questions are not numbered, or are poorly set out **they get savage!** | If you have not read the question properly **you get no marks!** |

This list gives the full names and addresses of the 53 Boards whose syllabus requirements are summarised on pp. 6–17. You can write to the Boards to buy complete syllabuses and past papers.

GCE Boards

1 AEB Associated Examining Board, Wellington House, Aldershot, Hampshire GU11 1BQ

2 Cambridge University of Cambridge Local Examinations Syndicate
Syndicate Buildings, 17 Harvey Road, Cambridge CB1 2EU

3 JMB Joint Matriculation Board, Manchester M15 6EU

4 London University Entrance and School Examinations Council
University of London, 66–72 Gower Street, London WC1E 6EE

5 Oxford Oxford Local Examinations
Delegacy of Local Examinations, Ewert Place, Summertown, Oxford OX2 7BX

6 O & C Oxford and Cambridge Schools Examination Board
10 Trumpington Street, Cambridge; and Elsfield Way, Oxford

7 SUJB Southern Universities' Joint Board for School Examinations
Cotham Road, Bristol BS6 6DD

8 WJEC Welsh Joint Education Committee (as No. 17), 245 Western Avenue, Cardiff CF5 2YX

9 NIEC Northern Ireland Schools GCE Examinations Council
Beechill House, 42 Beechill Road, Belfast BT8 4RS

SCE Board

10 SEB Scottish Examining Board
Ironmills Road, Dalkeith, Midlothian EH22 1BR

11 *Joint 16+* ALSEB/JMB/YHREB

CSE Boards
North

12 NREB North Regional Examinations Board
Wheatfield Road, Westerhope, Newcastle upon Tyne NE5 5JZ

13 NWREB North West Regional Examinations Board
Orbit House, Albert Street, Eccles, Manchester M30 0WL

14 ALSEB Associated Lancashire Schools Examining Board
77 Whitworth Street, Manchester M1 6HA

15 YHREB Former Yorkshire Regional Examinations Board
31–33 Springfield Avenue, Harrogate, North Yorkshire HG1 2HW

16 YHREB Former West Yorkshire and Lindsey Regional Examining Board
Scarsdale House, 136 Derbyshire Lane, Sheffield S8 8SE

Midlands and Wales

17 WJEC Welsh Joint Education Committee (as No. 8), 245 Western Avenue, Cardiff CF5 2YX

18 WMEB West Midlands Examinations Board
Norfolk House, Smallbrook Queensway, Birmingham B5 4NJ

19 EMREB East Midlands Regional Examinations Board
Robins Wood House, Robins Wood Road, Apsley, Nottingham NG8 3NH

20 EAEB East Anglian Examinations Board
The Lindens, Lexden Road, Colchester, Essex CO3 3RL

South

21 SWEB South Western Examinations Board, 23–29 Marsh Street, Bristol BS1 4BP

22 SREB Southern Regional Examinations Board, 53 London Road, Southampton SO9 4YL

23 SEREB South East Regional Examinations Board
Beloe House, 2/4 Mount Ephraim Road, Royal Tunbridge Wells, Kent TN1 1EU

24 LREB London Regional Examinations Board
Lyon House, 104 Wandsworth High Street, London SW18 4LF

Northern Ireland

25 NICSE Northern Ireland Schools Examination Council
See **9** for address.

The following list includes the requirements of Examination Boards for 1984. There may be changes of detail after that date, but the virtual unanimity across the whole range of GCE, SCE, CSE and 16 plus syllabuses with regard to composition and comprehension indicates that the central concern in written examinations is likely to remain with these two vital English skills, which are fully dealt with in Section II of this book.

GENERAL CERTIFICATE OF EDUCATION—**Ordinary Level (GCE)**

Board and syllabus	*Papers or other tests*	**Content**	*Time allowed*	**Marks**
1 **AEB** **Syllabus I**	Paper 1	(a) *Composition* – factual, descriptive, imaginative or controversial.	1 hour	35
		(b) Practical expression – description of object or operation, instructions or report, letter or article, factual information.	30 minutes	15
	Paper 2	*Summary* – of prose passage of 300–350 words. *Comprehension* – questions on another prose passage. Questions on usage.	1¾ hours	50

Note: A joint GCE/CSE syllabus is also available, based on the above, together with the South East Regional Examinations Board (No. 23) CSE syllabuses. See below (No. 23) for details.

Board and syllabus	*Papers or other tests*	**Content**	*Time allowed*	**Marks**
AEB **Syllabus II**	Paper 1	*Composition* – two subjects, one from each section: A factual or controversial; B narrative, descriptive and imaginative.	1¾ hours	50
	Paper 2	*Comprehension* – objective or multiple choice test, 25 items, including vocabulary questions.	50 minutes	25
	Paper 3	*Comprehension* – questions on character, mood, atmosphere, language (may include *summary*).	55 minutes	25
2 **Cambridge** **(1100)**	Papers 1 and 3	Both papers contain choice of subjects for *composition* – one subject to be chosen for each.	1 hour each	(25 each)
	Paper 2	Passage or passages of prose for *comprehension*. Some questions may involve *summary*.	1½ hours	50
Cambridge **(1101)**	School assessment	Five pieces of work done throughout the school year and marked in school (moderated externally).		50
	Paper 2	*Comprehension* and *summary* (same paper as 1100).	1½ hours	50
Cambridge **(1102)**	Paper (one only) (for adults only)	Q.1 *Composition* – one subject chosen from selection given.	1 hour	30
		Q.2 *Composition* – based on material supplied in paper, and involving logical, orderly presentation of argument, letter writing, etc.	¾ hour	20
		Q.3 *Comprehension* – based on passage of prose of approx. 500 words. Questions may also involve *summary*.	1¼ hours	50

Board and syllabus	Papers or other tests	Content	Time allowed	Marks
3 **JMB** **Alternative** **A**	Paper I	Section A *Comprehension* – short set passage, to test powers of understanding.	30 minutes	17
		Section B *Composition* – choice of subjects requiring a personal response.	1 hour	33
	Paper II	Section A *Comprehension* – longer set passage.	1 hour	30
		Section B *Practical writing* – choice of questions to test ability to communicate in a practical situation.	30 minutes	20
JMB **Alternative** **D**	Internal assessment	Type of scheme depends on school, but covers English skills as in other alternatives.		
JMB **Alternative** **E**	Paper (one only)	Part I		
		Comprehension. Two short passages, one of them factual, on *both* of which questions must be answered.	66 minutes	40
		Practical writing. One question based on given material, to test the ability to communicate in a practical situation.	34 minutes	20
		INTERVAL, during which scripts of Part I are collected.	10 minutes	
		Part II Composition Choice of questions, giving opportunities for imaginative writing.	50 minutes	40
		Note: JMB Alternative syllabuses B and C are no longer set.		
4 **London** **(160)**	Paper 1 (2 hours)	1 *Composition* – one subject from at least eight set: may involve narrative, descriptive, dramatic argument or letter-writing.	1 hour	40
		2 *Summary*/directed writing: based on set passages in form of dialogue, interview, court or other evidence, statistics, diary, letters or notes.	1 hour	30
	Paper 2	*Comprehension* – multiple choice objective test.	1¼ hours	30
London **(165)**	Spoken English (optional)	(Can only be taken if 160 is also taken.) Part 1 Reading (in groups of 3 candidates).	5 minutes approx.	
		Part 2 Conversation – group and individual.	15 minutes approx.	
5 **Oxford**	Paper 1	Part I *Composition* – wide choice of subjects		
		Part II *Practical writing* – one out of a choice of two exercises in clear and accurate communication, e.g. letter, report etc.	1½ hours	100
	Paper 2	*Comprehension and summary* – two passages set, one factual, the other more literary.	1¾ hours	100

Board and syllabus	Papers or other tests	Content		*Time allowed*	**Marks**
6 **O & C**	Paper 1	Section A	Questions, including *summary* and practical writing, based on given material.	2 hours	60
		Section B	*Comprehension* of passage of prose, or drama.		40
	Paper 2	Section A	*Comprehension* and appreciation of verse passage, or two passages (one or both verse).	2 hours	50
		Section B	*Composition* – continuous writing of 350–500 words, based on one subject out of a range of choices.		50

Note: As an alternative to Paper 2 schools may choose to set and mark their own internal examination.

Board and syllabus	Papers or other tests	Content	*Time allowed*	**Marks**
7 **SUJB**	Paper (one only)	(a) *Comprehension* and *summary* questions based on prose passages.	2½ hours (+15 mins)	35/20
		(b) *Composition* – including argument, and writing based on material given.		45
SUJB Alternative	Paper (one only)	Q.1 *Comprehension* – based on passage of up to 800 words. Two other questions out of a choice of six, based on topics (e.g. War and Conflict, The Town).	3 hours	30 50
	Course work	Five to ten pieces of work, totalling 5,000 to 10,000 words.		20

Notes: 1 This syllabus has been prepared for sixth formers, and is not available to private candidates.
2 Standard dictionaries may be brought to the examination.

Board and syllabus	Papers or other tests	Content	*Time allowed*	**Marks**
8 **WJEC**	Paper (one only)	Q.1 *Composition* – 500–600 words, choice of topic.	1 hour	40
		Q.2 *Comprehension* – may include questions on grammar, vocabulary and punctuation.		30
		Q.3 *Summary* – of passage given.	2 hours	20
		Q.4 Letter, speech or other form of everyday communication.		10
9 **NIEC**	Paper I	Q.1 *Composition* – a choice of subjects giving opportunities for narrative and other kinds of continuous writing.	1½ hours	
		Q.2 *Factual writing* – e.g. instructions, letters, interpreting statistics.		
	Paper II	Q.1 *Summary* of a given prose passage.	1¾ hours	
		Q.2 *Comprehension* – a range of questions based on a set prose passage.		

SCOTTISH CERTIFICATE OF EDUCATION – **Ordinary Grade (SCE)**

Board and syllabus	*Papers or other tests*	**Content**	*Time allowed*	**Marks**
10 **SEB**	Paper 1	*Composition and reading:* Section A *Composition* – one topic from a wide choice of narrative, descriptive, discursive, etc.	1 hour 50 mins	30
		Section B *Reading* – either Part 1 – two essay answers on general questions about Drama, Poetry, Prose, Media, or Part 2 – a single question geared to the thematic approach.		(10 each)
	Paper 2	*Interpretation and language:* Passage 1 Generally more literary material. Questions on general *comprehension,* gist-extraction, etc.	1 hour 30 mins	25
		Passage 2 Generally more factual or informative material. Questions more concerned with choice of expression, structure, punctuation, etc. Includes a *summary* worth 8 marks.		25
11 **16 plus** **(Joint ALSEB,** **JMB,** **NWREB,** **YHREB)**	Paper 1	*Expression* SECTION A Practical writing; one or more pieces of *composition* based on information given (e.g. articles, diagrams, maps etc.).		20
		SECTION B *Composition* – a piece of continuous imaginative writing based on one of a number of stimuli chosen to evoke an individual response.		20
	Paper 2	*Understanding (Comprehension)* SECTION A Questions based on one or more pieces of imaginative writing – prose or verse.		40
		SECTION B Extracting information from one or more passages.		

Notes: 1 Dictionaries may be used.
2 *Spoken English* is assessed within the school over a period of about a year.
3 As an alternative to Paper 1 a folio of coursework can be submitted.

CERTIFICATE OF SECONDARY EDUCATION – **Mode I (CSE)**

(Modes II and III of this examination involve fuller participation by the schools, and are too various to be summarised here. In general they are similar to Mode I, but depend more on course work; oral and aural English sometimes earn a higher proportion of total marks than in Mode I syllabuses).

The CSE examinations are organised on a regional basis, in order to make it possible to involve the schools more fully in certain parts of the examination, notably oral and aural tests and course work. We list them below as follows: numbers 12–16 NORTH; 17–20 MIDLANDS and WALES; 21–24 SOUTH; 25 N. IRELAND.

Board and syllabus	Papers or other tests	Content	Time allowed	Marks
12 **NREB**	Written Part A	Teacher's assessment.	—	20
	Part B Paper 1	*Composition* – three or four sides of continuous writing on one subject from choice of eight.	1¼ hours	32
	Paper 2	Letter/*comprehension*.	1¾ hours	
		SECTION 1 Letter – formal or semi-formal, two choices. Layout important. Not less than 10 lines.		8
		SECTION 2 *Comprehension* – three or four questions on passage of prose, verse, advertising, etc., or picture, statistical table, graph. May include *summary*.		40

Note: Dictionaries are not permitted.

	Oral Part A	Reading – candidate must read a prose passage fluently, with feeling and understanding.		15
		Conversation – to converse informally on topic of own choice.		25
		Teacher's assessment.		20
	Part B	Listening tests – up to four tests (longest 15 minutes). Candidates write answers to questions on pieces heard.	45 mins	40

Note: The Oral examination is *not* compulsory for candidates taking the Written examination.

13 **NWREB**	Paper 1	*Comprehension* – in three sections: A Passage of modern creative writing (if a poem is set, there will be prose as an alternative). Questions involve some continuous writing. B Multiple choice objective test on prose passage. C Questions on a piece of persuasive writing.	2½ hours (+15 mins)	40
	Paper 2	*Composition* (expression) – in two sections: A Imaginative writing, wide choice of subjects. B Writing based on information provided. (Letter may be set in either A or B)	2 hours (+15 mins)	40
	or Folio	Minimum of 15 pieces of writing done over at least two terms.		40
	Spoken English	Variety of possible forms tested, at discretion of school, e.g. conversation, discussion, reading, drama, debate.		20

Board and syllabus	Papers or other tests	Content	Time allowed	Marks
14 **ALSEB** **Alternative** **A**	Paper I	*Composition* – in three sections: A imaginative description; B logical presentation of information; C persuasion and argument.	1½ hours (+10 mins)	35
	Paper II	*Comprehension* and appreciation – three sections: 1 prose 2 poetry } passage of each kind, and 3 drama } questions on it.	2 hours (+15 mins)	35
	Spoken English	1 Communicating information or a viewpoint. 2 Communicating thoughts and feelings. 3 Responses to various speech situations.		30

Notes: 1 Dictionaries are permitted for the written examinations.

2 In Paper II 30 minutes extra time may be allowed.

3 The Spoken English test is administered by teachers in schools, and moderated externally.

Board and syllabus	Papers or other tests	Content	Time allowed	Marks
ALSEB **Alternative** **B**	Folio written work	Representing five terms' work, and including 24 pieces of unaided work, 12 of which are related to literature. (Assessed by teachers in school, externally moderated.)		70
	Spoken English	As in Alternative A.		30

Board and syllabus	Papers or other tests	Content	Time allowed	Marks
15 **YHREB** **(former** **YREB** **syllabus)**	Paper 1	1 *Comprehension* of a variety of types of information.	2 hours (+15 mins)	20
		2 Letter – formal or informal, or *comprehension* or short report.		15
		3 *Composition* – based on given stimuli, e.g. newspaper, advertisement, diagram.		25
	Paper 2	1 Appreciation of prose passage.	2 hours	25
		2 Appreciation of verse or drama (choice).	(+15 mins)	15

	School assessment	Based on five terms' work, and including:
		  (i) oral work;
		  (ii) *composition* and *comprehension*;
		  (iii) appreciation of literature.
				20
				50
				30

Notes: 1 Dictionaries may be used in written examinations.

2 School assessment carries equal marks to the rest of the examination.

3 This Board offers in addition an *English Studies* syllabus, assessed entirely on course work over five terms. A list of suggested reading is provided.

Board and syllabus	Papers or other tests	Content	Time allowed	Marks
16 **YHREB** **(former** **WY & LREB** **syllabus)**	A Written English	Form of examination, number of papers, etc. may vary, but will cover *composition, summary, comprehension,* letters, response to printed material, including appreciation of literature.	not more than 2½ hours	50
	B Spoken English	To include both individual and group work.		25
	C Course work	Any work from the beginning of the CSE programme.		25

Notes: 1 Dictionaries may be used for A.
2 B and C are assessed in school.

Board and syllabus	Papers or other tests	Content	Time allowed	Marks
17 **WJEC**	Paper I	Q.1 *Composition* – wide choice, including letters and other imaginative or practical writing. Q.2 *Comprehension* of given passage, including *summary.* Q.3 *Composition* based on stimuli of various kinds, e.g. pictures, news-items.	2¼ hours	40
	Paper II	Q. 1, 2 and 3 Appreciation of prose, poetry and drama, with given passages., Q.4 Relating to extracts used for Q.1–3. Q.5 (alternative to 4) Allowing candidates to write on literature–choice of subjects.	2¼ hours	40
	Listening test	Comprehension of passage(s) read aloud but not seen by candidate.	5 minutes per passage	10
	Oral examination	(i) passage to be read aloud by candidate (ii) questions to test comprehension of passage (iii) conversation.	10 minutes prep.	10

Notes: 1 A list of suggested reading is provided.
2 The Oral examination is conducted and marked by teachers in the schools.
3 Dictionaries may be used in both written examinations.

Board and syllabus	Papers or other tests	Content	Time allowed	Marks
18 **WMEB**	English Language			
	Paper 1	*Composition* – wide choice of subjects.	1½ hours	30
	Paper 2	*Comprehension* – including *summary,* of passages from various sources including newspapers. Includes some letter-writing.	2¼ hours	35
	Oral	Includes reading aloud and conversation.		5 15
	Aural	Written paper based on recording.	15 mins	10

Note: Dictionaries are permitted for Paper 1.

Board and syllabus	*Papers or other tests*	**Content**	*Time allowed*	**Marks**
	English			
	Paper 1	As for English Language.	1½ hours	20
	Paper 2	As for English Language.	2 hours	20
	Oral	As for English Language.		20
	Paper 3	Literature. *Either* (A) based on books chosen by school, *or* (B) based on set texts prescribed by Board. The examination will have three sections – prose, poetry, drama; candidates must answer three questions from at least two sections.	2 hours	40

Notes: 1 Dictionaries are permitted for all papers.

2 As an alternative to Paper 3 candidates may submit a folio of Literature course work, containing at least 12 pieces of work, of which four must be 600 words or more.

3 A separate examination in English Literature is provided.

19 EMREB	Part I	Oral English Based on an examination in two parts, (a) reading aloud, (b) discussion, together with continuous assessment.	—	30
	Part II	Written English: *comprehension*.	1¼ hours	35
	Paper I	(A) Aural comprehension – questions on a passage read by the teacher.	½ hour	
		(B) Questions on a prose passage.	¾ hour	
	Part III	Written English: *composition*.		
	Paper II	(A) Letter writing: two choices, formal letter.	1 hour	19¼
		(B) *Summary*, report, notes, etc. based on given stimulus.		
	Paper III	Continuous writing – about 300 words. One topic, from wide choice.	1 hour	15¾

Notes: 1 Dictionaries may be used for Part III.

2 A separate syllabus is provided in English Literature.

20 EAEB North	Paper I	Q.1 *Composition* – on one or two subjects from a wide choice: imaginative, factual, argument.	2 hours	20
		Q.2 A composite question involving *comprehension* of prose passage and/or diagram, letters, *summary*.		
	Paper II	Literature. Questions on three long passages, one each of prose, poetry and drama, involving appreciation and *comprehension*, and some *composition* based on the passages.	2½ hours (incl. 20 mins reading time)	30

Board and syllabus	Papers or other tests	Content	Time allowed	Marks
	Course work	A selection of work done throughout the course, including evidence of reading (at least eight prose works, three plays, a wide selection of poetry).		30
	Spoken English	Part 1 Course work – based on teachers' assessment.		10
		Part 2 Final test – conversation with the examiner.		10

Note: A list of recommended reading is provided.

Board and syllabus	Papers or other tests	Content	Time allowed	Marks
EAEB South	Paper I	Continuous writing (*composition*). Wide choice – imaginative, narrative etc., including questions relating to literature.	1¼ hours	17½
	Paper II	Understanding and interpretation. *Comprehension and Summary.* Questions based on one passage, or several related passages, which may be factual (e.g. newspaper item, diagram) or literary (e.g. drama, poetry). Questions will be in ascending order of difficulty, to be answered in sequence.	1¼ hours	17½
	Spoken English	School assessment – based on year's work.		10
		Examination – in three sections:		15
		section 1 – prepared passage of prose, verse or drama;	2–6 minutes	
		section 2 – personal project – talk of not less than three minutes on topic of own choice, *or* group project – shared talk (two or three candidates);	10–15 minutes	
		section 3 – conversation.		
	Course work	Written work from five terms, including evidence of wide reading (at least six prose works, two plays, wide selection of poetry); in two sections: section I – work based on literature; section II – creative writing and other language work, including *comprehension, summary,* notes and letters.		40

Note: A list of recommended reading is provided.

Board and syllabus	Papers or other tests	Content	Time allowed	Marks
21 SWEB	Paper I	*Composition* – single piece of writing, wide choice of subjects.	1¼ hours	25
	Paper II	*Comprehension and Summary* Section A Multiple-choice comprehension questions on a set passage.	1½ hours	30
		Section B One further question testing the ability to summarise, based on the same passage or an additional one.		
	Course work	Five pieces of writing, one of each of the following: description, fiction/creative, instructions, report, argument. Approx. 2,000 words in all.		

Board and syllabus	Papers or other tests	Content	Time allowed	Marks
	Oral work	(a) Continuous assessment during year. (b) Test, devised in consultation with candidates, including discussion.		25

Notes: 1 Dictionaries may be used for written examinations.

2 Course work and oral work are set and assessed by teachers, and externally moderated.

3 A separate syllabus is available in English Literature.

Board and syllabus	Papers or other tests	Content	Time allowed	Marks
22 **SREB** **Syllabus R**	Paper 1	*Composition* – wide choice of subjects, which may include writing in other forms than essay, e.g. letters, reports.	1½ hours	24
	Paper 2	One question to be answered from each section: 1 letter writing; 2 *comprehension,* interpretation, *summary;* 3 continuous writing on informative or factual topic.	2 hours	40
	Course work	A file containing five representative pieces of continuous writing.		60
	Oral assessment	Ability to communicate ideas and sustain a conversation.		40

Note: This Board also offers a separate syllabus in English Literature for which a list of recommended reading is provided.

Board and syllabus	Papers or other tests	Content	Time allowed	Marks
23 **SEREB**	Part I Paper 1	*Comprehension* – in form of multiple choice objective test of passage of modern prose.	1 hour	10
	Paper 2	Section A Creative writing – *composition* with a wide choice of topics.	1½ hours	20
		Section B Factual writing – *composition* of practical kind, e.g. letter, report, instructions.		10
	Part II Course work	To include work based on reading as well as creative and factual writing.		40
	Part III Oral and Aural	To include reading aloud, conversation and answering questions on a passage read aloud by the teacher.		20

Note: Parts II and III are teacher assessed.

Board and syllabus	Papers or other tests	Content	Time allowed	Marks
SEREB **Joint GCE/** **CSE Syllabus** **(in con-** **junction with** **AEB)**	Part I Paper 1 Paper 2	*Comprehension* – multiple choice. *Composition:* Section A – choice of six topics based on candidates' own experience, or imaginative; Section B – choice of four topics, including letter, report, instructions, etc.	1 hour 1½ hours	10 20

Board and syllabus	Papers or other tests	Content	Time allowed	Marks
	Paper 3	Aural *comprehension* – questions based on recorded passage.	½ hour	10
	Oral interview	Reading and conversation, either singly or in pairs.		10
	Part II Course work (Language)	A minimum of three assessments.		10
	Part III Course work (Literature)	A folio of written assessments based upon a study of four books including Poetry, Drama and Prose.		35
	Part IV	A minimum of three assessments.		5

Notes: 1 Each candidate gaining CSE grade 5 or above will receive a CSE certificate. If he/she achieves the appropriate standard the candidate will also receive a GCE certificate.

2 Parts II, III and IV are assessed within the school.

3 Books for Part III can be selected from lists of recommended reading provided by both Boards.

Board and syllabus	Papers or other tests	Content	Time allowed	Marks
24 LREB (former MREB syllabus)	Regional assessment	*Two written papers.* These may take various forms, but will seek to test:		
		(i) *comprehension* and response to a literary passage or poem;		10
		(ii) *comprehension* and *composition* of factual, informative writing;		7
		(iii) continuous writing – one longer or two shorter *compositions*;	1 hour approx.	10
		(iv) continuous writing in response to wide reading.		13
	Oral test	Group discussion with five or six candidates and an examiner, on topics supplied by candidates and selected by examiner.		15
		Teacher's assessment.		10
	Course work	A folder of work done during the course.		35

Notes: 1 Dictionaries may be used in the written examinations.

2 Written papers vary from year to year; the Board wish to discourage the working of past papers as preparation for the examination. One of the papers may be divided into two sections, with an interval.

3 A book list is provided. Section A lists eleven books from which candidates can choose one or more for close study. Section B gives a wider choice. Books may be taken into the examination room. No candidate is compelled to answer any of the questions set on recommended books.

Board and syllabus	Papers or other tests	Content	Time allowed	Marks
24 **LREB** **(former** **MetREB** **syllabus)**	Paper 1 Writing	Section A *Composition* – choice of eight topics	1¾ hours +	15
		Section B *Composition,* in form of report, letter, etc. based on a particular situation.	30 minutes (optional)	15
	Paper 2	Section A *Comprehension* and appreciation, based on a passage of imaginative prose.	1½ hours +	12½
		Section B *Comprehension* and *summary* questions based on a collection of materials.	30 minutes (optional)	12½
	Paper 3 Literature	Four questions to be answered (wide choice) on four set texts, including play, fictional prose, and poetry anthology.		30
	Oral test	Either individual or group, at discretion of school (tests conducted in schools).		15

Notes: 1 *Writing folder* consisting of 12 pieces of original writing may be offered as alternative to Paper 1 (but see Note 2).

2 *Literature folder* consisting of 12 pieces of writing, including four based on set texts (as in Paper 3), may be submitted as alternative to Paper 3, as long as Papers 1 and 2 have been taken (i.e. candidates may submit only *one* folder, as alternatives to either Paper 1 or Paper 3).

3 A list of set literature tests is provided.

Board and syllabus	Papers or other tests	Content	Time allowed	Marks
25 **NICSE**	Paper I	Questions based on six themes (e.g. Love, Authority, War). At least three to be answered from at least two themes. At least one to be based on recommended books.	2 hours	20
	Paper II	Section A *Comprehension* Section B Two questions requiring various modes of writing, based on stimuli like newspaper articles, forms etc. Questions may include letters.	2 hours	20
	Paper III	Two questions based on stimuli. One will be visual or aural stimulus, the other written (poem, dramatic etc.) and sent to schools in advance.	1¾ hours	20
	Folio	Six to ten pieces of work done during course.		20
	Oral	Continuous assessment throughout course.		20

Notes: 1 Dictionaries may be used in written examinations.

2 Candidates entering the examination as described above are eligible for a double award. Alternatively, the examination can be taken as two separate subjects, as follows:
General English: Paper II (33⅓%), Paper III (33⅓%), Oral (33⅓%)
English Literature: Paper I (75%). Folio (25%).

Section II (Core units 1–5)
Reading, understanding, writing
1 Composition

1.1 TYPES OF ESSAY QUESTION

Composition is a main question in all GCE English Language and SCE examinations, and in almost all CSE papers. (See p. 145 Self-test units and Section V.)

There are four types of essay question. Some can be written in the form of a story; some are topics for discussion; some are almost entirely descriptive – here you are sometimes asked to describe a skill, a science or an activity of which you have first-hand experience; some require you to look at a picture and write about it – would you have anything to say about the one below?

1.2 FICTIONAL ESSAYS

When *planning* your story:

(a) try to be original. Given the title 'A Close Finish' (from GCE paper, University of London, June 1977), consider possibilities other than the last five minutes of a football game. This idea will occur to so many boys that the examiner will welcome a less obvious story.

(b) positively avoid treating the subject as you may have seen it treated on TV, or written about in a magazine. For instance, if you are writing about family life, rid your mind of *Coronation Street*; if your story concerns crime and the law,

forget about *Starsky and Hutch*. Such programmes use 'formula' techniques, so to copy them will do nothing for your story except make it ordinary.

A story usually contains description, narrative and dialogue.

Description

Aim for brevity, clarity, vividness and above all liveliness in setting a scene or capturing a character. One or two memorable descriptive words are far more effective than a number of commonplace ones.

Which of these descriptions of a chess-player brings the character to life more?

(a) He picked up the little pawn in his large muscular hand and moved it, but did not let go his hold until he had looked all over the board and made sure that he wanted it to stay where he had put it, because he felt that this could be an important move. When he was sure, he took his hand away.

(b) Delicately his strong square hand retained the little pawn; behind his eyes his brain carefully weighed the wisdom of this particular move – so much could depend on it. Finally, satisfied, he withdrew the protection of his hand.

Narrative

The pace or speed of your narrative will be determined by what you are relating. If you vary the pace your story will be much more effective.

If what you are relating is leisurely, use leisurely words . . .

The village lay sleepy and quiet in the noon sunlight. The river, spanned by the old stone bridge, flowed peacefully over the pebbles in its wide, shallow bed. Thus it had flowed for centuries from the Welsh hills of its source down through the valleys to the broad Severn, and thence to the open sea.

But then . . . suddenly the peace was shattered. A shot rang out in the High Street, two men dashed from the post office and flung themselves into their waiting car. Doors slammed, engine leaped, and they were away. The car reached 50 in 15 seconds; the panic whine of their high gear tailed them down the road . . .

Dialogue

From what people say, we learn what they are like. By studying the way they say it we learn even more about them. (See Unit 5.2 for the special techniques of writing speech.)

GETTING STARTED

The more closely a writer is involved in what he is writing the more convincing the story is likely to be . . . so . . . use your five senses. They are tools and can be made to work for you.

Sample question

'Concentrating on atmosphere, write a story entitled *A Door into the Dark*.' (From GCE paper, Oxford and Cambridge Schools Examination Board, June 1977.)

Although I was clutching Karl's arm, feeling his comforting warmth through the rough sleeve of his sweater, holding tightly to the reassurance of his day-time self, I could still feel my heart pounding in near panic at the slow creaking of the door as it opened. (I think I had been praying that it would not.) Stone steps – we could see six or seven steps, uneven from use, curving away, leading downwards into total, terrifying blackness. 'Oh no, Karl, no!' I tried to pull him back. 'We must go on now,' he said.

The writer here placed himself or herself in the centre of the action at a dramatic moment, concentrating on the sense of *touch*.

Touch emphasises Karl's 'comforting', 'reassuring' presence and, by contrast, makes the 'heart pounding', 'near panic' more real.

Having started the story at the centre of the action, the writer can see clearly what the outline would have to be:

1 how the two people embarked upon their adventure;
2 where the stone steps led to, and what they found;
3 how the episode ended.

The story started with **2**, which is not yet complete. Next the writer could fill in **1** before continuing **2**.

But beware

A title like this may tempt you to use unoriginal ideas and obvious words and phrases, like this:

Suddenly the tunnel widened out into a space where we could stand upright. Karl shone his torch, and revealed a cobwebby, dusty room. In one corner we could see an old oak chest with brass hinges. I held my breath as he inched forward, and gingerly lifted the lid. What would he find?

What *could* he find? Treasure, charts, a skeleton? The tone of the writing, through the choice of words – not wrong but ordinary – makes us fairly certain that this won't be different from a hundred such stories examiners have had to read.

You lose marks by being dull.

PRACTICE

Use the opening just given (p. 19, col. 2) and continue the essay; concentrate on conveying atmosphere, both around you and within you, as you go down the steps. Use your *senses* to connect you with what is happening.

Sample question

'*The Day of the Party.* Describe such a day from your own experience. You may choose a recent party or a children's party you remember well.'(From GCE paper, JMB, June 1975.)

I put on my new dress, and stood admiring myself in the long mirror. Plain brown cord, with an Empire waist and long sleeves, frilled with cream lace at the neck and wrists. I turned this way and that, studying the effect.

'With your blonde hair and fair skin,' my mother said, 'it's just right for you'.

I liked myself in it. As I walked round to Sarah's house for her party I felt good; I was looking forward to the evening . . . until Sarah opened the door to me. She is also blonde and fair-skinned and – you guessed it – we stared at each other's brown cord dresses in disbelief.

'We look like twins!' Sarah laughed. She did not seem to mind too much. But I was mortified . . .

By using the sense of *sight* the writer has started to portray a girl who cares about colour and design, who likes plain things, and who is insecure in a situation which she sees as embarrassing. She will describe the people at the party *subjectively*, as they affect her. This essay subject is more 'open-ended' than the first example, and so less predictable. You would have a better chance of writing a story that will be new to the examiner.

Details drawn from your own experience can be used effectively; a single incident, insignificant in itself, can colour one's whole feeling towards people at a party:

I heard Sarah's younger sister – she's in the fourth form at our school – saying to Graham: 'She'll have bought it on purpose to copy Sarah'.

She did not know I heard her. After that Graham seemed to keep away from me. I *hated* my wretched brown dress. Everybody seemed to be absorbed, laughing, playing records. 'I'm not enjoying this party one little bit,' I said to myself miserably.

PRACTICE

If the suggested opening appeals to you, use it, and finish the essay. Your rough plan could be:

1 your expectations of the party;

2 a description of an encounter or encounters there;

3 how the attitudes and behaviour shown to you affect your enjoyment;

4 your reflections on it all afterwards.

And now . . . a complete short story for you to read. Story-tellers have been in demand ever since civilisation began. If you doubt their popularity now, take a look at the fiction section of your nearest library or bookshop. Why do people enjoy reading stories? There are good reasons for enjoying this one:

● Readers who have ever been fishing can identify with the feelings of the boy or the girl.

● Those who have never gone fishing can take part, through their imagination, in what is happening.

After you have read it you will find more reasons suggested.

Something gets to them

'Are you ever coming?' asked the boy.

'Soon,' she said. She knew he would not go fishing without her. He had bought bait, made sandwiches, filled a bottle with lemonade, sorted his tackle—everything was put ready by the open door. He was waiting outside the door in the sunlight.

'Come on, it's late.'

'It's not.'

'What are you doing?'

She was at the mirror by the sink fixing her hair into a pony tail with a new tortoiseshell clip. Trying to.

'I'll go alone.'

She just knew he wouldn't; it was for her to watch him bait up, watch him cast; to wait patiently, clamping her lips together not to make a noise, to defer to his patience, knowledge and skill, to fix her eyes upon the striving line. He wanted someone to wail his disappointment if he lost a fish, to leap and shout his satisfaction if one swung clear of the water and fell twitching silver upon the green at their feet. And he preferred that she should be the one to relate to his father in the evening, sipping his mother's lovely sweet cocoa by the fire—'I watched Peter catch two trout.'

Or three—or four—or five—once I caught a fish alive— she sang the rhyme as they walked along. She'd had to leave her hair loose, it was like a black mane, too thick and wiry for the new clip; she was used to it round her shoulders but it made her hotter. Today it was sweating hot and there were a lot of flies—the high strong sun, no wind, no clouds—

'Peter, let's stop here.'

'We're going to the loop,' said Peter. His father's farm had water meadows, but Peter had planned that they should cross by the road bridge and fish away from home on the opposite bank on Ron Evans' land. The fishing was better; in fact Ron had let it to a Birmingham doctor—'you'll be all right, he only comes down weekends,' Ron had said. A public footpath ran along his bank, skirting two meadows before the river curled back on itself in a wide, deep loop. Ron's Herefords were grazing in the second meadow.

'Lysander's out,' she said. Lying on the grass with the cows, lazy in the heat, the old bull was obviously not going to stir; old and slow and docile, Lysander frightened nobody except visitors.

They reached the place where Ron's meadow bordered the inner curl of the loop. The high bank here jutted out almost like an island; to the right and left of it black alder trees stuck their angular branches out over the shining mirror beneath them. This jutting grassy knoll commanded a fine curving stretch of water, deep under this bank and in mid-stream, levelling out to stony shallows by the farther bank, where yellow willows drooped in suspense above the still water. These shallow pools under the willows were great places for resting trout, likewise the deep water under the overhang on which they were standing. The almost imperceptible current, unfortified by any breath of wind, hung merely a transparent veil between the rocks and roots of the river bed proper and the shafts of sunlight which cleaved clear to the bottom. In this clarity the children's sharp eyes missed nothing.

'By Christ there's a big 'un!' She also had seen a large fish lying along the current in mid-stream. Quickly and excitedly Peter dumped the gear. He began to fix up his rod.

'Get us a worm out.'

She found a piece of flat slate from a place where the bank fell away, and went for the bait tin. She so hated the warm feel of the tin and the stirring of the white grubs within; and worse, as she prized the lid up, the familiar nauseating smell which made her stomach heave. She shut her eyes and held her nose with her free hand, offering him the tin at arm's length.

'Yuk!' she said, 'ugh, horrible!'

Peter knew but he didn't care. He picked out a worm, fixed it to the hook, reeled out sufficient line.

'Keep still.'

'I'm putting the tin back.'

'He can see us easy. It's too bright.'

He cast quite skilfully up-river from the resting trout; they watched the white blob of worm wriggling its way down the current. Peter reeled in gently, bringing the bait within striking distance. The fish ignored it as it floated past.

'Try again,' said Peter. He tried a dozen times. She sat on the dry grass, relaxed, quietly absorbing the rhythm of his movements; today she felt treacherously withdrawn and careless of his success or failure. She was thinking, 'I'm never going to open the bait tin again.' And she was thinking, 'That fish lives there, it's his home'— when suddenly the fish was there no longer.

Peter looked up. 'Bloody cows,' he said. Upstream from them the Herefords were ambling into the water at a shallow muddy place. Some stooped to drink, others stood aimless— cooling their heels, staring—

'Stupid bloody animals. Go and chase them off,' Peter said.

'You go,' she said. She held his rod while he ran along the bank shouting and waving at the cows. While he was gone she saw a small fish jump. Also she saw the incredible lightning-blue flash of a kingfisher; he skimmed the water's surface in front of her, travelling the surprising curve of the loop with brilliant precision. She thought, he must know all the winding shapes of the river; before he got to the loop he must have remembered the shape of it, to go so fast.

Peter came back, hot.

'I saw a kingfisher,' she said.

'I wish Ron didn't turn his cows into that meadow.' He took the rod from her. They both saw a fish jump, near the other bank.

'Only a little one. There's not enough wind, the big 'uns are all lying close. There'll be a few lying under this bank.' He dropped the worm straight down in front of where they both crouched. Quite soon, a smallish fish ventured out from beneath their feet; Peter swayed the rod tip, the worm danced obediently to his baton, weaving a tiny pattern in the water.

'Come on, come on!' He moved the rod a little more, the worm responded and the fish darted away.

'You ought to hold it still.'

'I know what I'm doing. They're used to things moving. They're all fed already, they've had plenty.'

'There's not many mayfly.'

'That's why they're not jumping.'

'They don't jump for mayfly, they wait till they get waterlogged.'

'What do they jump for then?'

'They jump for joy.'

'Oh don't talk daft!'

'They do. I read it.'

'They jump for bloody mayfly. Everyone knows that.'

She pointed. A sizeable trout had leaped some distance downstream; the rings lapped gently wider.

'I'll try there.' She made no move to follow him.

'I'm going to have a drink.' The lemonade Peter had mixed was weak and tepid, but she was thirsty. And hungry. She opened the sandwiches. Brown bread with honey in. She counted them; he had made four double slices and cut them in half.

'Four halves each,' she called to him.

'It's not tea time.'

'I'm hungry.'

'Shut up shouting.'

She lay on her stomach on the warm grass munching sandwiches and staring into the water. The big trout they had first seen was back again. She tried to imagine herself looking out, from his angle, at the sun, the alders, the willows, at her own self looking down. She reckoned he was big enough to defend the place that was his home against all other fish; and at night it would be a safe place, no poachers along the bank could reach him there. Fish were wily and wary, but fishermen were crafty and skilful—she hoped that the big trout could feel the altered flow of the current at his back when a strong nylon fishing line sliced the water in two, that he could also see the line like a thin crack in his watery window as he stared through it up at the sunlight. She hoped he knew the danger of it.

Peter was making his way back—he looked tall, striding along. His jeans were tucked into his wellingtons, and his check shirt was tucked into his jeans at the front —it was out at the back. Before he reached her she picked up a stone and threw it into the water.

'What you doing? What you chucking stones for?' He sounded peevish. She glanced at where the big fish had been.

'You should know not to chuck stones.'

'Have a sandwich,'—she held the packet out. He took one and ate it absent-mindedly, staring into the water.

'They're just not interested. Not a single bite. It's no good today.'

She knew his mood—blaming the sunshine, the lack of wind, blaming the scarcity of mayfly, blaming her for speaking, for moving—

'D'you want to go home?' she asked.

'We only just got here.'

'If you didn't want to fish we could bathe. It's hot.'

'It's too bloody bright; we need a bit of wind. If you hadn't have shouted at me up there—I nearly had a bite—'

'It's no fun if you can't talk.'

'You better bloody go home then.'

A bathe, she thought. A lovely cool bathe.

'Hey, look,' said Peter, 'there's that big 'un again.'

'He's too wily; you'll never catch him.'

'Want to bet?'

She clenched her fists and stared at the line where it entered the water, willing the fish to sense danger. She did not watch the bait as it drew nearer to the fish; she watched the motionless fish himself, willing him to stay still, to ignore it—not to feel hungry, not to feel tempted—no, no, no—Peter kept drawing the worm across his field of vision—'he doesn't want to know'—ten times, and each time she had counted, she had breathed 'no' under her breath—Peter had tried ten times, ten skilful, careful attempts, and each time no—

'You've tried ten times. He doesn't want to know.'

Peter cast again. Get past thirteen, let him get past thirteen. She picked up a small stone. Tense and nervous, she held it. She held her breath—

'Fourteen,' she said, fingering the stone.

'Quit counting. You've got to have patience, you've got to spend hours. Quit that stupid counting.'

But she still counted. Twenty casts. Then the hook caught itself in a piece of weed and the worm came off.

'Get the bait tin.'

'You get it,' she said. She jumped up and walked away a little.

'You're no help. What d'you come out for I wonder?' Peter was cross. He put his rod down and went for the tin. While his back was turned she quickly threw the little stone. Peter heard the splash, turned and saw the rings in the water, and saw that the fish was gone.

'He's gone! You threw another stone!'

'No I didn't!'

'You bloody did. I heard it.'

'Something fell into the water.'

'Oh yes, bloody likely, out of the skies, right by my fish, scared him off—'

'It must have.'

'You try to fool me—'

I don't like Peter.

'You chuck stones—'

I don't like him.

'—and then tell lies you didn't.'

I hate him.

'I hate you,' she said.

'Well, I hate people who tell lies. You're no fisherman.'

'No I'm not. I hate fishing. I'm glad I scared him off.'

'Well hard luck,' said Peter, 'because he's back. If you're stopping, keep your hands in your bloody pockets.'

Miserable, she now hated the fish. She didn't care what happened to him. He deserved to be caught—good riddance to him; another fish could have his place. All she had done for him, and there he was, stupid, back in the same place, mesmerised by the stupid horrible worm. Persistently, Peter repeated the same routine. She lost count—hundreds of times—for ever—

'Oh so boring!' she said loudly. 'I think fishing is so stupid!'

But she failed to goad him because just then the fish moved slightly. Peter was holding the worm steady about four inches from his nose and he altered his position fractionally.

'Come on, come on,' muttered Peter, 'come on, come on—'

'He won't,' she said, again loudly.

'Shut up!' Peter's voice was muted and savage. The fish moved again, but still maintaining the same distance between him and the bait.

'He will. Come on.' Peter moved the worm a half inch closer. Nothing.

Suddenly a much smaller fish darted from some distance away and took the worm in its swift forward path; the line travelled and tightened. Peter easily controlled his puny catch and landed it on the bank. She laughed unkindly at it.

'Better than nothing,' said Peter.

'It's not. You'll have to throw it back.'

'It's big enough, just about.'

'Oh, nowhere near, it's tiny. You know it's too little.'

Peter extricated the hook, and gripped the fish in his hands. It flipped strongly.

'You're no fisherman if you keep that.'

'I caught it didn't I—'

'Whatever d'you want it for?'

Peter had no answer. The fish arched itself frantically.

'You just want it to prove something, to prove you can catch something. It's so young it doesn't know anything; you don't prove anything unless you'd caught the big one—'

'You didn't want me to.'

'No. but if you had you'd be a good fisherman—I'd respect you even if I do hate fishing. I'd tell them at home, I'd even tell I tried to scare him off. Anybody can catch little ones; they're for kids.'

'I landed it.'

'It just took the bait; you weren't trying for it.'

'When you're fishing you're trying to catch a fish, stupid.'

'You just had to land it to get the hook free; it got itself caught. You've held it; now put it back. You know you don't want it.'

Obstinately he still held it tight. The poor thing opened its bleeding mouth pitifully.

'It'll die in a minute. I shan't say at home you caught a fish. I shan't say anything. You can show it to your father.'

The fish was almost at its last gasp.

'You won't want to show him. He'll be angry, and Ron Evans will—Ron thought you were a proper fisherman. And I did; I'll never come with you again.'

'Big deal!'

Her eyes were hot and sharp with tears. The little fish lay limp in Peter's hand.

'What a baby, crying for a fish!'

'I'm not. I'm crying for—because—'

She couldn't say why. But something she knew suddenly found its only expression in loud childish sobbing. Peter went to the water's edge and flung the fish as far as he could. It disappeared with a small splash.

Gradually, as the hard lump in her chest eased and melted, her tears ceased. She heaved a big sigh. Peter sat down without speaking and unwrapped what was left of the sandwiches; presently she sat down beside him and together they finished them, and the lemonade.

'D'you want to have a go for him?' asked Peter, 'You see Mister Big 'Un's back again. D'you want to try for him?'

She nodded. He got to his feet and baited the hook for her; in a short while she became as absorbed as Peter had been. She asked his advice but he didn't give her much. 'He's a crafty bugger, I reckon we won't catch him in a hurry,' he said.

The kingfisher flew down the river again, and almost immediately flew back past them—they both saw it. Presently she gave the rod back to Peter. They sat side by side on the bank; Peter just dangled the worm out of sight under the bank. A slight breeze sprang up, ruffling the river's surface at the farther side; the willows moved trailing their sun-yellow fingers in the water.

'A bit of wind. Let's have some action,' said Peter. He bounced his rod up and down in an amateurish manner, flicking the worm in and out of the water. He made her laugh; he was funny, fooling about. In one movement he looped the worm into the air and flipped it carelessly over at the big fish. She thought it landed right on him.

With an incredible outraged turbulence of the water in which he had lain so still for so long he flashed up, showering spray from his galvanised body. Peter couldn't believe it. He leaped up too, nearly dropping the rod. Both the children were desperately excited—she screamed in surprise, clapping her hands, jumping up and down, and Peter's hands shook as he began to reel in; it was a bigger fish than he had ever caught before.

'What if he gets away! Oh, don't let him!' She chewed her fingers, she was sweating. So far, the trout was still hooked—

'What if he breaks the line?' Peter was sweating too.

The tip of the rod bent to the water; the woodpecker rattle of his reel clocked up a timeless period of suspense. Peter drew his catch relentlessly closer, and closer— till he judged the time was right and swung the big fish up in a triumphant arc on to the bank.

'Oh Peter, if you could see your face!'

'And yours—' he grinned at her. They were both crouching by his panting catch. A huge confidence born of success out of failure wrapped them both in unutterable content.

'He's swallowed the hook right down.'

'Can you get it out?'

'Sure.' While she waited for Peter to unhook the fish the wind swayed in the willows again; the river seemed to be coming alive. Many fish were growing active; several random sets of rings appeared on the surface. She imagined the urgent upward fling of solid bodies made light in the water by a strange compulsion. Peter came and stood by her.

'He's heavy. I reckon he weighs a pound and a half, maybe.'

'Look at them jump! They must feel so light and cheerful to jump like that.' They could clearly see many fish darting and gliding the length of the loop.

'Something gets to them,' said Peter.

'The rings only show where they've been, not where they are now.'

'They're all over the bloody place.'

'I wonder what it is that gets to them—'

They didn't feel like going home. Peter took a fresh worm. He had some luck; he had several strikes and landed two more fish. She watched him, watched the fish swimming, watched the willows and the river. She went a little way along the bank, took her sandals off and played about in the water. She crouched on the rocky floor of a small pool fringed with weed, where boatmen skated and a school of tiny minnows flickered.

The sun beat down upon her head and upon her back—the breeze blew more strongly—she was conscious of no time but now, no place but here—the stream flowing cold round her bare feet might well have had neither source nor destination—this day might well have had no dawning—nor be approaching any nightfall—

Hilary Tunnicliffe, printed by permission of the author.

If you have enjoyed this story, it is partly because:

● there is enough **description** included to enable the reader to imagine the pleasant country setting;

● the writer has made sure that the **narrative** tells us how the boy and girl feel as well as what they do;

● the **dialogue** is natural (some might think it *too* natural in places!), and helps to bring the characters to life.

These are general reasons; any careful reader could have found them. There may also be personal reasons, unique to each reader

— a detail that awakens a vivid memory

— a feeling that is echoed in your own experience

— a turn of phrase that has a special association for you alone.

If you choose a fictional essay subject you too need to *make contact* with your reader, the examiner, and you have less time to do it than most short story writers. Think about any points of contact between you and this writer, or a writer whose work you have enjoyed.

For the record
This short story is between 4,000 and 5,000 words long. You will be expected to write one in 500 to 600 words.

1.3   DISCUSSION ESSAYS

A frequent method of setting these is to give one or more comments on a particular problem— social, political, educational, even personal—and then to ask you to state your views on the subject.

If you attempt this type of essay you must have some well thought-out personal views on the subject.

'Gold watch at sixty.
Retired so early?
What's living for:
a torch left burning in a drawer?'

What are your views on the problems of old people? You may, if you wish, write about the way of life and the problems of one or more old people known to you. (From CSE paper, East Anglian Examinations Board, April 1977.)

Here is one pupil's first attempt:

I don't really know any old people to speak to, but I don't think it can be much fun to be old. All the things you like to do when you are young, you are maybe too lame or out of breath to do them. And the younger generation maybe don't have much time for you, so you get to thinking 'I might as well be dead, they never come to see me'. . . .

This is called 'writing out of the top of your head'. There is no plan; the writer is carelessly jotting down very immature ideas as they come into his head. If the essay continued in the same way it would earn very low marks indeed.

Advice If you choose this subject

● think about the quotation for a few minutes;
● note down some ideas, and organise them into a plan. Here is a possible one:

Introduction Large numbers of old people. What is done for them? What should be done?

Main part Problems of retirement (comment on poem). Compensations of growing old. Everyone's concern—we may all live to be old.

Conclusion A real life anecdote—perhaps about one of your grandparents (or other relation or acquaintance), chosen to show that being old can be worthwhile and dignified.

It is helpful in topics of this kind to have some detailed information, for example: how the problem is dealt with, or on what scale it exists, in your own town or village.

Essays of this type lend themselves to careful planning. Here is a possible plan for many discussion essays:

1 Introduction

(i) State the nature of the problem.

(ii) List the points to be discussed.

(iii) If you can, comment on a recent event that has to do with the topic being discussed.

Example (for the subject just given): a death from hypothermia (dangerously low body temperature) reported locally; the coroner's comments at the inquest emphasise the urgent need for a voluntary system of house visiting for the elderly.

(iv) State your own attitude to the problem— perhaps in a single positively worded sentence like this: 'My own view is that not nearly enough public money is set aside for the special needs of the aged.'

2 Personal slant

Start a new paragraph, linking it with **1** (iv). Argue your case, giving evidence to support your view. (Hint: if the ideas are complicated, keep your sentences simple and direct.)

What's wrong with this as an example?

'I think that more money should be spent on training welfare and social workers and visitors so that old people could be visited more often. If more money was spent there would be more social workers, and old people would not die from hypothermia because they would be visited more often. They would not be so lonely because there would be more people to visit them.' (Answer on p. 184).

3 Other points of view

State them clearly, and if you disagree with them give good reasons; don't just dismiss them.

4 Conclusion

(i) Sum up the main points discussed;

(ii) Suggest possible measures, remedies or solutions;

(iii) Re-state the need to recognise the problem.

Does this describe you?

● You have an interest in contemporary problems and current affairs.

● You watch television current affairs documentaries and serious news programmes.

● You regularly read your local paper and/or a national paper.

● You have a good memory for facts.

● You have a clear brain for reasoned argument, or good experience in debates and public discussions (e.g. in school or class debates).

If so, this type of essay should suit you well.

PRACTICE

TV broadens the mind,
stifles conversation,
makes people lazy,
befriends the lonely,
is politically biased,
encourages violence.

Write your views on the way television affects people's lives, referring, if you wish, to the above comments. (From GCE paper, Joint Matriculation Board, June 1975.)

Alternatively: write an essay on the topic concerning old people given above. Try using the suggested plan.

For fictional essays we gave you a complete story to show you what could be done. For discussion-type essays we print here a complete essay on a controversial subject in sport

Muhammad Ali takes a swing at Richard Dunn

George Orwell is well-known for his hard-hitting journalism and his defence of the English language, as well as for his two best-sellers, *Animal Farm* and *1984*. He wrote the essay below more than 30 years ago. Whether or not you like football you should find the argument, and Orwell's way of presenting it, interesting.

Be warned! It is not easy reading; forceful, well-supported argument that is closely reasoned rarely is. But it is worth the effort of reading it carefully.

The sporting spirit

Now that the brief visit of the Dynamo football team* has come to an end, it is possible to say publicly what many thinking people were saying privately before the Dynamos ever arrived. That is, that sport is an unfailing cause of ill-will, and that if such a visit as this had any effect at all on Anglo-Soviet relations, it could only be to make them slightly worse than before.   5

Even the newspapers have been unable to conceal the fact that at least two of the four matches played led to much bad feeling. At the Arsenal match, I am told by someone who was there, a British and a Russian player came to blows and the crowd booed the referee. The Glasgow match, someone else informs me, was simply a free-for-all from the start. And then there was the controversy, typical of our   10
nationalistic age, about the composition of the Arsenal team. Was it really an all-England team, as claimed by the Russians, or merely a league team, as claimed by the British? And did the Dynamos end their tour abruptly in order to avoid playing an all-England team? As usual, everyone answers these questions accord-

* The Moscow Dynamos, a Russian football team, toured Britain in the autumn of 1945 playing against leading British clubs.

ing to his political predilections. Not quite everyone, however. I noted with 15
interest, as an instance of the vicious passions that football provokes, that the
sporting correspondent of the russophile *News Chronicle* took the Anti-Russian
line and maintained that Arsenal was *not* an all-England team. No doubt the
controversy will continue to echo for years in the footnotes of history books.
Meanwhile the result of the Dynamos' tour, in so far as it has had any result, 20
will have been to create fresh animosity† on both sides.

And how could it be otherwise? I am always amazed when I hear people
saying that sport creates goodwill between the nations, and that if only the common
peoples of the world could meet one another at football or cricket, they would have
no inclination to meet on the battlefield. Even if one didn't know from concrete 25
examples (the 1936 Olympic Games, for instance) that international sporting
contests lead to orgies of hatred, one could deduce it from general principles.

Nearly all the sports practised nowadays are competitive. You play to win, and
the game has little meaning unless you do your utmost to win. On the village green,
where you pick up sides and no feeling of local patriotism is involved, it is possible 30
to play simply for the fun and exercise: but as soon as the question of prestige
arises, as soon as you feel that you and some larger unit will be disgraced if you lose,
the most savage combative instincts are aroused. Anyone who has played even in
a school football match knows this. At the international level sport is frankly
mimic warfare. But the significant thing is not the behaviour of the players but the 35
attitude of the spectators: and, behind the spectators, of the nations who work
themselves into furies over these absurd contests, and seriously believe—at any
rate for short periods—that running, jumping and kicking a ball are tests of
national virtue.

Even a leisurely game like cricket, demanding grace rather than strength, can 40
cause much ill-will, as we saw in the controversy over body-line bowling and over
the rough tactics of the Australian team that visited England in 1921. Football,
a game in which everyone gets hurt and every nation has its own style of play which
seems unfair to foreigners, is far worse. Worst of all is boxing. One of the most
horrible sights in the world is a fight between white and coloured boxers before a 45
mixed audience. But a boxing audience is always disgusting, and the behaviour of
the women, in particular, is such that the army, I believe, does not allow them to
attend its contests. At any rate, two or three years ago, when Home Guards and
regular troops were holding a boxing tournament, I was placed on guard at the
door of the hall, with orders to keep the women out. 50

In England, the obsession with sport is bad enough, but even fiercer passions are
aroused in young countries where games playing and nationalism are both recent
developments. In countries like India or Burma, it is necessary at football matches
to have strong cordons of police to keep the crowd from invading the field. In
Burma, I have seen the supporters of one side break through the police and disable 55
the goalkeeper of the opposing side at a critical moment. The first big football
match that was played in Spain about fifteen years ago led to an uncontrollable
riot. As soon as strong feelings of rivalry are aroused, the notion of playing the
game according to the rules always vanishes. People want to see one side on top
and the other side humiliated, and they forget that victory gained through cheating 60
or through the intervention of the crowd is meaningless. Even when the spectators
don't intervene physically they try to influence the game by cheering their own side

† animosity — active enmity. (See *Vocabulary*, p. 33) [Ed.]

and 'rattling' opposing players with boos and insults. Serious sport has nothing to do with fair play. It is bound up with hatred, jealousy, boastfulness, disregard of all rules and sadistic pleasure in witnessing violence: in other words it is war minus   65
the shooting.

Instead of blah-blahing about the clean, healthy rivalry of the football field and the great part played by the Olympic Games in bringing the nations together, it is more useful to inquire how and why this modern cult of sport arose. Most of the games we now play are of ancient origin, but sport does not seem to have been   70
taken very seriously between Roman times and the nineteenth century. Even in the English public schools the games cult did not start till the later part of the last century. Dr Arnold, generally regarded as the founder of the modern public school, looked on games as simply a waste of time. Then, chiefly in England and the United States, games were built up into a heavily-financed activity, capable of attracting   75
vast crowds and rousing savage passions, and the infection spread from country to country. It is the most violently combative sports, football and boxing, that have spread the widest. There cannot be much doubt that the whole thing is bound up with the rise of nationalism—that is, with the lunatic modern habit of identifying oneself with large power units and seeing everything in terms of competitive   80
prestige. Also, organized games are more likely to flourish in urban communities where the average human being lives a sedentary or at least a confined life, and does not get much opportunity for creative labour. In a rustic community a boy or young man works off a good deal of his surplus energy by walking, swimming, snow-balling, climbing trees, riding horses, and by various sports involving cruelty to   85
animals, such as fishing, cock-fighting and ferreting for rats. In a big town one must indulge in group activities if one wants an outlet for one's physical strength or for one's sadistic impulses. Games are taken seriously in London and New York, and they were taken seriously in Rome and Byzantium: in the Middle Ages they were played, and probably played with much physical brutality, but they were   90
not mixed up with politics nor a cause of group hatreds.

If you wanted to add to the vast fund of ill-will existing in the world at this moment, you could hardly do it better than by a series of football matches between Jews and Arabs, Germans and Czechs, Indians and British, Russians and Poles, and Italians and Jugoslavs, each match to be watched by a mixed audience of   95
100,000 spectators. I do not, of course, suggest that sport is one of the main causes of international rivalry; big-scale sport is itself, I think, merely another effect of the causes that have produced nationalism. Still, you do make things worse by sending forth a team of eleven men, labelled as national champions, to do battle against some rival team, and allowing it to be felt on all sides that whichever   100
nation is defeated will 'lose face'.

I hope, therefore, that we shan't follow up the visit of the Dynamos by sending a British team to the U.S.S.R. If we must do so, then let us send a second-rate team which is sure to be beaten and cannot be claimed to represent Britain as a whole. There are quite enough real causes of trouble already, and we need not add to them   105
by encouraging young men to kick each other on the shins amid the roars of infuriated spectators.

George Orwell, from *Collected Essays, Journalism and Letters*, reprinted by permission of
Mrs Sonia Brownwell Orwell and Martin Secker & Warburg Ltd.

This has between 1,400 and 1,500 words, so it is again a good deal longer than most examination essays. It is a good idea to get used to estimating the number of words in a piece of writing. Do you know how many you normally write on one page of this size? It will probably be between 150 and 250 words, but you should get to know what 100 words looks like in your normal hand-writing.

VOCABULARY

Whenever you write you take it for granted that your intended reader will understand you. Orwell assumed that readers of *Tribune* (a socialist weekly, in which the essay appeared) would understand such words as:

> *predilections* (line 15)
> *russophile* (line 17)
> *animosity* (line 21)

The last of these is a key word. Unless you understand it a central point in Orwell's argument is obscured.

DICTIONARY PRACTICE

(see also *Using a Dictionary*, p. 137) Establish the meanings of the two words not explained,

and of these four from later in the essay:

> *obsession* (line 51)
> *sadistic* (line 65)
> *cult* (line 72)
> *sedentary* (line 82)

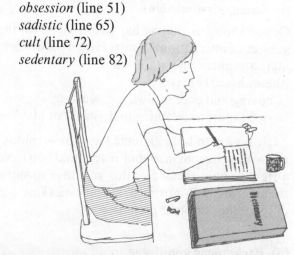

A shop steward reports back to union members

BBC copyright photograph

Notice how a full understanding of their meaning helps you to follow Orwell's argument and to understand his feelings more clearly. (When you have found the dictionary meaning of each word, check that it makes sense in the passage.)

Here are the two main ingredients of a good discussion essay:

(i) Strong personal views

Orwell shows us that he has strong views on the subject of international sport. He makes deliberately argumentative statements:
'these absurd contests'
'a boxing audience is always disgusting'
'serious sport has nothing to do with fair play'.

It is easy to hold extreme views or opinions; not so easy to convince your reader that you have a right to hold them. For this you have to show that you are well-informed, and not speaking out of ignorance or blind prejudice.

(ii) Background knowledge

There is plenty of evidence here that Orwell has thought about his subject, and that he knows the facts that will support his views:
e.g. the 1936 Olympic Games;
the visit in 1921 of the Australian cricket team;
first-hand evidence of violence in football in Burma;
a knowledge of the history of sport.

STRUCTURE

This kind of essay gains greatly from careful planning. Let's see how Orwell does it. He uses nine paragraphs for his 1,450 or so words— about three times the length you may be expected to write in an examination. The essay is planned in two main parts:

Part A (about 1,000 words)
Paragraphs 1 to 6, stating the facts, and the writer's views on them.

Part B (about 500 words)
Paragraphs 7 to 9, explaining the history of the subject, and making recommendations based on the writer's views.

Notice the linking sentence between part A and part B:

'Instead of blah-blahing about the clean, healthy rivalry of the football field and the great part played by the Olympic Games in bringing the nations together, it is more useful to inquire how and why this modern cult of sport arose.' (Lines 67–69.)

We can see the structure clearly if we examine it paragraph by paragraph.

Part A

1   *Introduction* (short)
(a) The news-item on which the essay is based.
(b) Orwell's view on it.

'Even the newspapers . . .'
2   *Facts* to support view given in 1
— carefully selected details.

'And how could it be otherwise?'
3 & 4 *General principles*
The argument developed; his view derived from general principles.

'Even a leisurely game . . .'
5   *Further illustrations*
Extending the argument to other sports.

'In England . . . bad enough, but . . . in young countries . . .'
6   *Context enlarged*
Effects of competitive sport in other countries; opportunity for personal reminiscence.

Part B

'Instead of blah-blahing . . . it is more useful . . .'
7   *Historical background*
Tracing development of phenomenon.

'I hope, therefore, that we shan't . . .'

8 & 9 *Conclusion*

Case fully made; suggestions for remedy.

Notice how Orwell holds the essay firmly together by means of linking words and ideas—a useful tip for your own discussion essays.

PRACTICE

Using some of the ideas in Orwell's essay, together with your own knowledge and observation to support your view, write an essay on this topic: 'International sporting events promote goodwill between nations.'

1.4 DESCRIPTIVE ESSAYS

1 Write about the pleasure that you personally derive from *one* of the following: astronomy, archaeology, colour photography, cooking, making your own clothes, taking part in a play, mountaineering. (From GCE paper, Joint Matriculation Board, June 1974.)

2 'The familiar sounds of home.' Describe some of the sounds which are typical of your home and the people in it; show how they express its special atmosphere and reveal the activities and characters of those who live there. (From GCE paper, University of London, June 1977.)

3 Describe the process of some craft in such a way as to give a clear impression of what the craftsman is doing and what he might be feeling. (From GCE paper, Oxford & Cambridge Schools Examination Board, June 1977.)

These essay topics have four things in common:
● they do not require a story line;
● they all need to include *facts* as a main ingredient
● they need little or no dialogue;
● they will involve close observation and attention to detail

If these points appeal to you consider choosing this kind of essay subject. Here are some suggested ways of going about it.

1 MAKING YOUR OWN CLOTHES

Plan

Introduction (100 words)

Set out briefly the points you will be dealing with in the essay. They might include:

— need for special teaching,
— own designs v. patterns,
— boys learning sewing,
— handling a sewing machine,
— personal qualities needed,
— advantages as a hobby.

Main part (300–350 words)

Deal in some detail with all the points listed. Here is an example: My young brother's class were given four choices of craft in their second year at school: metalwork, woodwork, cookery or needlework. Quite a number of the boys chose needlework. My brother soon became proficient in the use of our sewing machine. He loved making things, turning up his new jeans and patching his old ones—with some startling choices of material—, even mending towels and pillowcases for my mother. He made a really professional-looking shirt at school: I was quite envious . . . (80 words). Four or five such points will be plenty for this part.

Conclusion (150 words)

An anecdote about a garment you have made recently; your success with it; your family's and friends' reactions to it.

2 THE FAMILIAR SOUNDS OF HOME

'My older brother plays the trumpet. What we should do if his room were not at the far end of our old house, with 18 inches of solid stone wall between him and the nearest room, I do not know. Fortunately, too, that room is the bathroom. My mother once had a bath after midnight. She told us next day how, as she lay relaxing, ghostly echoes of Haydn's Trumpet Concerto came floating upon the night air as if from outer space.'

Plan

Introduction

Here are some topics you might deal with:

— the members of your family.
— ordinary, routine sounds. (Sit in your bedroom and list the sounds as you hear them.)
— sounds special to your family, perhaps unusual.
— effect of your house's layout on sounds.
— effect on visitors.
— your own feelings about the sounds.

Main part

Cover more closely some or all of the points in your introduction.

Conclusion

A comment on whether your house would really be 'home' for you if the sounds were not there.

3 THE CRAFTSMAN AND HIS CRAFT

Plan

Introduction

How, when, where and why you came to know this craftsman.

Main part

Comment on all aspects of the work: the workshop, the craftsman's tools and how he keeps them, materials and how they are stored. Describe what he has told you of his apprenticeship or training, and any details about the history of the craft. Use your powers of *observation* to describe his processes, his hands and how he uses them, his working position—standing, sitting, squatting cross-legged (e.g. a tailor). Move from the man to his product—how long it takes to complete, where it will go, how much it will cost; and whether its maker gets satisfaction from that, or from making it well.

'Today I watched him sharpening the blade of the plane he uses for shaping fingerboards. They are made of ebony and need a good sharp tool. He took a flat piece of smooth stone from his right-hand drawer and wetted it by dipping his fingers in a jar of water that had been at the back of his bench for a week. Then he unscrewed the blade and circled it flat upon the stone. The firm pressure bent his broad fingers concave, and their tips curved outwards. The steel made wet black rings on the stone. When he had finished he reached for a piece of cotton-wool and wiped the stone clean before putting it away. After wiping the blade as well he stropped it on a strip of hard black leather from his left-hand drawer—up and down, long strokes, twice each way. Finally he tested it for sharpness by shaving some hairs off the back of his hand.

'That'll do,' he said.'

(A violin-maker)

Conclusion

Imagine yourself in his place. Think, and describe what must be satisfying, or tiring, or frustrating about this particular job—perhaps comparing it to other crafts.

We have outlined three typical descriptive essays similar to ones you may be asked to write in an English examination. Let's think about them one by one.

Making Your Own Clothes will be more successful the keener you are on the subject. You will be able to show that you know specialised terms and equipment, practical dangers and difficulties, short cuts. In short, your enthusiasm will convey a professional attitude to the subject. Which of these writers do you think is the keener dressmaker?

(a) I would advise any inexperienced dressmaker to use a bought pattern—*Style* or *Simplicity* are the easiest—because the step-by-step instructions are straightforward. The cutting layout saves wasting material; they remind you to notice the grain of the stuff, and to check that the pattern is the right way up. They show you where to make alterations to fit your own figure—and all this nowadays in French, German and Spanish as well as English! It's almost like having someone beside you giving you the benefit of her professional know-how.

(b) I love dressmaking; it is nice to be able to tell somebody you have made the dress you are wearing. Even if the clothes have a home-made look, at least nobody else will have one the same. I am not too bothered if my efforts do not turn out very professional-looking; I like casual clothes, loose or tunic styles, gathered skirts. I don't like pleated or tailored skirts.

The Familiar Sounds of Home will be more successful if your home gives you plenty of scope for describing varied sounds. A small, fully carpeted house with only two or three careful occupants may not be the best material for this subject.

The Craftsman and his Craft could be the most successful essay of the three—but only if you know a craftsman and enjoy watching him at work. Your special relationship with the craftsman and your enjoyment in watching his skill will make it easy for you to transmit your interest to a reader. It would be hard to write an imaginary essay on this subject.

We showed you what could be achieved in writing essays of the fictional and discussion types (pp. 18, 28) by printing complete pieces by British writers. For essays of the descriptive type we have chosen an extract from an autobiographical novel by an American poet, Sylvia

Plath. This is to show that descriptive writing can serve many different purposes, and need not be just an end in itself.

In the Amazon Hotel

There were twelve of us at the hotel.

We had all won a fashion magazine contest, by writing essays and stories and poems and fashion blurbs, and as prizes they gave us jobs in New York for a month, expenses paid, and piles and piles of free bonuses, like ballet tickets and passes to fashion shows and hair stylings at a famous expensive salon and chances to meet successful people in the field of our desire and advice about what to do with our particular complexions.

I still have the make-up kit they gave me, fitted out for a person with brown eyes and brown hair: an oblong of brown mascara with a tiny brush, and a round basin of blue eye-shadow just big enough to dab the tip of your finger in, and three lipsticks ranging from red to pink, all cased in the same little gilt box with a mirror on one side. I also have a white plastic sun-glasses case with coloured shells and sequins and a green plastic starfish sewed on to it.

New York by night

I realised we kept piling up these presents because it was as good as free advertising for the firms involved, but I couldn't be cynical. I got such a kick out of all those free gifts showering on to us. For a long time afterwards I hid them away, but later, when I was all right again, I brought them out, and I still have them around the house. I use the lipsticks now and then, and last week I cut the plastic starfish off the sun-glasses case for the baby to play with.

So there were twelve of us at the hotel, in the same wing on the same floor in single rooms, one after the other, and it reminded me of my dormitory at college. It wasn't a proper hotel—I mean a hotel where there are both men and women mixed about here and there on the same floor.

This hotel—the Amazon—was for women only, and they were mostly girls my age with wealthy parents who wanted to be sure their daughters would be living where men couldn't get at them and deceive them; and they were all going to posh secretarial schools like Katy Gibbs, where they had to wear hats and stockings and gloves to class, or they had just graduated from places like Katy Gibbs, and were secretaries to executives and junior executives and simply hanging around in New York waiting to get married to some career man or other.

These girls looked awfully bored to me. I saw them on the sun-roof, yawning and painting their nails and trying to keep up their Bermuda tans, and they seemed bored as hell. I talked with one of them, and she was bored with yachts and bored with flying around in aeroplanes and bored with skiing in Switzerland at Christmas and bored with the men in Brazil.

Girls like that make me sick. I'm so jealous I can't speak. Nineteen years, and I hadn't been out of New England except for this trip to New York. It was my first big chance, but here I was, sitting back and letting it run through my fingers like so much water.

I guess one of my troubles was Doreen.

I'd never known a girl like Doreen before. Doreen came from a society girls' college down South and had bright white hair standing out in a cotton candy fluff round her head and blue eyes like transparent agate marbles, hard and polished and just about indestructible, and a mouth set in a sort of perpetual sneer. I don't mean a nasty sneer, but an amused, mysterious sneer, as if all the people around her were pretty silly and she could tell some good jokes on them if she wanted to.

Doreen singled me out right away. She made me feel I was that much sharper than the others, and she really was wonderfully funny. She used to sit next to me at the conference table, and when the visiting celebrities were talking she'd whisper witty sarcastic remarks to me under her breath.

Her college was so fashion-conscious, she said, that all the girls had pocket-book covers made out of the same material as their dresses, so each time they changed their clothes they had a matching pocket-book. This kind of detail impressed me. It suggested a whole life of marvellous, elaborate decadence that attracted me like a magnet.

The only thing Doreen ever bawled me out about was bothering to get my assignments in by a deadline.

'What are you sweating over that for?' Doreen lounged on my bed in a peach silk dressing-gown, filing her long, nicotine-yellow nails with an emery board, while I typed up the draft of an interview with a best-selling novelist.

That was another thing—the rest of us had starched cotton summer nighties and quilted housecoats, or maybe terry-towel robes that doubled as beachcoats, but Doreen wore these full-length nylon and lace jobs you could half see through, and dressing-gowns the colour of skin, that stuck to her by some kind of electricity. She had an interesting, slightly sweaty smell that reminded me of those scallopy leaves of sweet fern you break off and crush between your fingers for the musk of them.

Sylvia Plath, from *The Bell Jar*, reprinted by permission of Faber and Faber Ltd.

American: 'bawled me out', 'Bermuda tans', 'talked with'—and many of the ideas, e.g. 'hats and stockings and gloves to class'.

The novel this piece is taken from is about a girl of 19—the narrator—who is, by American standards, very unsophisticated for her age. Description is used here to help us to share the girl's new experiences, so the writer appeals to our *senses* by, for example,
— the look and the feel of things in the make-up kit;
— the appearance and the voices of the other girls;
— the appearance, the voice and even the smell of Doreen;

— the feel of her cotton nightdress contrasted with Doreen's nylon and lace negligee.
 If the story is to come to life we, the readers, must be helped to see what an unsophisticated 19-year-old girl would see. Good descriptive writing depends on careful selection of details: here everything selected is important to a young person. For example,
— all the free bonuses, ballet tickets, hair styling, etc.;
— the make-up box in all its details;
— the admission that she 'got a kick out of' all the free gifts;

— the comparison of the hotel with her college dormitory;

— her envious attitude to the richer girls;

— her pride at being singled out by Doreen and her fascination with Doreen's behaviour, wit, clothes;

— her anxiety to do well in her work.

Good writing, like good building or good joinery, stands or gains its strength from the care and skill that has gone into its construction. Even

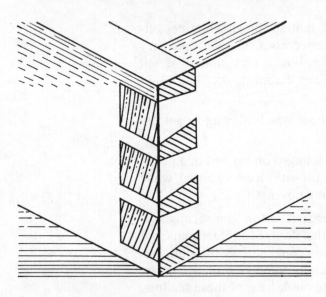

in so short a piece, taken from a 250-page novel, we can see some methods of *construction*. Three sentences are given paragraphs to themselves— three plain facts, like firm planks to build on. Ideas stem from each one, which can be coloured in the speaker's own personal, American way.

'There were twelve of us at the hotel.'

'I guess one of my troubles was Doreen.'

'The only thing Doreen ever bawled me out about was bothering to get my assignments in by a deadline.'

The writer does not need to state background information outright; instead we are allowed to discover it *obliquely*.

How do we know . . .

1 the colour of her hair and eyes?

2 that she is a writer?

3 that all the twelve in the group were girls?

4 that she had had some illness after this award?

5 that she now has a baby?

(Answers on p. 184)

DESCRIPTIVE WRITING—ways of setting to work

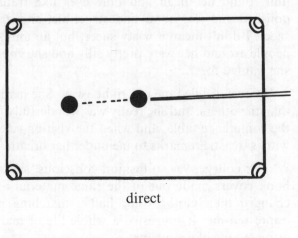

direct

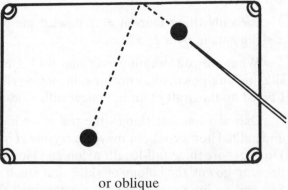

or oblique

Here are some choices:

1 Completely plain, bare, straightforward statement of fact. e.g. 'As it happened, on that particular day I was wearing a bright red woollen sweater.'

2 Straightforward, but with more descriptive words. e.g. 'On that memorable Saturday I decided when I was dressing to put on my new sweater. It was pure wool, bright red and very warm.'

This is what we have done for these two kinds of writing:

1 particular day . . . was wearing a . . . woollen sweater

2 memorable Saturday . . . decided when I was dressing to put on my new sweater . . . pure wool . . . and very warm.

3 Obliquely, connecting the fact to something else. e.g. 'By the time the sun reached its height there was no cloud in the sky, no breath of wind. I had stripped off my woollen sweater, and it lay a splash of brilliant red on the white sand by the rocks.'

4 More obliquely, i.e. stressing the other item so that the original fact seems of casual importance. e.g. 'We were startled to hear voices nearby. At first we thought nothing of it, until a woman's voice said: "But I'm known to the police; I'd be recognised." We crept as close as we dared, fascinated. She and her companion were behind some rocks; we could get closer without being seen—or so we thought until the woman said: "There's something red moving." They stood up, a man and a woman, and sauntered casually away, not glancing in our direction. The others glared at my red woolly sweater accusingly.'

Sight is the sense being used here—a good choice because the title of the essay set was *A Red Woollen Sweater*.

PRACTICE

Here are four plain, bare statements—like the first of our four choices. Each concerns one particular *sense*. Using this as a tool, write versions **2**, **3** and **4** for each in turn, on the lines of *A Red Woollen Sweater*.

(i) The grandfather clock in the corner of the room struck eight o'clock. (hearing)

(ii) I thought I was in an empty house until I heard the sound of someone hammering. (hearing)

(iii) The postman handed me a small but heavy parcel. (touch or feel)

(iv) People who have a weight problem need a calorie-controlled diet. (taste)

Picture A

BBC copyright photograph

Picture B   *copyright Press Association*

1.5 PICTURE-BASED ESSAYS

Write a story or a description or a number of thoughts suggested by one of the pictures.

Is this a new type of essay at all?

— 'a story'... (fictional)
— 'a description'... (descriptive)
— 'thoughts'... (discussion)

Yes it is, because there is an important new element—the need to use your *eyes* and your brain along with them, before you start writing.

Here are some suggestions based on the two pictures and the question above:

Story
One way to start is to *be* one of the people you see in the picture (or the person taking the photo). Use your senses again.

in A Does the man standing behind look as though he will speak out to back up his mate?

in B Is the sit-down peaceable?
in A Are the man's eyes afraid or steady?
in B Are most of the sitters occupied while they wait?
both Where might the photographs have been taken? What time of year? Or time of day?
in B What could be the purpose of the sit-down?
both What might there be nearby, but off the picture?
both Where is the camera situated? Do the people in the picture react to being photographed?

A 'I stood behind Jack, backing 'im up like. I knew the way he would play it—cool, with his trap tight shut and his eyes wide open. I was fair hugging myself against the moment when the gaffer would run out of steam. Pick your time, Jack, let him have it, straight from the shoulder. I'm right behind you ...'

B 'On the morning of the sit-in my grandpa got dressed in his best suit. "Got to show them we're not riff-raff," he said. And when we went out, he sat in the middle of the road, at the front ...'

Description
If there is plenty of detail in the picture (as in picture B) *one way* of starting your description is to describe first the parts furthest away, and work towards those nearest to you. This brings the picture closer:

e.g. the walkers,
the parked van,
the one readable poster,
the spread plastic seating,
then the two lads at the back of the group,
the man leaving, front right.

Another method is to fasten on to the particular feature or detail that strikes you most, and to let that lead you further into the ideas suggested by the picture ...
e.g. in picture A it might be the two men's caps.

Thoughts
The third choice in the question gives more freedom for the *imagination*. As long as the thoughts spring directly from something in the picture they need not be confined to what is in the picture. Thus:

● Picture A might lead you to consider other clashes between workers and officialdom.
● Picture B might lead you to write about the way a common cause such as fighting for a new by-pass helps people to forget 'the generation gap'.

PRACTICE

Find an open-air scene in a newspaper or magazine, *or* an old family photograph at home, and write an essay using the question we have quoted. If you choose a photograph, ask one of the people in it to read and comment on your essay.

Using your eyes

A simple description of what is before your eyes may seem an easy thing to write. Don't be deceived! To be both *accurate* and *interesting* in such a plain piece of writing is far from easy. You need to be observant and you need to be able to find the right words.

Heath Robinson, 'Plucky attempt to rescue a family overtaken by the tide', from *Absurdities*, reproduced by permission of Duckworth & Co. Ltd.

Heath Robinson's balancing acts

The design, the draughtsmanship and the content of these humorous drawings are worth some consideration. For instance, 'Plucky Attempt to Rescue a Family Overtaken by the Tide': the drawing shows the unhappy father standing on a tide-encircled rock at the bottom of a high cliff, holding his fat wife in his arms with their two children sitting on her back. The rescue apparatus consists of a motor cycle tied to the back of a motor car which is strapped to the back of yet another motor car. This conglomeration projects over the top of the cliff and is held in precarious position by eleven stout helpers and a twelfth beneath, who is supporting it with his umbrella. A back wheel of the motor cycle is being used for a pulley and the line from this supports a little man who dangles near the marooned family. He is holding two forked branches to act as tweezers and is in the process of lifting the first child off its parent's back. It could work, except that the three vehicles could never have remained balanced in this precarious manner, and anyhow, how did they get on top of one another? The little man with the sticks could never have lifted the child from its mother's back, let alone have landed it safely on the top of the cliff . . . and so on. The more detailed the description of the drawing, the more improbable the whole thing becomes. Yet, looking at the drawing, because of its precise and careful delineation of all the factors, including the chopped-down telegraph pole from which the willing helpers have collected their rescue lines, one is convinced that this is a viable but complicated method of rescue. The precarious balance, the literal cliff-hanger, provides the tension and at least part of the humour.

Unlikely balancing feats seem to feature in Heath Robinson's comic drawings. Another drawing (not shown here) is called 'Narrow Squeak of an Alpine Touring Party'. In this a car that had plunged vertically over a precipice is balanced on the horns of a chamois perched on a pinnacle of rock. The car is steadied by one of its back tyres which has conveniently stretched out like a rubber band and is looped round the branch of a miserable bush that had a precarious foothold on the edge of the precipice. Another cartoon of the Ark balancing on a pointed rock on which her stern has grounded is a masterpiece of mechanics. All the heavy animals and a few light ones have been crowded into the stern to provide an equilibrium. The onlooker's belief in the balancing act is never in doubt. Heath Robinson was to use the same balancing joke for various of his 'Flat Life' absurdities and particularly in the drawing of 'How the Tenant of the Top Flat can Enjoy the Amenities of a Back Garden'. Here on the most precariously cantilevered framework, a contented gent sits in his armchair smoking a pipe, while his wife does a tight-rope act bringing out his afternoon tea. The equally contented baby in its cradle is suspended from beneath the chair.

John Lewis, from *Heath Robinson, Artist and Comic Genius*, reprinted by permission of Constable Publishers.

In this description the writer has managed to explain just what makes the pictures funny. He has done so by exact attention to detail, as well as by describing how they might (or might not) work. His common-sense approach and plain language match the crazy precision of Heath Robinson's drawings. Here are some of the exact words used here:
tide-encircled
conglomeration
projects
precarious
pulley

Test the writer's observation (and your own!)

● Has he left anything important out in describing the 'cliff-hanger'?

● Has he noticed any details that you would have missed?

Three more of Heath Robinson's drawings are briefly described. Try to find a copy of one or more of them, and test the accuracy of the description. Most public libraries will have some of his illustrations in stock.

2 Comprehension

2.1 WHAT IS COMPREHENSION?

A frightening word? It needn't be, because it refers to something you practise daily. For instance:

> You travel to school or to work by bus. One day the bus takes a different route. Why? Before realising that you are doing it, your mind starts listing possible reasons—road repairs? accident? new pick-up points? a driver unfamiliar with the road? The evidence for each in turn will be considered by you (e.g. 'Oh yes, I remember, Oak Road was being dug up yesterday.'), and after checking and perhaps comparing your ideas with others, you arrive at conclusions.

At the end of such thoughts you may say to yourself, 'Ah, now I understand.' You have successfully completed an exercise in comprehension.

To **comprehend** a situation, or a piece of writing, means to **understand** it fully, to grasp the essential points.

Let's look at the stages of this particular instance:

  I Observation You notice the bus is taking a different route. (If you'd been asleep, or reading, or fooling about, you probably wouldn't have.)

 II Comparison You compare what is happening with what normally happens, the less familiar with the more familiar, the unknown with the known.

III Reflection You think of all possible reasons for the change. Here your memory can be particularly helpful.

IV Selection You choose reasons that fit the facts best, comparing one with another, rejecting those that seem improbable or inappropriate.

 V Conclusion You draw conclusions, arrive at certain decisions based on the facts you have observed and your thoughts about them

In English studies what you are asked to comprehend usually comes in the form of writing. (Occasionally it may be a diagram or a picture, or a set of statistics. Where these need special skills we shall look at them separately.) Writing usually deals with more than one idea or situation at a time, so needs closer attention than you might give to a changed bus route. But you will think in a similar way to the one we have described when you answer a comprehension question. The examiner setting the question is like the person who, in the situation we have described above, might ask you why you are later than usual.

Now let us apply all this to your English comprehension test, which usually consists of several questions based on a written passage:

Observation

Your first reading will tell you what the passage is about. You may be asked to set out the **argument**, i.e. the line of thought or reasoning, to show how one point depends on another. Sometimes particular points may be dealt with in separate questions, to see whether you have noticed them.

Comparison

Your full understanding of the passage will involve comparing things. The commonest and most useful kind of comparison will concern the actual words used, the writer's **vocabulary**. Words you have used before, or seen used in your reading, provide you with meanings to compare with the ones you are asked about. Even when a word seems quite new to you, you can compare the way it is used with expressions, sentences, contexts familiar to you. Many comprehension questions test your word skill, often by asking you to put the words in sentences of your own —an active comparison, so to speak—, or to provide synonyms (i.e. words closely similar in meaning).

Reflection

This gets to the heart of comprehension. When we are dealing with writing it includes **drawing inferences**. (see p. 54) (In the example used earlier the passenger might have correctly inferred the reason for the change by linking his observation of the change with his recollection of the road under repair.) Thinking about writing takes us further. We may be expected to notice the way something is written, and relate it to the writer. Is he being serious here? Does he mean just what he says? What kind of person is he? Or what kind of person is he describing?

Selection

Many comprehension questions test your ability to select the appropriate points. From your close reading and observation of the passage you will be able to select the features that illustrate different aspects of the subject written about, or of the writer's methods.

Conclusion

Once the preliminary work has been done you can draw conclusions about the passage as a whole, what it is aiming at, and the way it is written.

Two words of warning . . .

1 A comprehension exercise is also a writing exercise *for you*. You must not only answer the questions correctly but also write your answers in clear, careful English, paying attention to spelling and punctuation. Above all, be concise. The person who wanted to know why you were late wouldn't want to know all your speculations about the route change, nor what the shops were selling *en route*. An important part of any comprehension exercise is KEEPING TO THE POINT.

2 'Own words'— When a question instructs you to write 'in your own words' you must *not* include in your answer key words and phrases from the passage. Obviously unimportant words like 'and', 'if', 'the', etc. do not matter, nor do common words like 'space' for which there are no satisfactory substitutes. But no credit will be given to an answer which merely repeats phrases and important words from the passage. (This useful warning is included in the instructions on certain English Language papers.)

2.2   TYPES OF COMPREHENSION QUESTION

Let us now relate the general points discussed above to the kind of questions you will face in an English examination after reading the passage set for comprehension. The following model questions are all based on ones that have been set in recent examinations (see also Self-test units 11-15 and Section V):

Type I (Observation)

   (i) Summarise in x words the argument of the second paragraph.
  (ii) Basing your answer on information given in the passage, state what different occupations A has.
 (iii) Mention briefly the *four* ways in which . . .
  (iv) Explain the meaning of '. . .' on line x.
   (v) List three ways in which, according to the author, . . .

Questions of this type are all testing your powers of intelligent observation of what you have just read. Keep a clear head, and all the material for your answers is there in front of you.

Type II (Comparison)

   (i) Explain why the word '. . . ' is used on line x.
  (ii) Give the meaning of *five* of the following words as used in the passage . . .
 (iii) Express in your own words '. . .' (line x).
  (iv) Give one word or one short phrase meaning the same as each of the following as used in the passage: . . .

In this type of question you are often reminded that the meaning sought is the one used in the passage. This is because words take much of their meaning from the context they are used in. You may be allowed a dictionary in your English examination—many CSE examinations allow them—, but will still need your own powers of comparison and selection to catch precisely the meaning required. Small dictionaries may even be a hindrance, misleading you in your answers. For instance: in the passage starting on page 50 the word 'usurp' is used (line 24). A small dictionary will give just one meaning—'seize wrongfully', but the right meaning here is 'take over' or 'adopt', because the word is being used metaphorically.

Type III (Reflection)

   (i) Describe the tone in which A speaks.
  (ii) Say why B thinks it would be better if he did grumble?
 (iii) Describe the relationship of C and D as demonstrated by the passage.
  (iv) What does the expression '. . .' (line x) tell us about the general public's attitude to B?
   (v) How does the writer indicate to us that A has not been seen before?
  (vi) (This question is a combination of Types I and III.) Explain the meaning, and comment on the effectiveness of . . .

Questions of this type are often set on extracts from stories or novels.

Type IV (Selection)

   (i) Select two statements in the passage which indicate . . .
  (ii) Quote three sentences or phrases which mean the same as . . .
 (iii) What details suggest that E has been carefully prepared and might be dangerous?

Type V (Conclusion)

   (i) Summarise A's and B's attitudes to writing novels. (on a passage portraying two contrasting approaches to writing)

(ii) Say whether you think the author is right.

(iii) Is . . . necessarily true? Explain why or why not.

A little practice will make it possible for you to recognise what kind of question you are being asked—an important step towards answering it properly.

Most passages given for comprehension will either be from a fictional work (story or novel) or set out a discussion or argument, often including a good deal of 'evidence' in the form of factual statement. Here is a piece of the second kind. It comes from a book about serious music—how it is written, what effects it can create, and so on. You may not have much interest in music, but if you concentrate you should be able to follow the writer's argument. Some of the less familiar words are explained at the end of the passage.*

Passage A

There are three ways in which music can represent physical objects. First, by *direct imitation* of something which emits a sound of definite pitch, such as a cuckoo, a shepherd's pipe, or a hunting horn. Here the parallel with painting is almost exact: the painter can represent the visual but not the aural aspect of the object, the composer the aural 5 but not the visual.

The second way is by *approximate imitation* of something which emits a sound of indefinite pitch, such as a thunderstorm, a rippling brook, or rustling branches. Here the composer's representation is inevitably less faithful than the painter's;. a painting of a storm strikes 10 the eye as a more or less exact reproduction of the appearance of a storm, but a musical representation of a storm strikes the ear as only an approximate reproduction of the sound of a storm. The definite sounds of music are different from the indefinite sounds of nature: rolls on the timpani do not sound exactly like thunder, nor chromatic scales on the 15 violins exactly like the wind. Nevertheless, even here, the composer has a certain compensatory advantage: he can reproduce the sensation of physical movement which the painter can only suggest.

The third way in which music can represent physical objects is by the *suggestion* or *symbolisation* of a purely visual thing, such as lightning, 20 clouds or mountains, using sounds which have an effect on the ear similar to that which the appearance of the object has on the eye. Here music at once approaches closest to painting, and recedes farthest from it. In its attempt to stimulate the visual faculty, it seeks to usurp the very function of painting; but in so far as it lacks the power of direct communication— 25 being unable to represent the object so that it can be immediately identi-fied without recourse to an explanatory title—it is less analogous to painting than when it confines itself to the imitation of aural phenomena. Knowing, as we do, that the first of Debussy's 'Three Nocturnes' is entitled *Nuages* (clouds) we are persuaded into interpreting the shifting 30 patterns of sound in terms of the visual imagination—shifting patterns of light, such as we experience from the movement of clouds. But if Debussy had not given the Nocturne its title, we should have been uncertain what the composer intended to represent, if anything at all.

Frequently, music's three methods of tone-painting are fused, or 35 superimposed on one another, in a single composition. In Beethoven's

Pastoral Symphony, for example, the direct imitation of bird-calls (cuckoo and quail) interrupt the approximate imitation of a murmuring brook, while the third bird-call (nightingale) is only approximately imitated; the thunder in the storm movement is approximate, the lightning and rain   40 are suggested, and these are followed by the direct imitation of a shepherd's pipe.

Deryck Cooke, from *The Language of Music,* reprinted by permission of Oxford University Press.

*pitch – place (of a note or sound) within the total range of audible sound; *inevitably* – necessarily; *timpani* – drums; *chromatic scales* – using all the notes, moving up or down in semitones; *analogous to* – like, comparable with; *tone-painting* – using musical sounds to convey pictures.

This is factual. It presents an interpretation of certain facts about music. Obviously some examination candidates will know more about music than others. Don't worry if you have no special knowledge of the subject-matter; the examiners know this, and the questions will not draw on any outside knowledge of the subject beyond what can be assumed to be general knowledge. (**Warning** If you do have special knowledge of the topic dealt with in a comprehension passage, don't be tempted to show it off: it may lead to inaccurate or over-long answers.)

Here is a selection of the questions that might be asked about this passage:

Q.1 *In your own words explain briefly the three kinds of descriptive music referred to.* This is straightforward observation (Type I). The passage is set out so logically that it is easy to see the answer. It may be less easy to use your own words. Remember the rule: do not include key words from the passage unless there is no alternative. Thus the italicised phrases *direct imitation, approximate imitation, suggestion* or *symbolisation* must not appear in your answer. A possible answer might be:

Ans. The first kind of music copies natural sounds very closely, for example a cuckoo's call. The second kind gives a general musical representation of less exact sounds, like wind or water. The third kind uses music to convey an impression in sound that we recognise to be like something we see, lightning for instance.

This answer has avoided using the three main key words and phrases, as well as others like *definite/indefinite pitch, visual/aural, to stimulate the visual faculty, the imitation of aural phenomena, tone-painting.*

Q.2 *Give words or short phrases as close as possible in meaning to: (i) faithful (line 10); (ii) compensatory advantage (l.17); (iii) recedes (l.23); (iv) usurp (l.24); (v) fused (l.35).*
This question does not need full sentence answers. If the words are lettered or numbered (as they are here), don't waste time writing them out again. A good answer might look like this:

Ans. (i) close to the original
(ii) ways of making up (for being less exact)
(iii) goes away
(iv) take over
(v) closely combined

Notice that by setting out your answers in a column rather than along a single line the examiner's marking task is made easier. This may be worth a mark or two, and in any case shows consideration for the examiner.

Q.3 *Comment on the effectiveness of any three examples given by the writer to illustrate his argument.*

Which do you think is the better of the two following openings to an answer for this question? (Our answer is on p. 184)

● The writer chooses many apt examples to support his ideas . . .

● In explaining the second kind of imitation the writer says 'rolls on the timpani do not sound exactly like thunder'. This makes his point much clearer, drum-rolls and thunder being familiar to most people . . .

Q.4 *What 'indefinite sounds of nature' (line 14) are imitated by Beethoven in his Pastoral Symphony?*

The answer is straightforward again, but it requires careful **selection** of the right details from the final paragraph. It would be acceptable in answering simply to state the sounds; there is no need for a full sentence of explanation. Try writing your own answer before looking up ours (p. 184).

Q.5 *The writer frequently compares music with painting. (a) Do you find this comparison helps your understanding of his main theme? Give reasons for your answer. (b) Do you think his conclusions about serious music can also be applied to pop music?*

Your answer to a question of this sort involves making up your own mind, because *your* views or opinions are sought. For part (a) you do not have to pretend; two candidates, one saying the comparison helped, the other saying it hindered, could gain equal marks, *providing they gave intelligent reasons* for their conclusions. The second part (b) is more open-ended. If no guidance is given regarding the length of your answer (e.g. number of words or lines or sentences, or marks allocated), three or four sentences should be adequate. Which of these is likely to become the better answer? (see p. 184)

● 5(b) Personally I can't stand pop music. It sounds like machinery most of the time . . .

● 5(b) Pop music uses so many electronic gimmicks that it would be impossible to follow these three simple types of imitation in describing them all. One record by *Pink Floyd,* for instance . . .

That was a factual, explanatory piece of writing. You may also have to answer comprehension questions on more imaginative writing—a poem, or an extract from a novel or story. Basically the method is the same, but there will be some changes of emphasis in the questions you are asked. As an example we can look more closely at the short story *Something gets to them* (see Unit 1).

First, let us select a part of the story which might be set as a passage for comprehension. It would probably have a few words of introduction:

(This passage comes from a short story about a boy and a girl who go fishing in a river near their home. The boy has spotted a big trout.)

Passage B

'Suddenly a much smaller fish . . .' (p. 25) to '. . . it was a bigger fish than he had ever caught before.' (p. 26)

Q.1 *There are five short sentences at different points, describing the fish in Peter's hand. Quote three of them and say what they add to the story.*

Once again this is a matter for **observation** and **selection** first. But the second part of the question demands more careful **reflection**. Here is an adequate answer:

Ans. (i) It flipped strongly.
    (ii) The fish arched itself frantically.
    (iii) The poor thing opened its bleeding mouth pitifully.

The wording of these three helps the story in two ways: first, it describes vividly the gradual exhaustion of the fish; secondly, it shows the fish through the girl's eyes—especially (iii)—and helps to express her feelings.

Notice that this answer does not quote the other two sentences about the fish—'The fish was almost at its last gasp.' and 'The little fish lay limp in Peter's hand.' They are purely descriptive, and illustrate only the first of the two points given in the answer. A good answer to this question involves selecting the three that you can say most about.

Q.2 *Why does the girl say—'You're no fisherman if you keep that.' and '. . . even if I do hate fishing . . .'?*

Make up your own mind about this question before looking up the answer on page 184, and jot down an answer in rough.

Q.3 *What is the tone of Peter's words 'Big deal!', and what does this tell us about his thoughts?*

'Tone'—the way words convey attitudes and feelings—is always an important part of the meaning in imaginative writing. From it you can often **draw inferences** (see next page) about the characters and their feelings, or about the writer's intentions. A satisfactory answer to this question would be:

Ans. Peter responds sarcastically to the girl's threat never to come fishing with him again, because at this moment he is antagonistic to her, and wants her to know that, far from feeling threatened, he would be pleased if she never came again. The slang expression 'Big deal!' also carries a note of contempt that suits the boy's mood.

Q.4 *The paragraph starting 'The kingfisher flew down . . .' adds a number of descriptive details—the kingfisher, the breeze, the willows, etc. Why are they given at this point in the story?*

This question demands careful **reflection** on the placing of this paragraph rather than its actual content. Decide which of the following openings would lead to the better answer (see p. 184), and try completing the answer for yourself.

Ans.
● This paragraph comes immediately after the children have made up their quarrel and are on good terms again . . .
● The paragraph describes how Peter dangled the worm under the bank, and how the willows dangled in the water too . . .

Q.5 *What words or phrases bring out the change of atmosphere when the big fish is hooked? Comment on their appropriateness.*

Obviously this is first a matter of careful **selection**.

In the following list
two are wrongly chosen.
Which are they? (Answer on p. 184)

    incredible outraged turbulence
    lain so still
    flashed
    showering spray
    galvanised
    leaped
    screamed in surprise
    began to reel in

The second part of the question—'Comment on their appropriateness'—asks you to draw **conclusions** about the way the paragraph is written. Conclusions are also needed for the final question; this time you are expected to draw on the passage as a whole in your answer:

Q.6 *How old do you think the boy and the girl are? Sum up their relationship as revealed in this passage.*

Try answering this question for yourself. An adequate answer would require between 50 and 70 words. Ours is on page 184, but don't look at it until you have written your own.

2.3   Drawing inferences

What you were being asked to do in question 6 was to draw inferences, to select and weigh up the evidence in the passage, think about it, and arrive at conclusions. As this is very frequently asked of you in English, we shall look at it a bit more closely. This time we shall use the whole story of *Something gets to them* (p. 21) as our source material, and examine how to arrive at conclusions on this aspect of it:

Q. *What can you gather from the story as a whole about both children's attitude to fishing, and about the girl's attitude to Peter?*

The word 'gather' in this question is synonymous with 'infer'. It will be as well to establish clearly what this word means:

infer (verb), **inference** (noun)
A Was it a good dance?
B Yes, terrific, I met this really nice boy who works at————. He's taking me out again tonight.
C I think it was dead boring. The group played all old stuff—not a single number that's in the charts.

    From this conversation we get certain **information**: B and C both went to a dance which A did not go to; B made a new friend. We can also **deduce** (i.e. arrive at a logical conclusion) that C is interested in pop music. But if we are alert to the tone of the remarks we might also **infer** that B is an extrovert, fond of good company, whereas C is a bit of a 'loner'. The inference about B, being based on slightly fuller evidence, is more likely to be accurate; further talk with C may establish other reasons for her boredom. But the conclusions about both girls are

inferences drawn from the tone of their replies as much as from what is said. (**Warning:** Don't confuse **infer** with the similar sounding and often misused word **imply** (noun: **implication**). To imply something is to suggest or hint at it without stating it outright, e.g. 'Are you implying that I'm a liar?')

Some comprehension questions ask for the meanings of individual words and phrases; others give you an opportunity to show how much more you understand by asking what you can infer from the passage. This is one reason why you are always advised to read the passage first, and then answer the questions. It is impossible to draw valid inferences from a piece of writing until you have read the whole thing; something at the end may change the way you look at it. If you read only as far as the point where the girl bursts into tears, you might infer that she hated fishing and thought it cruel. Read on and it becomes clear that she can be as enthusiastic and as engrossed as Peter, as they try for the big trout.

The girl's attitude to fishing is a mixture of like and dislike; what about her attitude to Peter? The author does not need to give an answer to this question in an explanatory paragraph, because the reader can find it in what she does and says. But we are given special insight into the girl's thoughts and feelings. How? From whose point of view is the story told? Not exclusively from the girl's, but we are taken inside her head more than Peter's.

The girl knows Peter well; he depends on her support so she can afford to make him wait. But she does what he says:

> 'Peter, let's stop here.'
>
> 'We're going to the loop,' said Peter.

She brings him the bait but makes him go and chase the cows. They are close as they argue about mayfly, apart as he goes to find a better place to fish and she begins to sympathise more with the fish than the fisherman. Their quarrel reaches its climax partly in the girl's mind:

> I don't like Peter . . .
>
> I hate him.
>
> 'I hate you,' she said . . . .
>
> '. . . I hate fishing. . . .'
>
> Miserable, she now hated the fish. . . .

Her mood changes but the quarrel continues until she bursts into tears; he finally throws back the undersized fish; they share the rest of the sandwiches, and he offers her the rod, which she accepts. The big fish is caught.

A huge confidence born of success out of failure wrapped them both in unutterable content.

The story ends on a note of complete satisfaction and tranquillity.

After a careful reading, or a fully absorbed reading (letting the story have its full effect on you), many of these points will be filed away in the mind and the memory; a quick re-read will recover enough material for a good answer to this question.

2.4   CLOZE PROCEDURE TESTS

On pages 153 ands 154 you will find short comprehension tests (nos. 13–15) of a different kind. Here we explain how to set about them. Work through this unit with Test 15 on page 154.

Cloze procedure involves a test in which every tenth word is omitted from a short passage, except for the first and last sentences, which are left in full. (The passage should not be too short; take 100 words as a minimum.) You can measure your degree of comprehension by your skill in filling the gaps; more or less exact synonyms count full marks. Sometimes the omissions are more frequent, e.g. every ninth, eighth etc, thus increasing the difficulty of the test.

Practise your skill on the examples in this book; then make up more tests with a friend, and you can test each other. Only single words are left out, but when you are doing the tests it is better to insert a group of words which make sense rather than a single word that doesn't. Work out a way of scoring to take this into account. *A score of 50% or more is a good indication of your skill in comprehension.*

Read the whole passage first, even if it doesn't make much sense; clues can often be found from repeated words or ideas.

In Test 15 on page 154 the first word omitted must be in the same group of things as factories and houses because it is sandwiched between them in a list; and it must be something you see in a city. How about 'tenements' or 'blocks of flats'? Not bad, but they are similar to 'houses' which comes straight after. Is there something more distinctive? The best word is 'offices'.

There is only one possible word for the next gap. Which word in the sentence must it be linked with?—'eating'. Therefore it can only be 'into'. ('In' doesn't make sense; it is possible to 'eat *up*', but not to 'eat further and further up . . .')

Look at the twelfth gap. Can you tell that it must be some sort of opposite to 'ease'? The blank after this, in the same sentence, follows a 'but', so there an opposite to an opposite to 'ease' is needed! To put this more simply, the thirteenth gap requires a word expressing something more than 'ease'.

That should give you a lead into this kind of quiz. Do the rest for yourself. All the answers are on page 205-206, but don't cheat!

Before we leave you with more practice material to get on with, there are *three* other types of comprehension test that sometimes form part of an English examination. All of them demand the same basic technique that we have already set out for you; by giving you a typical example of each we can demonstrate this clearly, and you will know what to do if one of them is included in your examination.

Passage C

Readership[1] of National Newspapers by Social Grade, Age, Education: All Adults, 1974–1975.

Estimated Population[2] (thousands)	Total 41,500	Social Grade[3]						Age when education completed			Age					
		A 1,061	B 4,379	C1 9,380	C2 13,696	D 9,207	E 3,777	15 or under 27,736	16–18 10,669	19 or over 2,904	15–24 4,980	25–34 5,338	35–44 4,753	45–54 5,081	55–64 4,185	65+ 5,344
		percentages						percentages			percentages					
Daily																
Daily Mirror	32	7	13	26	40	41	22	35	27	15	39	34	33	34	29	20
Sun	29	5	11	23	38	39	17	32	26	12	42	35	32	28	24	14
Daily Express	21	24	23	25	20	17	17	20	23	19	17	16	21	23	25	23
Daily Mail	12	15	16	17	11	9	9	11	16	13	11	12	11	13	14	13
Daily Telegraph	9	42	28	14	4	2	3	4	17	28	8	9	11	10	10	8
Guardian	3	7	9	5	1	1	—	1	4	16	4	4	3	3	2	1
The Times	3	20	9	4	1	1	—	1	5	13	3	3	3	3	3	1
Financial Times	2	14	7	3	1	1	—	1	4	7	2	3	3	2	2	1
Sunday																
News of the World	36	7	13	26	43	49	31	41	27	12	42	39	35	35	35	27
Sunday Mirror	31	9	14	28	39	37	18	33	31	15	41	38	33	32	25	16
Sunday People	30	5	12	25	36	37	26	34	25	9	33	27	28	34	32	25
Sunday Express	23	47	39	33	19	14	14	19	33	32	20	20	24	26	27	24
Sunday Times	10	42	28	14	5	2	2	4	16	37	12	13	12	10	7	4
Observer	2	22	17	9	4	2	1	3	10	27	8	8	6	6	5	3
Sunday Telegraph	6	25	16	8	3	2	2	3	10	16	5	5	6	6	6	5

Source: National Readership Survey (JICNARS), July 1974 — June 1975.

Notes:
[1] 'Readership' is defined as 'reading or looking' at a copy of the newspaper in question either on the day before the interview in the case of a daily, or in the past seven days in the case of a Sunday.

[2] 'Estimated populations' are the total number of people in Great Britain (excluding those living north of the Caledonian Canal), aged 15 and over, estimated to be covered by each category.

[3] The social grade is normally based on the occupation of the head of the household. The grades are defined by JICNARS as follows:—

Social Grade	Social Status	Head of Household's Occupation
A	Upper middle class	Higher managerial, administrative or professional
B	Middle class	Intermediate managerial, administrative or professional
C1	Lower middle class	Supervisory or clerical, and junior managerial, administrative or professional
C2	Skilled working class	Skilled manual workers
D	Working class	Semi- and unskilled manual workers
E	Those at the lowest levels of subsistence	State pensioners or widows (not other earners), casual or lowest grade workers

2.5   INTERPRETING STATISTICS

At first this kind of test looks very different from comprehension as we have explained it so far. Instead of a passage to read you are faced with a mass of facts, often in the form of a table like the one on page 57.

This is simply a different way of presenting factual information. It is doing a similar job to the passage about imitative music that we have already examined (p. 50). Once you have understood its layout, comprehension work usually consists first in selecting the relevant facts. To go back to our five steps in comprehension: tests of this kind tend to concentrate on **observation** (I) and **selection** (IV). Sometimes you are also asked to draw **conclusions** (V) on what you have found out.

Here is a typical question you might be asked about the table given on page 57.

Q.   *What, according to the table, is the total number of people of 15 and over in Great Britain?*

This question concerns only one fact—the *age* of the population. The answer is not difficult to find. The top line consists, as we are told in the first box, of 'estimated population in thousands', and our attention is drawn to an explanatory note by the little figure [2]. We see from this that the table is concerned *only* with people of 15 and over. So our answer is in the next box, headed 'Total': 41,500,000.

Try this for yourself. The answers to the ten questions that follow are on page 185, so you can easily check your accuracy.

Q.1   How many people completed their education at 19 or over?

Q.2   Which is the most popular daily paper with those who left school at or before the age of 15?

Q.3   Which is the most popular daily paper with those who left school at 19 or over?

Q.4   What three types of work are done by those among whom the *Times* and *Guardian* find most of their readers?

Q.5   Put the Sunday papers in the order of their circulation.

Q.6   What daily newspaper is read most by your own age-group?

Q.7   Which of the dailies is read most by elderly people?

Q.8   How can one tell from a study of the percentages that some social grades read no newspaper and some more than one newspaper?

Q.9   How many readers are there in the 45-54 age-group?

Q.10   How many of the last-mentioned age-group read *The Daily Telegraph*?

Sometimes you may be expected to go a little further, and **interpret** or give an opinion on the statistical information you have drawn out. Here, for instance, you might be asked to comment on the reading habits of your own age-group compared with the over-55s; or you might be asked whether you find anything surprising about the information which relates the types of newspaper to particular social groups. Once you have grasped the method used to present the facts this is an exactly similar comprehension exercise to ones already dealt with.

2.6   PERSUASIVE WRITING

Advertisements usually have some factual ingredients, but their main aim is, of course, to persuade you to buy a particular product. As the differences between two or three or 20 brands of mass-produced consumer goods get smaller and smaller, so the techniques of persuasion become more sophisticated. Advertising copy-writers make considerable use of psychology, and a full understanding (or comprehension) of this kind of writing involves drawing conclusions about its real, as opposed to its apparent or stated intentions. Once again our standard comprehension practices can be employed; but this time the emphasis will be on **reflection** (III) and on drawing your own **conclusions** (V).

The following made-up advertisement demonstrates some of the more familiar advertising methods, and the questions that follow are characteristic of ones you could be asked in an examination. Read the advertisement and then answer the questions.

Passage D

Don't ask for soap—
insist on Coolstream!

Already millions of satisfied users know just how welcome is new *Coolstream* to sensitive skins . . . country-fresh *Coolstream*.

No soap brings such thrilling over-all freshness to you. *Coolstream* has all the sparkle of spring to keep you fresh and confident all the day long. Its lasting natural fragrance is as fresh as the flowers of the field, its lavish lather so mild yet so refreshing.

For you—for him—for all the family —get *Coolstream* today!

Q.1 Why is it suggested that millions use the product?

Q.2 If this advertisement persuades someone to buy the soap, what has he or she been made to think of? Quote your evidence.

Q.3 How can soap be said to bring 'confidence'?

Q.4 Find an example of alliteration, and say why it is used.

Q.5 What actual information are we given about the soap?

Q.6 Why is it stated that Coolstream is not soap?

Your answers need to be brief and lucid. An answer to the first question could be:

> The purpose of the (unverifiable) claim that there are already millions of *satisfied* users is to reassure readers who are unfamiliar with the product name. It plays on the well-known human traits of wanting to be like others, and fearing to miss out on benefits others are getting.

Try answering the other questions for yourself. There is a set of answers on page 185 (including a shorter answer to Q.1), but in questions of this sort there can never be a particular answer that is the only right one. There is another advertisement comprehension exercise in Test 12 on page 185. You can make up others for yourself by picking up the nearest colour supplement, or by reading advertisements more critically next time you are travelling by public transport or walking down the street.

Finally, here is a type of comprehension exercise set out in a rather different manner. As you can see from the questions, the difference is in layout and presentation; you need to bring to it just the same kinds of skill we have already explained.

2.7   OBJECTIVE OR MULTIPLE CHOICE TESTS

The tests are given this name, because they are supposed to be entirely free from markers' errors of judgment and to allow them no scope for personal ('subjective') opinion. A passage of prose is set, followed by (say) 20 questions, each of which is provided with four or five answers, of which one is correct. The candidate is asked to choose, and to mark his choice in such a way that papers can be marked automatically.

Some of the answers offered for consideration may seem rather silly at times, but it is often difficult to choose between two answers, both of which appear at first glance to be on target. These need care in making sure which meaning best fits the context.

It is worth doing one of these tests to familiarise yourself with the way they work. There is no point in working right through a practice book of multiple choice tests.

Read the passage below carefully; decide which of the four answers is correct in each case and put a mark against the answer you have chosen.

Passage E

There is no doubt that the sensational increase both in the size of individual lorries and in the number of the lorries themselves has caused severe social damage. A main response to this has been to build bigger roads, both in an effort to reduce the damage and to increase the efficiency of the lorries themselves. But this measure has been met by the production 5
of bigger lorries (in 1972, 32-ton axle weight) and the proposal of even bigger ones ($41\frac{1}{2}$-ton, if we agree to EEC conditions). Going along as these increases have done with the quite fabulous increase in car ownership, the next response on the part of local and national government has been to keep the dominant industries where they are, and to build more roads for 10
the traffic to occupy. This practice is then justified both by economic and practical arguments. It is held that traffic jams waste money; that road-building helps to make money (increases liquidity, investment, regional development etc); that in any case traffic must be kept moving and people must get to their destinations. But these beliefs are held and these argu- 15
ments offered in such a way as to make refutation almost impossible. We have a situation in which the fanatics of profitability and their serfs fight to conserve a set of arrangements which can be shown convincingly to be squandering huge sums of money. And when their spokesmen are challenged not in the name of decency and social justice, but in the name 20
of their own totems, cost effectiveness and profit, to do their sums better, they react not by rational argument but, in the classic manner of bureaucracy, by threats, black magic, and by suppression.

Fred Inglis, from *The Black Rainbow*, edited by P. Abbs, published by Heinemann Educational Books Ltd.

Q.1 *sensational* (line 1) means much the same as:
    A startling   _____
    B unnatural   _____
    C causing excited interest   _____
    D recognisable   _____

Q.2 *social damage* (line 3) refers to:
    A the influence of socialism   _____
    B the harm done to people's lives together   _____
    C the effect on the ruling class   _____
    D the influence of societies on individuals   _____

Q.3 How would the *efficiency* (line 4) be increased?
    A by enabling the lorries to maintain a higher speed   _____
    B by causing the roads to be much less bumpy   _____
    C by reducing the damage to buildings   _____
    D by making the roads pleasant to the drivers   _____

Q.4 *this measure* (line 5) refers to:
    A the reduction of damage   _____
    B the limit of size imposed   _____
    C the improved efficiency of lorries   _____
    D the building of bigger roads   _____

Q.5 *EEC* (line 7) stands for:
    A Eastern Electricity Council   _____
    B Eastern Economic Committee   _____
    C English Electric Company   _____
    D European Economic Community   _____

Q.6 What does the writer mean to convey by *fabulous* (line 8)?
    A the unexpectedness of the increase   _____
    B it was almost unbelievable   _____
    C it was admirable   _____
    D it was the sort of thing that happens only in legends   _____

Q.7 As applied to industries what does *dominant* (line 10) mean?
    A consuming large amounts of raw material   _____
    B the most important   _____
    C belonging to the ruling class   _____
    D the longest lasting   _____

Q.8 *economic arguments* (line 11) are those that:
    A cost the least money   _____
    B lead to a saving of money   _____
    C are based on the financial aspect   _____
    D cost a great deal of money   _____

Q.9   Which of these is the most *practical* (line 12) argument in favour of
       more roads?
       A they keep traffic moving
       B they eventually save money
       C they promote regional development
       D they are a good investment

Q.10   *destinations* (line 15) refers to the travellers':
       A homes
       B places of work
       C intended arrival points
       D journeys' end

Q.11   What is the meaning of *refutation* (line 16)?
       A clear reasoning
       B contradiction based on reason
       C common sense
       D failing to heed them

Q.12   *fanatics* (line 17) could be replaced by:
       A religious maniacs
       B people with a considerable knowledge
       C very eccentric people
       D enthusiastic believers in

Q.13   *profitability* (line 17) means:
       A the likelihood of being proved right
       B excessive gains
       C money-making
       D the scale of profits

Q.14   *serfs* (line 17) means:
       A supporters
       B followers
       C close friends
       D slaves

Q.15   *conserve* (line 18) could be replaced by:
       A maintain unaltered
       B keep in reserve
       C improve
       D reshape

Q.16   *squandering* (line 19) implies that those in favour of building more
       roads and bigger are:
       A idealistic
       B wasteful
       C mean
       D generous

Q.17 *totems* (line 21) suggests that the road supporters are:
    A like North American Indians   _____
    B mad   _____
    C placing unreasonable faith in certain ideas   _____
    D not open to suggestion   _____

Q.18 *cost-effectiveness* (line 21) means:
    A spending money wisely   _____
    B financial efficiency   _____
    C economical spending   _____
    D expenditure that gets the desired result   _____

Q.19 *bureaucracy* (line 23) means:
    A control by officials   _____
    B management   _____
    C departmental planning   _____
    D local government   _____

Q.20 *suppression* (line 23) means:
    A injustice   _____
    B concealing the truth   _____
    C over-ruling   _____
    D discouragement   _____

The correct answers are on page 185.

2.8   Further practice

In the rest of this unit dealing with comprehension skills we give you nine more passages to practise on. Many of the answers (or in some cases suggested answers) are to be found later in the book (pp. 185-192) so that you can check your work. Once you have studied the following pieces, together with the extracts we have already examined, you will have had first-hand experience of all the types of writing you are likely to meet in the comprehension section of an English Language examination.

Passage 1

Television as a source of information

We are surfeited with information. The day starts with a mélange of news, weather forecasting, evangelism and chat from the radio. At the same time, some of us are scanning the back of the cornflake packet and skimming the daily paper, while others, listening on car radios, are exposed to road signs, traffic lights and hoardings. We 'see' hundreds of   5
advertisements a day, in addition to worksheets, memos, recipes, knitting patterns, bills and computerised warnings from the bank and the Inland Revenue.

It seems probable that most of us are overloaded with information, supercharged with signals through all our senses. The mental damage   10
would be worse if we did not have a psychological cut-out switch, as a result of which we do not notice a great many of the impulses making for our ears and eyes. We tend only to see what we want to see; what is necessary for survival, satisfaction or self-esteem; what is essential to get on with the task in hand.   15

Despite this protective device, we are easily distracted, and when we are distracted information fails to get through. There are many experiments which show this happening. After a lesson punctuated by loud bangs outside the classroom or the lecture hall, children and students are less able to remember what they were being told at the moments of 20 explosion.

The power of television to inform is also severely diminished by its domestic situation. The home is an area of maximum distraction—a centre of family responsibility to be discharged, an arena in which emotional tension tends to be high, where there are many other calls on 25 time and attention, often trivial but with the force of habit behind them. The washing up needs to be done, the baby is crying, the insurance man is at the door, the lads from across the road have dropped in for a beer. To be well informed by television requires determination in the viewer and a domestic regime which is sympathetic to such earnest, autodidactic 30 purposes. What most of us do is to focus our attention on the undiscriminated stream of stimuli only when something special comes up— racing results, news which directly affects our lives (will there be a food shortage as a result of a dock strike, is there a traffic hold-up on the A3?).

There are considerable variations between viewer and viewer which 35 complicate the picture. The more you know already, the more media you will consume to add to what you know: the better informed you are, the better the context into which to fit what will for other viewers be isolated incomprehensible scraps of information. It is a chronic problem for broadcasters to know what degree of previous knowledge to assume in that vast 40 heterogeneous audience; and despite the simplicity of the language in which they are presented many current-affairs items or news reports on matters important enough to be worth paying attention to conceal their significance within some allusion to concepts which are familiar intellectual baggage for only a minority and which only a handful of 45 specialists really understand.

Brian Groombridge, from *Television and the People: A Programme for Democratic Participation,* pp. 129–131, copyright © Brian Groombridge, 1972, reprinted by permission of Penguin Books Ltd.

When you have read the passage carefully *at least twice,* answer the questions below:

marks

Q.1 Give one word or short phrase for each of the following as used in   5
the passage:

      surfeited (1.1)   chronic (1.39)

      regime (1.30)   allusion (1.44)

      context (1.38)

Q.2 Quote two words in the first paragraph each meaning 'reading super-   2
ficially'.

Q.3 Why is 'see' (1.5) in inverted commas?   3

Q.4 Explain and comment on the effectiveness of the metaphor in the   5
    following (1.10):

> 'The mental damage would be worse if we did not have a
> psychological cut-out switch . . .'

Q.5 What have the findings of the experiment described in lines 18-21   3
    to do with TV programmes?

Q.6 'The home is an *area* of maximum distraction' (1.23). Quote two   6
    words in the same paragraph each having a similar meaning to
    'area'. In each case explain the reason for using that particular word.

Q.7 What is the source of the 'undiscriminated stream of stimuli' (1.31)?   2

Q.8 Explain briefly in your own words what makes it difficult for the   14
    producer of a television current affairs programme to prepare his
    material.

                                                    total 40

Note of advice Here, as often happens in comprehension questions, you have been told how the total of 40 marks is allocated. Make the most of useful information of this kind. Don't waste time writing a paragraph of detailed explanation to Q.3, for instance. If you are short of time in an examination, *concentrate on the questions carrying most marks*. Here questions 1, 4, 6 and 8 account for 75% of the total marks. (Answers to the above questions are on pp. 185–186.)

Passage 2

Excerpt from 'Roots'

Below is part of Act II of Arnold Wesker's play *Roots*. Beatie is 22, and is visiting her parents (who live in an isolated cottage in Norfolk) after working in town. She turns on the radio and listens to part of Mendelssohn's Fourth Symphony.

MRS BRYANT *(switching off radio)*: Turn that squit off!

BEATIE *(turning on her mother violently)*: *Mother!* I could kill you when you
    do that. No wonder I don't know anything about anything. I never heard
    nothing but dance music because you always turned off the classics. I
    never knowed anything about the news because you always switched off   5
    after the headlines. I never read any good books 'cos there was never any
    in the house.

MRS BRYANT: What's gotten into you now gal?

BEATIE: God in heaven Mother, you live in the country but you got no—no—
    no majesty. You spend your time among green fields, you grow flowers and   10
    you breathe fresh air and you got no majesty. Your mind's cluttered up
    with nothing and you shut out the world. What kind of a life did you give
    me?

MRS BRYANT: Blust gal, I weren't no teacher.

BEATIE: But you hindered. You didn't open one door for me. Even his mother   15
    cared more for me than what you did. Beatie, she say, Beatie, why don't
    you take up evening classes and learn something other than waitressing?
    Yes, she say, you won't ever regret learnin' things. But did you care what
    job I took up or whether I learned things? You didn't even think it was
    necessary.
                                                                 20

MRS BRYANT: I fed you. I clothed you. I took you out to the sea. What more d'you want? We're only country folk you know. We ent got no big things here you know.

BEATIE: Squit! Squit! It makes no difference country or town. *All* the town girls I ever worked with were just like me. It makes no difference country or town—that's squit. Do you know when I used to work at the holiday camp and I sat down with the other girls to write a letter we used to sit and discuss what we wrote about. An' we all agreed, all on us, that we started: 'Just a few lines to let you know', and then we get on to the weather and then we get stuck so we write about each other and after a page an' half of big scrawl end up: 'Hoping this finds you as well as it leaves me.' There! We couldn't say any more. Thousands of things happening at this holiday camp and we couldn't find words for them. All of us the same. Hundreds of girls and one day we're gonna be mothers, and you *still* talk to me of Jimmy Skelton and the ole woman in the tub. Do you know I've heard that story a dozen times. A dozen times. Can't you hear yourself Mother? Jesus, how can I bring Ronnie to this house?

MRS BRYANT: Blust gal, if Ronnie don't like us then he—

BEATIE: Oh, he'll like you all right. He like people. He'd've loved ole Stan Mann. Ole Stan Mann would've understood everything Ronnie talk about. Blust! That man liked livin'. Besides, Ronnie say it's too late for the old 'uns to learn. But he says it's up to us young 'uns. And them of us that know hev got to teach them of us as don't know.

MRS BRYANT: I bet he hev a hard time trying to change you gal!

BEATIE: He's *not* trying to change me Mother. You can't change people, he say, you can only give them some love and hope they'll take it. And he's tryin' to teach me and I'm tryin' to understand—do you see that Mother?

MRS BRYANT: I don't see what that's got to do with music though.

BEATIE: Oh my God! *(Suddenly)* I'll show you. *(Goes off to front room to collect record-player and a record.)* Now sit you down gal and I'll show you. Don't start ironing or reading or nothing, just sit there and be prepared to learn something. *(Appears with player and switches on.)* You aren't too old, just you sit and listen. That's the trouble you see, we ent ever prepared to learn anything, we close our minds the minute anything unfamiliar appear. *I* could never listen to music. I used to like some on it but then I'd lose patience, I'd go to bed in the middle of a symphony, or my mind would wander 'cos the music didn't mean anything to me so I'd go to bed or start talking. 'Sit back woman,' he'd say, 'listen to it. Let it happen to you and you'll grow as big as the music itself.'

MRS BRYANT: Blust, he talk like a book.

BEATIE: An' sometimes he talk as though you didn't know where the moon or the stars was. (BEATIE *puts on record of Bizet's* L'Arlésienne *Suite.)* Now listen. This is a simple piece of music, it's not highbrow but it's full of living. And that's what he say socialism is. 'Christ,' he say. 'Socialism isn't talking all the time, it's living, it's singing, it's dancing, it's being interested in what go on around you, it's being concerned about people and the world.' Listen Mother. *(She becomes breathless and excited)* Listen to it. It's simple isn't it? Can you call that squit?

MRS BRYANT: I don't say it's all squit.

BEATIE: You don't have to frown because it's alive. 70

MRS BRYANT: No, not all on it's squit.

Arnold Wesker, from *The Wesker Trilogy*, reprinted by permission of Jonathan Cape Ltd.

marks

Q.1   Why is Beatie so angry with her mother? 2

Q.2   Why is she anxious about bringing her fiancé (Ronnie) to the house? 2

Q.3   How can you tell that Beatie is not very sure about the right words, but that she is struggling to find them and has a feeling for them? 3

Q.4   What does Beatie mean by 'majesty' (1.11)? 4

Q.5   What is the effect of Beatie's repetitions in her first speech? 5

Q.6   Is Beatie fair to her mother? 5

Q.7   In what ways were the girls Beatie worked with just like her? 2

Q.8   'I could kill you when you do that.' (1. 2) Does this represent Beatie's real feeling for her mother? Find evidence for your answer in her speech starting 'Oh my God!' 5

Q.9   How does Mrs Bryant show that her mind is not entirely closed? 2

Q.10 Which of these is (or are) the most important lesson(s) learned by Beatie from Ronnie? Give reasons for your choice: 10
    (i) socialism should be cheerful and not dull;
    (ii) it is no use trying to change the ideas of the old;
    (iii) an idea of what life is and how to live it;
    (iv) love is the mainspring of all that is best in the world.

total 40

Note We have included this excerpt from a play to give you practice in a different kind of reading. At first it may seem more difficult to make out what is happening. Listen to the different voices in your head and try to visualise the characters.

Questions 1, 2, 3, 7 and 9 are straightforward tests of careful reading. Questions 4, 5 and 8 need more thought; and questions 6 and 10 involve you in making up your own mind and giving your own response to the passage. (Answers to all the above questions are on pp. 186–187.)

The next piece is a short one, which you should be able to complete in about 20 minutes. Use it for practice when you can limit your time carefully; it is worth reminding yourself that most written English examinations have a strict time-limit.

Passage 3

Natural enemies

.I am fortunate enough—some people might say *un*fortunate—to have a large garden extending up the hill behind my house. When we moved in, the garden was quaintly old-fashioned, with tiny paths lined by miniature box hedges—shelter for thousands of slugs and other creepy-crawlies—, numerous ill-tended herbaceous borders, and an overgrown 5 kitchen garden complete with fruit-cage full of diseased currant bushes.

It was with some alacrity that I accepted the suggestion a few years later that my wife's parents should build a bungalow for themselves at the top of this voluntary labour camp. The plan involved the drastic use of a bulldozer, the wholesale slaughter of comfortably ensconced pests, 10 and—eventually—the welcome liberation of the owner into an orderly and spacious enclosure. This now comprised a large lawn dominated by an umbrageous tulip tree—much appreciated during the long hot summer; a manageable vegetable garden segregated by a (notional) beech hedge— no more than a row of saplings for several years, but promising an annual   15 colour-display of green and gold; and a series of small terraces setting off a neat cottage in warm brown brick.

This restored Eden was not without its serpent. The new building altered the configuration of the slope and was beset, in the following winter, by an icy air current round one side, which blasted tender, newly   20 planted shrubs and in its more violent moments tore flowers bodily from the soil. Instead of insidious infiltration by the silent army of aphids, slugs and other guerillas I now had to combat a frontal attack. It took a hefty piece of masonry and a cunningly angled fence to defeat it. We are braced for the next challenge.   25

The answers to questions 1 to 3 need not be in complete sentences. Answer *in your own words* as far as possible. (For answers, see p. 187.)

marks

Q.1 Give *two* disadvantages of the garden when the owner first came to it.   2
Q.2 Explain what is meant by
    (a) voluntary labour camp (1. 9)
    (b) restored Eden (1.18)
    (c) guerillas (1. 23)   6
Q.3 Why did the owner plant slow-growing beech for his hedge?   2
Q.4 Quote a single word later in the passage which suggests a deliberate contrast with 'labour camp', and explain the comparison implied by the two terms.   4
Q.5 As briefly as you can, give the meanings of *six* of the following words *as they are used in this passage*. Start each answer on a fresh line: 6

    ill-tended (1. 5)   alacrity (1. 7)   drastic (1. 9)
    ensconced (1. 10)   umbrageous (1. 13)   segregated (1. 14)
    configuration (1. 19)   insidious (1. 22)

total 20

Passage 4

Dating pottery by thermoluminescence

Thermoluminescence is the light emitted when a crystalline substance (often found in pottery) is heated to around 500°C; and this light appears in addition to the incandescence that is normally produced at so high a temperature. The light is caused by a release of energy stored in the crystalline material as a result of many years' exposure to nuclear radia-   5 tion; this radiation goes on all the time in the earth. Consequently minerals such as quartz, calcite and the various feldspars emit vast quantities of thermoluminescence when heated—and this is a direct result of the long dosage of radiation they have received in the ground.

The light however is very faint—too faint to be seen, except in some   10 very ancient limestones. It is sometimes possible to see the thermo- luminescence from such limestones by heating some pieces in a frying-pan in a dark room. But pottery cannot be older than about ten thousand years, compared with the millions of years since the limestone was deposited, and so the light emitted when a sherd is heated is correspond- 15 ingly less.

The minerals we mentioned above were frequently added to the potter's material of raw clay to give his pot a 'breathing' capacity and strength to face the rigours of firing in a kiln. This firing, usually to temperatures between 700°C and 1100°C, would drive out any geological 20 thermoluminescence in the mixture. Thus when the finished pottery began its life, perhaps as a cooking vessel or storage unit, it would contain no stored-up thermoluminescent energy whatsoever. Such wares would probably survive only a decade, at most, before damage and disposal. The greater part of its archaeological life-time will have been spent not 25 in being used but lying buried in the soil.

Here it would be subject to a very long period indeed of radiation. The natural radioactivity in the pottery fragments ('sherds') and in the material in which they are buried supplies a fresh and steady source of radiation dose year after year right up to the present day. Gradually a 30 store of thermoluminescent energy is built up; and this we can measure in the laboratory by means of very sensitive electronic devices. The amount measured is now directly related to the total radiation the ceramic material has received since a 'time zero' was set by the original firing.

Read the passage above carefully; and then answer these questions *in your own words*. (Our answers are on pp. 187–188.)

                                                                                    marks
Q.1 Think of single words or short expressions that could be used to   7
    replace these words in their context above:

emitted	(1. 1)	incandescence	(1. 3)
deposited	(1. 15)	rigours	(1. 19)
survive	(1. 24)	decade	(1. 24)
related	(1. 33)		

Q.2 Explain why the light is 'correspondingly' less (1. 15).   4
Q.3 '. . . its archaeological life-time' (1. 25). What *other* life-time would the pot
    have had?   4
Q.4 What does the 'original firing' (1. 34) do to set the time scale at nought?   5
Q.5 How is thermoluminescence caused?   10
Q.6 What use is thermoluminescence to the historian or archaeologist?   10
                                                                         ——
                                                            total 40

Passage 5

The new castle

The seat of Colonel Hector Campbell of Mugg was known locally as 'the New Castle' . . . The exterior was German in character . . . of moderate size but designed to withstand assault from all but the most modern weapons. The interior was pitch-pine throughout and owed its decoration more to the taxidermist than to the sculptor or painter.   5

Before Guy and Tommy had left their car, the double doors of the New Castle were thrown open. A large young butler, kilted and heavily bearded, seemed to speak some words of welcome but they were lost in a gale of music. A piper stood beside him, more ornately clothed, older and shorter; a square man, red bearded. If it had come to a fight between them   10
the money would have been on the piper. He was in fact the butler's father. The four of them marched forward and upward to the great hall.

A candelabrum, consisting of concentric and diminishing circles of tarnished brass, hung from the rafters. A dozen or so of the numberless cluster of electric bulbs were alight, disclosing the dim presence of a large   15
circular dining table. Round the chimney-piece whose armorial decorations were obscured by smoke, the baronial severity of the rest of the furniture was mitigated by a group of chairs clothed in stained and faded chintz. Everywhere else were granite, pitch-pine, tartan and objects of furniture constructed of antlers. Six dogs, ranging in size from a couple   20
of deerhounds to an almost hairless pomeranian, gave tongue in inverse proportion to their size. Above all from the depths of the smoke cloud a voice roared.

'Silence, you infernal brutes. Down, Hercules. Back, Jason. Silence, Sir.'   25

There were shadowy, violent actions and sounds of whacking, kicking, snarling and whining. Then the piper had it all to himself again. It was intensely cold in the hall and Guy's eyes wept afresh in the peat fumes. Presently the piper, too, was hushed and in the stunning silence an aged lady and gentleman emerged through the smoke. Colonel Campbell   30
was much bedizened with horn and cairngorms.* He wore a velvet doublet above his kilt, stiff collar and a black bow tie. Mrs. Campbell wore nothing memorable.

The dogs fanned out beside them and advanced at the same slow pace, silent but menacing. His probable destiny seemed manifest to Guy, to be   35
blinded by smoke among the armchairs, to be frozen to death in the wider spaces, or to be devoured by the dogs where he stood. Tommy, the perfect soldier, appreciated the situation and acted promptly. He advanced on the nearest deerhound, grasped its muzzle and proceeded to rotate its head in a manner which the animal appeared to find reassuring.   40
The great tail began to wave in the fumes.

Evelyn Waugh, from *Sword of Honour,* reprinted by permission of A. D. Peters & Co. Ltd.
* *cairngorms*—semi-precious stones [Ed.]

Now answer the following questions. (Our answers are on p. 188.)

marks

Q.1 Provide a suitable title for this passage.   2
Q.2 Explain why the butler *'seemed* to speak some words of welcome' (1. 8)?   3
Q.3 Give two details which suggest that the interior of the great hall was not well looked after.   4
Q.4 Which three factors contributed most to Guy's discomfort?   6
Q.5 Why do you think the author says 'Mrs Campbell wore nothing memorable' (1.32)?   4

Q.6 Which dogs made the most noise? Quote the evidence for your answer.   4

Q.7 Describe in your own words the action Tommy takes with one of the dogs. What effect does it have?   5

Q.8 Write a description of 'the New Castle', using your own words as far as possible. It may help you to look up in your dictionary the meanings of: 12

pitch-pine   taxidermist   candelabrum   concentric
tarnished   armorial   mitigated

     —

total 40

Passage 6

Engineering training

We have included the following passage as a reminder that comprehension is a skill required in many different occupations. The engineering apprentice who fails to grasp its meaning could be at a serious disadvantage.

The procedure is that at the end of the first year course of training a choice is made of one or more Stage II modules on the combined basis of the firm's need and the trainee's aptitude. Training in the chosen module will proceed in accordance with the appropriate training specification and to the standards prescribed by the skill specification. During the training the work carried out will normally consist of items of production which have been carefully selected by the training staff in consultation with the production departments to give the range of training prescribed. Close attention must be given to such matters as accuracy, finish, time and safe working practice, and periodic testing in accordance with the prescribed standards must be carried out.

Module training may take place on or off the job but in all cases it will be a requirement for recognition of approved training that the trainee is responsible to a supervisor who has been trained in the techniques of instruction manuals and testing procedures. The supervisor will be required to certify the entries of training in the trainee's log book and record the assessments carried out.

From *Training for Engineering Craftsmen, The Module System,* reprinted by permission of the Engineering Industry Training Board.

     marks

Q.1 What special term in this passage needs to be understood before the meaning of the passage as a whole can be fully grasped?   2

Q.2 What will a second year trainee's work consist of?   5

Q.3 When the training staff are choosing what work trainees should do, what do they have to keep in mind?   4

Q.4 Mention two things that a trainee will be expected to pay particular attention to during his second year?   2

Q.5 What is compulsory before a trainee's work in his second year can be officially recognised?   3

Q.6 In about 80 words describe what is required of a second year trainee.   14

     —

total 30

(Our answers are on p 189.)

Passage 7

The football game

[This extract is from *Kes*. Billy Caspar is the boy who keeps and trains a kestrel. He enjoys little of his school life and certainly not football, for which he has none of the right kit and no sympathy from the teacher.]

Mr Sugden used the lengths of bandage to secure his stockings just below the knees, then he folded his tracksuit neatly on the ground, looked down at himself, and walked on to the pitch carrying the ball like a plum pudding on the tray of his hand. Tibbut, standing on the centre circle, with his hands down his shorts, winked at his left winger and waited for Mr Sugden to approach.

Sugden (teacher): 'Who are we playing, Tibbut?'

'Er . . . we'll be Liverpool, Sir.'

'You can't be Liverpool.'

'Why not, Sir?'

'I've told you once, they're too close to Manchester United's colours aren't they?'

Tibbut massaged his brow with his fingertips, and under this guise of thinking, glanced round at his team.

'We'll be Spurs then, Sir. There'll be no clash of colours then.'

'. . . And it's Manchester United v. Spurs in this vital fifth-round cup-tie.'

Mr Sugden (referee) sucked his whistle and stared at his watch, waiting for the second finger to twitch back up to twelve. 5 4 3 2. He dropped his wrist and blew. Anderson received the ball from him, sidestepped a tackle from Tibbut then cut it diagonally between two opponents into a space to his left. Sugden (player) running into this space, raised his left foot to trap it, but the ball rolled under his studs. He veered left, caught it, and started to cudgel it upfield in a travesty of a dribble, sending it too far ahead each time he touched it, so that by the time he had progressed twenty yards, he had crash-tackled it back from three Spurs defenders. His left winger, unmarked and lonely out on the touchline, called for the ball. Sugden heard him, looked at him, then kicked the ball hard along the ground towards him. But even though the wingman started to spring as soon as he read its line, it still shot out of play a good ten yards in front of him. He slithered to a stop and whipped round.

'Hey up, Sir! What do you think I am?'

'You should have been moving, lad. You'd have caught it then.'

'What do you think I wa' doin', standing still?'

'It was a perfectly good ball!'

'Ar, for a whippet perhaps!'

'Don't argue with me, lad! And get that ball fetched!'

Back in the goal, Billy . . . touched the ball for the first time. Tibbut, dribbling in fast, pushed the ball between Mr Sugden's legs, ran round him and delivered the ball out to his right winger, who took it in his stride, beat his full back and centred for Tibbut, who had continued his run, to outjump Mr Sugden and head the ball firmly into the top right hand corner of the goal. Billy watched it fly in, way up on his left, then he turned round and picked it up from under the netting.

'Come on Caspar! Make an effort, lad!'
'I couldn't save that, Sir.'
'You could have tried.'
'What for, Sir, when I knew I couldn't save it?'
'We're playing this game to win you know, lad.'
'I know, Sir.'
'Well, try then!'

He held his hands out to receive the ball. Billy obliged, but as it left his hand the wet leather skidded off his skin and it dropped short in the mud, between them. He ran out to retrieve it, but Sugden had already started towards it, and when Billy saw the stare of his eyes and the set of his jaw as he ran at the ball, he stopped and dropped down, and the ball missed him and went over him, back into the net. He knelt up, his left arm, left side and left leg striped with mud.
'What wa' that for, Sir?'
'Slack work, lad. Slack work.'

He retrieved the ball himself, and carried it quickly back to the centre for the restart. Billy stood up, a mud pack stuck to each knee. He pulled his shirt sleeve round and started to furrow the mud with his finger nails.
'Look at this lot. I've to keep this shirt on an' all after.'

The right back was drawn by this lament, but was immediately distracted by a chorus of warning shouts, and when he turned round he saw the ball running loose in his direction. He ran at it head down, and toed it far up field, showing no interest in its flight or destination, but turning to commiserate with Billy almost as soon as it had left his boot. It soared over the halfway line and Sugden started to chase. It bounced, once, twice, then rolled out towards the touchline. He must catch it, and the rest of his forward line moved up in anticipation of the centre. But the ball, decelerating rapidly as though intended to be caught, still crossed the line before he could reach it. His disappointed forwards muttered amongst themselves as they trooped back out of the penalty area.
'He should have caught that, easy.'
'He's like a chuffing carthorse.'
'Look at him, he's knackered.'
'Hopeless tha means.'
Tibbut picked the ball up for the throw in.
'Hard luck, Sir.'

Sugden, hands on hips, chest heaving, had his right back in focus a good thirty seconds before he had sufficient control over his respiration to remonstrate with him.
'Come on, lad! Find a man with this ball! Don't just kick it anywhere!'

The right back, his back turned, continued his conversation with Billy.
'SPARROW'
'What, Sir?'
'I'm talking to you, lad!'
'Yes, Sir.'

'Well pay attention then and get a grip of your game. We're losing lad.'
'Yes, Sir.'

[Manchester United equalised soon after when the referee awarded them a penalty. Sugden scored.]

Barry Hines, from *A Kestrel for a Knave,* reprinted by permission of Michael Joseph Ltd.

When you have read the extract carefully, look at it again to find answers to these questions.

Q.1 What parts does Mr Sugden play and how good do you think he is at each of them?

Q.2 How do the boys respond to Mr Sugden?

Answer both these questions from information in the extract. (Our answers are on pp. 189–190.)

Passage 8

The zoo

Everything is happening all at once, like a film projector gone crazy. There are not only all the different animals; the architecture is just as much of a bizarre jumble. Neo-Georgian pavilions, utilitarian galleries, cosy kiosks, the colossal mock rocks of the Mappin Terraces, and the witty *jeu d'esprit** of the Penguin Pool. All sorts of new shapes are now going up, equally diverse, from Sir Hugh Casson's concrete elephant house to Lord Snowdon's aviary, which turns out to be far more robust than it looked in the model. It would be a pity if the Zoo ever became too uniform, because it makes such a good match for nature's craziness. The whole thing could float off down the Thames as Noah's Ark and the Tower of Babel combined. Some of the oddest effects occur from outside the Zoo, in Regent's Park itself. By day, a mountain goat high up on the terraces where you least expect it. At night, a terrifying set of squeals and snuffles to liven up a walk home to Swiss Cottage.

It may be a silly thing to say, but the Zoo is one of the most under-used amenities in London. It seems to be regarded as a place to bring the kids and not much more. In fact it would be a good place to get to know someone, to talk over all but the most hard-headed business, or simply to drown one's indignation at human imbecility in the antics of the rest of Nature's jokers. After all, it costs no more than the price of a scotch and soda, which is a more usual remedy. And if the baboons and the sea-lions don't work, you can always have the scotch and soda anyway, in the Zoo's bar. London offers unlimited opportunities for pleasure, but so many of them drive you slap up against man's pettiness—a fashionable play, for example, or a meal in the King's Road. It is good to have a place which takes the mickey out of architecture, the animal world, and its human visitors simultaneously.

Ian Nairn, from *Nairn's London,* p. 103, copyright © Ian Nairn, 1966, reprinted by permission of Penguin Books Ltd.

* *jeu d'esprit* — joke. [Ed.]

(Answers to the following three questions are on pp. 190–191.)

marks

Q.1 What does the author like about the Zoo? Answer in about 50 words.   14

Q.2 Give the meaning of the following words from the first paragraph as   8
they are used in the passage:

      utilitarian   robust

      diverse   uniform

Q.3 In your own words, explain the three examples given by the author in   18
paragraph 2 of using the Zoo other than 'as a place to bring the kids'.

                                                    total 40

Passage 9

Moorings

In a salt ring of moonlight
The dinghy nods at nothing.
It paws the bright water
And scatters its own shadow
In a false net of light.

A ruined chain lies reptile,
Tied to the ground by grasses.
Two oars, wet with sweet water
Filched from the air, are slanted
From a wrecked lobster creel.

The cork that can't be travels —
Nose of a dog otter.
It's piped at, screamed at, sworn at
By elegant oyster catcher
On furious red legs.

With a sort of idle swaying
The tide breathes in. Harsh seaweed
Uncrackles to its kissing;
The skin of the water glistens;
Rich fat swims on the brine.

And all night in his stable
The dinghy paws bright water,
Restless steeplechaser
Longing to clear the hurdles
That ring the point of Stoer.

Norman MacCaig, from *A Round of Applause*, copyright © Norman MacCaig, 1962, reprinted by
permission of Chatto and Windus Ltd.

Now answer these questions. Our answers are on pp. 191-192.

marks

1 Explain the comparisons suggested by *two* of the following: 4
reptile (line 6)   *Filched* (line 9)   *breathes in* (line 17)

2 What is the effect of the third or middle stanza on the poem as a whole?   6

3 Choose two descriptive words or phrases from different parts of the poem   2
that you find particularly effective, and explain why.

4 There is one central image or comparison in the poem. Say what it is, and   8
show how it is sustained.   —

total 20

2.9   CHECK-LIST OF COMPREHENSION PASSAGES

Here is a check-list of the comprehension practice we have provided for you. The
first five passages are discussed quite fully as you go along; the other nine are for
you to practise on. Suggested answers, and some ideas about ways of arriving at
them, are given later in the book (pp. 184-192). See also Self-test units 11-15.

Marking your work

Be severe on yourself! Mark strictly, using the suggested marks for each question.
It is a good idea to time yourself strictly for some of the work, to get an idea of
examination time-limits. If you can't decide whether your answer deserves a good
mark, ask a friend to read it and decide for you.

I *Examples of types of passage, with comments*

A Imitative music   factual
B Something gets to them   fiction
C Statistics—newspaper readers   factual
D Advertisement—'Coolstream'   persuasive
E Heavy traffic   argument

II *Further practice, with comments and answers on pp. 185-192*

1 Television as a source of information   factual/argument
2 Excerpt from *Roots*   drama
3 Natural enemies   factual/descriptive
4 Dating pottery by thermoluminescence   factual/scientific
5 The new castle   fiction
6 Engineering training   factual/technical
7 The football game   fiction
8 The zoo   factual
9 Moorings   poetry

3 Summaries and notes

3.1 HOW TO SUMMARISE

One of the most useful of all skills in the handling of English is the ability to **select**

from a piece of writing just those facts, ideas or opinions—and no others—that we need for a particular purpose. We do this all the time in our listening to spoken English—or, if we are lazy or uninterested, we let others (reporters, newscasters, TV personalities, even our parents or friends) do it for us. Here is an example:

> A boy's father has agreed to take him for his first camping holiday. They have planned to drive to the Brecon Beacons in Wales, then garage the car and hike for a few days, carrying their gear in rucksacks. The evening before the day they had planned to set off the weather seems uncertain. They turn on the radio, and the father says to his son: 'Let me know what they have to say about the weather over the week-end. We don't want to be drowned.'

The son has to listen very closely, first isolating from nation-wide reports and forecasts only the items that might apply to the Brecon area; then deciding which particular forecasts are likely to affect camping conditions. When his father says: 'What did they say?' he must be ready with his **summary.** In his own interest he is probably alert and careful; a missed item may mean a soaking, or at least a very uncomfortable night.

Let's compare this boy's experience with an English examination candidate's, faced with a 'summary' question. A radio or television weatherman may speak between 100 and 150 words a minute, and his weather report may last five minutes—the equivalent of a written passage from 500 to 700 words long. (Many English examinations have passages for summarising of just that length.) You will be faced with a similar task to the boy's, with regard to length and content. Like him, too, you may be asked to select for a particular purpose, or to pick out information on one particular aspect of the topic. Alternatively, you may be asked to summarise the whole passage, either in a set number of your own words, or in about one-third or a quarter of the length of the original.

If someone said to you: 'What's in the paper today?' or 'Did you watch the news? What's been happening?' he would again be asking you to summarise. Your replies are not likely to be very carefully planned; after all, no marks are awarded for **accuracy** and **completeness** in our daily life. Both are expected of the good examination candidate when he is producing written summaries.

Here is an example of a summary question, followed by an explanation of how it can be summarised in about one-third of its original length.

Question

Read the passage below carefully, and then summarise the ways in which wolves resemble human beings. Your answer should be in the form of continuous prose and should not exceed 90 words in length.

Most of the great carnivores of Africa and Asia form family groups, but it is the pack hunters whose social system bears the closest similarity to that of man. It may come as a surprise to those who are acquainted with the promiscuous behaviour of our domesticated canines to learn that in their natural state wolves form permanent male-female pair relationships, and that wolf packs are in fact extended families.

Wolf packs have now been recognised as family or kinship units that hunt co-operatively. They grow up around a pair of adult wolves and their offspring. Adult males pair off with adult females, establishing a permanent or semi-permanent pair-bond, each pair possessing their own 'den' in which, as a nuclear family, they raise their own litter. Since the females have to care for offspring during the 'denning' season, hunting becomes the responsibility of the male at this time, and food sharing develops on a family basis because of a basic dichotomy of role—a basic division of labour—between the paired male and female. At times when the female is unable to join the chase, the male, on his return from a successful hunt, will regurgitate sufficient food for her sustenance. On occasion, adults leave the parental pack to set up their own pack. Having a permanent family-type society, wolves take a great interest in their offspring, extending much care not only to the nourishment and protection but also to the socialisation and education of their young. Wolf fathers share their consorts' interest in the litter and appear to educate the cubs in the techniques of hunting.

Roger Pearson, from *Introduction to Anthropology*, published by Holt, Rinehart and Winston.

Method

Read through fairly fast. Don't stop at difficult words or points not understood.
Re-read more slowly, ticking or underlining points that seem important.
If time allows, jot down the points in note form. This makes it easy to spot repetitions and irrelevant material.
See how many words your jottings amount to.
Write your summary. It will probably need a rough copy then a re-write. The passage is short enough for you to have time for this.

This is how the method worked with us. First the jotted points:

> Male and female wolves stick together.
> Wolf packs are big families—they hunt co-operatively and they are formed round an adult pair, with a den.
> When female has to stay at home in breeding season the pair divide up the necessary work; the male hunts for food while the female looks after the young.
> Sometimes adults leave to start up a pack on their own.
> As well as nourishing and protecting their young, wolves take an interest in educating their young.
> The father teaches the cubs the technique of hunting.

When it came to writing our continuous prose, we made a false start. It was much too long-winded:

> Male and female wolves pair off, often permanently; and round them is formed a large family group, which also forms the pack for hunting purposes.

So we scrapped it and began afresh. Finally we produced this:

> Male and female wolves pair off, like human beings, and start a big family, which hunts as a pack. The pair has a den; and the female shares with the father the responsibility and work of looking after the cubs—he hunts and fetches food home while she looks after the family. (Sometimes members of the family leave and start packs of their own.) Again like human parents, wolves not only feed and protect their young, but also educate them, with the father helping the mother and teaching the cubs how to hunt.

Notes

1 In line 1 of our version we've put in 'like human beings' because the question set asks for this.
2 We have hardly used paragraph 1 at all; the two relevant points, about pairing, and about the pack being a big family, are repeated in the main paragraph.
3 We've left out technical language like 'pair-bond', 'nuclear', 'basic dichotomy', 'socialisation'.
4 Also omitted are the details about providing sustenance.
5 We've left in the piece about wolves setting up on their own because, though it's not in the main stream of argument, it is something which human beings do (see question again).
6 Near the end we have inserted 'Again like human parents' to show that all the time we have kept in mind the resemblances of wolf to man.

We are three words over our ration of 90. Where could we lose three words?

PRACTICE

Now use the same method to summarise the main points of the following passage, which comes from a book for home handymen. There are about 470 words here; aim at 150 in your summary. Allow yourself no longer than 50 minutes. (We have done a summary for you (p. 193) but don't look at it until you have finished your own.)

The domestic water supply

When you turn on a tap, you expect the water (hot or cold) to come out, and it nearly always does. However, it is as well to know something about the things that actually cause this to happen so that you can decide what to do on the millionth occasion when it doesn't.

As a rule, the householder's responsibility for the water arrangements begins at the point where the service pipe from the mains crosses the boundary of his land. There may be a stop-cock in the garden here, but if not there will certainly be a stop-cock or main tap just inside your house.

The usual place is under the kitchen sink, since the cold tap (for drinking water, etc.) here is connected to the rising cold main. When this stop-cock or main tap is turned off, no more water from the main will come into your house. Consequently it is the tap to make for and turn off if there is a burst anywhere. In many houses the cold water (drinking water) tap is taken direct from the incoming rising main, as it is called: this makes it easy to check whether you have found the right stop-cock and whether it is in working order or not. Simply turn on the cold-water tap and then screw down the stop-cock. The flow from the cold-water tap should quickly cease. If it does not, it may be because the stop-cock is defective or it may be (in the older houses) because the cold-water supply to the tap is taken from a storage cistern and not from the rising main. Whatever the reason, you must find out why the water still runs. You must stop the water in order to check it, so look for an external stop-valve that can be closed. If you can't discover one yourself ask the water company to send a man round to explain things.

Next in importance to the inside stop-cock is the 'draw-off' tap. Somewhere in your house is a tap which, if you turn it on after the stop-cock has been closed, will draw off all the water left in the rising cold-water main. This is often the cold-water tap at the kitchen sink. It is important to be able to do this, not only for full protection when the house is unoccupied in the winter, but also to enable repairs to be made.

The common water supply arrangements are usually as follows: there is a mains cold supply to the kitchen for cooking and drinking purposes, and to a storage tank or cistern in the loft. The storage tank supplies the cistern in the w.c. and also provides the cold water for the hot-water system, if any. The cold-water supply to bath and wash-basin is almost invariably taken from the storage tank and not direct from the main.

J. Wheeler, from *The Awful Handyman's Book*, reprinted by permission of Wolfe Publishing Ltd.

TYPES OF WRITING FOR SUMMARY

The two passages we have just looked at are factual rather than imaginative. The skill of summarising as tested in English examinations is usually concerned with fact or opinion, rather than with stories or imaginative prose. This makes sense: fictional and imaginative writing are meant for enjoyment, and this is not likely to be increased if we are expected to approach them in the closely analytical way we need for summarising. It is also true that factual summaries are easier to assess in examinations. (To some extent, however, you *are* expected to apply the art of summarising to stories, when writing book reviews. See p. 111.)

3.2 UNDERSTANDING THE QUESTION

The next passage and question show the close link between summary and comprehension and the importance of understanding the question.

(Between 1964 and 1967 Dr Colin Turnbull, an anthropologist, lived with an African tribe called the Ik. They had been forced to live in one corner of the area they formerly hunted in, and successive droughts had brought famine and the virtual destruction of their society. In his book *The Mountain People* Dr Turnbull described his experiences, which he believes are relevant to certain trends in our own society. This is from a chapter with the title 'Self and Survival'.)

Question

Using information given in the passage, explain in 80 to 100 words what Dr Turnbull means when he says that 'the family is not such a fundamental unit as we usually suppose.'

The Ik seem to tell us that the family is not such a fundamental unit as we usually suppose, that it is not an essential prerequisite for social life except in the biological context. The circumstances that have brought this about . . . are admittedly extreme, but they are circumstances into which we could all conceivably fall, and the potential for what we might care to call the inhumanity that we see in the Ik is within us all . . .

Under the circumstances that surround the Ik, the larger a family grows, the less security it can offer. The ideal family, economically speaking, is a man and his wife and no children. Children are useless appendages, like old parents. Anyone who cannot take care of himself is a burden and a hazard to the survival of others. I found it difficult to see why they bother having children, the likelihood of their being able and willing to contribute to the family as a whole being as small as it is. There is always the chance of a good year in the fields during which the family proper—that is to say, parents with children—finds mutual advantage in cooperation, which is the only reason conceivable to the Ik. The family, otherwise, is for the insane, for it spells death, not life . . .

So we should not be surprised when the mother throws her child out at three years old. I imagine the child must be rather relieved to be thrown out, for in the process of being cared for he or she is carried about in a hide sling wherever the mother goes, and since the mother is not strong herself this is done grudgingly. Whenever the mother finds a spot in which to gather (i.e. berries, roots etc.), or if she is at a water-hole or in her fields, she loosens the sling and lets the baby to the ground none too slowly, and of course laughs if it is hurt. Then she goes about her business, leaving the child there, almost hoping that some predator will come along and carry it off. This happened once while I was there—once that I know of, anyway— and the mother was delighted. She was rid of the child and no longer had to carry it about and feed it, and still further this meant that a leopard was in the vicinity and would be sleeping the child off and thus be an easy kill. The men set off and found the leopard, which had consumed all of the child except part of the skull; they killed the leopard and cooked it and ate it, child and all. That is Icien economy, and it makes sense in its own way. It does not, however, endear children to their parents or parents to their children.

Colin Turnbull, from *The Mountain People*, published by Jonathan Cape Ltd.

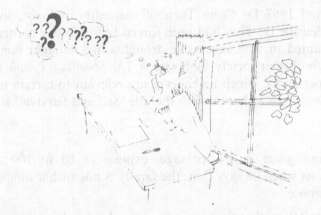

Your summary here is to be compressed into less than a quarter of the original passage. The question directs your attention to the opening remarks. Before you start your summary you need to be sure you understand what is being asked. This is where we see that **summary** and **comprehension** are linked skills: you cannot successfully summarise a passage you don't understand.

The expression likely to cause difficulty here is 'a fundamental unit'. Look a little further and the idea is re-stated different —'an essential prerequisite for social life'. It is obvious that the words 'fundamental' and 'essential' express closely similar ideas. The word 'prerequisite' simply means 'requirement' or 'necessity', so we might re-write the question thus:

Summarise any facts or information in the passage showing that family bonds are not necessary for the survival of a society.

Once we have understood the question we can tackle the passage more purposefully. Here is our first jotted-down list of points:

1 Children cannot help with survival, because they don't support themselves.
2 Similarly, old parents are a burden.
3 Icien mothers abandon children at the age of 3.
4 Icien mothers are careless with younger children, even leaving them where predators can carry them off.
5 It is normal for mothers to laugh when their children are hurt.
6 The Ik are prepared to hunt, kill and eat leopards that have just eaten their own children, i.e. they survive by neglecting parental bonds.

It is clear that point 6 is the most relevant one for us. For this reason we can put it first in our summary, which might begin:

When a hunting leopard carried off an Icien baby its mother was pleased to be freed from looking after it. The tribe was able to track and kill the sated

A strong family bond between happy mother and child

leopard, which meant food for them. Family bonds were ignored in the interest of survival. (45 words)

We used the unfamiliar word 'sated' (i.e. whose hunger had been satisfied, full of food) to save words. Even so this has already used almost half the permitted number of words. So we look more carefully at the rest to see what is most relevant. Point 5 can be scrapped; it doesn't relate to survival. The other points can be paired, 1 and 2 together, then 3 and 4, each pair containing a single idea. We continue our summary:

Relatives unable to support themselves, like children and old parents, are not cared for. Mothers look after their children only to the age of 3, and are careless and grudging even about that. (33 words)

We have used 78 words, so still have some in hand. If we now put our two parts together it is evident that the sentence starting 'Mothers...' logically follows our opening statement. So we re-arrange and expand a little. Here is our final version.

When a hunting leopard carried off an Icien baby while its mother was working, she was pleased to be freed from looking after it. The tribe was able to track and kill the sated leopard, which they then cooked and ate in spite of the nature of its last meal. Family bonds were ignored in the interest of survival. Mothers accept responsibility for their babies unwillingly, and treat them carelessly. At three the children must fend for themselves. In the interests of survival, ties to family members unable to support themselves, i.e. old parents and young children, are ignored. (99 words)

Notice that by using more of the permitted number of words we have been able to add useful details—the mother working when her baby was carried off, the gruesome nature of the leopard's meal.

PRACTICE

These three linked news items appeared in *The Times* during January 1978. Read them carefully, then, using the method we have just demonstrated, answer this question (see p. 193 for notes and suggestions):

In about 200 words explain the need to control pollution in the Mediterranean, and the difficulties in agreeing what measures should be taken.

I

The first concerted international effort to clean up the Mediterranean will almost certainly be agreed on during the week-long conference of 18 countries which begins in Monte Carlo in the morning.

Two years of preparatory work has already been done by delegates from these countries, all with a Mediterranean coastline. A great deal of scientific research has been undertaken and coordinated by the United Nations Environmental Programme (Unep).

Nations long in dispute, such as Morocco and Algeria, Turkey and Greece and Israel and Lebanon, will be sitting down to sign the agreement. If one or two are not represented it will be merely for domestic reasons. The chances are that they will certainly sign before long.

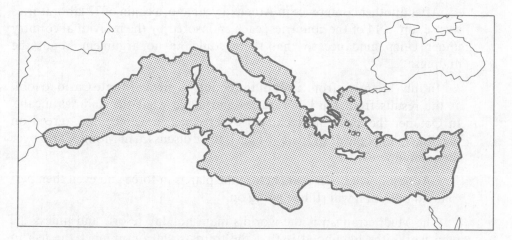

Something like 120 cities pump their sewage into the Mediterranean and 90 per cent of it is untreated. Factories far inland producing every possible combination of poisonous matter simply tip their waste into the nearest river and let it carry the pollution out to sea. For years ships have cleaned their crude oil tanks out at sea.

The Mediterranean has only a minute tide so that it takes something like a century for the Atlantic to get in through the Pillars of Hercules and completely change the water. The main rivers feeding the sea, like the Rhone, Po and Nile, are so polluted that their waters merely add to the problem.

Scientists have calculated that one swimmer in seven can be sure to pick up a virus infection. In 1973 a cholera outbreak in the Bay of Naples killed 22 people. The level of mercury in fish is so high that Adriatic fishermen have been found to have retained enough of it in their bodies to kill a cat. Researchers say that eating 5lb. of Mediterranean-caught fish a week is a sure way to commit suicide—although it will take about 20 years.

Stringent controls about pollution by oil spillage and dumping from tankers and aircraft were quickly agreed at a conference in Barcelona. A monitoring headquarters on the Maltese island of Manoel has been functioning since the end of 1976.

Land-based pollution is the main problem now. The countries involved agreed that something had to be done to stop the dumping of heavy metals, chemicals and pesticides and that sewage treatment plants were essential everywhere.

They agreed on a 'black list' of substances such as mercury and radio-active waste that should never be put into the sea and a 'grey list' of chemicals such as arsenic and cyanide which could be dumped only under special licence.

But the cost of implementing this Mediterranean Action Plan was pro-hibitive. An estimated £2,800m was needed, equivalent to around £4 a head for every citizen of every country involved.

Blaming the richer countries for causing most of the pollution, the poorer nations felt they should contribute less. The negotiations developed into something of a north-south dialogue.

After another conference in Athens a year ago, a chain of 72 laboratories was set up in 14 of the countries, each sponsored by the individual country under Unep guidance so that there could be no argument about the findings.

In July, scientists from most of the countries met in Monte Carlo to look at the results from the laboratories and agree what the findings meant. In October the legal and technical experts met in Venice and agreed on the principles of the draft treaty which is to be discussed in Monte Carlo over the coming week.

At best it will be 20 years before the plan is in force and even then permitted pollution will still be going on.

The Mediterranean is the world's main holiday resort, and unless the plan works the likelihood is that the tourists will outnumber the fish in five years' time. Small wonder, therefore, that traditional rival countries are prepared to bury their differences in facing this common danger to their livelihoods.

Ian Murray, 'Rivals on land bury differences to bale out Mediterranean', reproduced from *The Times* by permission.

II

Fish are becoming smaller in the Mediterranean, Commander Jacques Cousteau, the under-water explorer, told the 17-nation conference on the sea's pollution during its session in Monaco today.

He outlined the findings of a survey he carried out in 10 areas of the sea between last July and early December.

These showed that the polluted area around the coast had started to extend into the centre, he said, and chemical pollution was 'enormously' high around the mouth of the Rhône. His complete report would not be ready until the end of this year or the beginning of next.

Ian Murray, 'Explorer finds fish shrinking in Mediterranean', reproduced from *The Times* by permission.

III

The task of reaching an agreement on stopping pollution in the Mediterranean has proved too great for the inter-governmental conference of 17 of the 18 countries with a coastline on the sea.

The conference ended in Monaco yesterday with nothing signed despite the optimism in which the delegates had arrived there the previous weekend. The stumbling block proved to be reaching agreement on a protocol

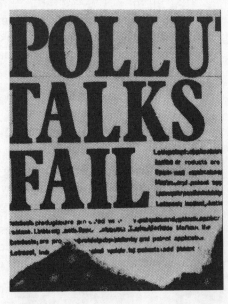

covering all forms of pollution which originate on land. Behind the difficulties of definition lay the immense problems of finance, for it will cost something in the region of £2,500m to clean up the Mediterranean.

With the need to raise this sort of money paramount in their minds, the poorer countries were very keen to see procedures laid down which would more clearly identify the sources of pollution. For this reason the conference has agreed to split up the different causes for separate study.

The draft proposals drawn up by experts from the different countries under the auspices of the United Nations Environment Programme meeting in Venice last October have been found to be too ambitious. Instead of one agreement to cover all land-originated pollution there will probably have to be several and each one will take time.

It is, nevertheless, hoped that the first one can be agreed on the most important cause of pollution—industrial waste or sewage being pumped straight into the sea or into rivers emptying into the sea. Agreement on that may be ready before the end of the year.

Scientific study on pollution poured into the atmosphere from the chimneys of industry will probably delay an agreement which will be more difficult and complicated to reach. Research into pollution that reaches the sea by subterranean water courses or sea pumping platforms is also likely to take time.

The difficulties go further than finding the necessary money. With so many different countries involved, each with its own legal system and industrial infrastructure, the problem of finding an agreement which is common to all is immense.

Nevertheless the good will is there, as is shown by the fact that the delegates were able to discuss the matter together at all, even though in several cases their countries have very poor relations on most other matters.

Ian Murray, 'Mediterranean countries unable to reach agreement on how pollution should be curbed', reproduced from *The Times* by permission.

3.3   MAKING NOTES

You will have noticed that making notes is often a good first step towards summarising a piece of continuous English. Note-making and summary are closely linked skills, which is why English examinations often set out to test your ability to provide a set of notes on a passage. Sometimes they will be related to the whole passage, sometimes to one particular part or aspect of the subject.

Notes need few words but plenty of thought. Remember Bernard Shaw's apology to a correspondent for sending such a long letter: 'I didn't have time to write a shorter one.' In note-making time for thought is needed to

– grasp the main points of an argument or a story;

– sort out the points that matter from those that don't;

– decide the best way of setting out the notes.

Really good note-making, like other skills, needs a lot of practice; but from the word 'go' you can make notes that look good.

It should be possible to read notes *at a glance*. Page layout is therefore worth thinking about carefully.

DON'T be *miserly* over space. Cramped, crowded writing, with no room for the eye to rest, makes for difficult reading.

Here are some more points to keep in mind:

1 Give each new point a fresh line (as we are doing here).

2 Number the points. If any of them includes subsidiary points number or letter these in turn, using a different style of number or letter.

       Suggested styles
       I II III IV V etc.
       i ii iii iv v
       1 2 3 4 5
       A B C D E
       a b c d e

Keep the series separate by placing them underneath each other, like this:

    1 ....
    2 (a) ....
       (b) ....
       (c) (i)...................................
          (ii)...............................
    3 (a) ....
       (b) (i)...............................

3 You are not writing continuous prose. Leave out any words you can, as long as the meaning is still clear to you (even after you have forgotten the original).

4 Use shortened forms of words wherever you can, and use initials for names, titles, etc.

5 Use numbers (nos.)—8 not 'eight', 64 not 'sixty-four'.

6 Emphasise by <u>underlining</u> or using CAPITAL LETTERS.

A piece of writing like the following could well appear in your English Language paper. We shall use it to show you how to prepare a set of notes.

Most gardeners, faced by the abundance of weeds that take root in any patch of newly turned soil that has been allowed to lie fallow for a few weeks, have asked themselves where on earth weeds come from. The answer, of course, is that each has grown from a seed that could have been deposited in the soil in one of an astonishing variety of ways.

The biggest culprit when it comes to spreading weeds is the bird. Whether it is the humble sparrow or the exotic waxwing, almost every bird eats seeds in large quantities. Some of these seeds pass right through the bird's body; those which fall on suitable ground germinate readily.

Secondly we must blame the wind. Apart from seeds adapted for wind-borne travel, like the familiar dandelion 'parachute', a lot of seeds are tiny enough to blow about on their own. The minute, soot-like spores of ferns are an extreme example. Water, too, must take its share of the responsibility —and not just the sea water which deposits coconut shells around the fringes of tropical islands. Streams, rivers, and the tiny rivulets which flow everywhere after heavy rain, all carry seed and deposit it on their banks or where they dry up.

Wild animals pick up seeds on their feet and transport them this way. Some seeds are covered with spines which adhere to animal fur and wool and are later rubbed off. Smaller animals (the squirrel is one) collect edible seeds such as acorns and stockpile them for winter foodstuff, or carry them back to an underground lair. If the animal is killed in the meantime, the seeds may eventually sprout. Certain insects, including ants, frequently carry seeds about.

As if all this were not enough, many plants have their own unusual ways of spreading seed. Quite a number do it by exploding their seed capsules violently, scattering their contents far and wide. Others, such as sycamore, fit wings to their seed so that it flutters well away from its source.

This is a gift to the note-maker. It sets out a *problem*, asks a *question* and provides a detailed *answer*. So the main points are easy to pick out. (We leave out detailed examples; they would only confuse the notes.)

Problem: weeds

Question: where from?

Answer: 1 birds (a) feet
         (b) undigested ss. in droppings germin.
       2 wind (a) spec. evolved (e.g. dandel.)
         (b) v. small ss.
       3 water—sea, rivers & streams (esp. after rain)
       4 wild anim.—feet, fur, hoarding (e.g. squirr.)
       5 insects (e.g. ants)
       6 plants self-spr.—e.g. explod., winged ss.

You will notice that we have reduced words, particularly repeated words, as much as we can, to save space and time. The whole passage is about seeds, so s. (plural ss.) should be enough to remind us of the word. v. = very; spec. = specially; esp. = especially; squirr. = squirrels; spr. = spreading; explod = exploding.

Test yourself!

It is easy to test your own note-making skill. Prepare notes on a passage (any of the ones here or in the comprehension unit; or choose a topic that interests you and make notes from an encyclopaedia). Put them aside for a day or two. Then, without referring to the source, try expanding your notes into a piece of continuous writing. Check your result with the original, or ask a friend to check it. If you have forgotten important points in your re-write, or got the wrong idea, or muddled the argument, your notes were not clear enough. Decide what went wrong, and try again.

You may get practice in making notes in other subjects you are studying. History, Geography and English Literature *always* involve finding some ways of condensing a mass of material and so do many other school subjects when you are preparing them for examinations.

Hint If the piece you are making notes on has key words or names that are unfamiliar, make a spelling list of them as part of your set of notes.

It is worth remembering that making notes or a summary is a useful skill not only for examinations. If you want information about a hobby, a holiday place, a do-it-yourself activity, you can find plenty of books or helpful advice. But not all that you hear may be relevant to your situation so you train your mind to pick out the bits that you need.

Suppose, for instance, that you need factual information about red deer. Here is a method of collecting it from an article, which is not confined solely to that topic. Anything about photography, for example, can be skipped. Have a dictionary handy, possibly for 'indigenous', 'vociferous', 'belligerent'.

Read the article first and then make notes of any factual information.

Finding and photographing the red deer

We have two indigenous species of red deer in Britain. The Red Deer, large and handsome, and the Roe Deer, diminutive and dainty. Of the other species which are to be found in the wild state, Fallow Deer are said to have been introduced from the continent and the rest, Sika, Mountjac and Chinese Water Deer, are escapees from captivity.

The Red Deer is our largest wild mammal and outside of Scotland the largest concentration is to be found, though not easily, on Exmoor. Inspired local guesswork puts the total number of Exmoor deer at between five hundred and one thousand. Exmoor National Park covers some two hundred and sixty-five square miles. Discounting the area around the perimeter of the Park which is also used by the deer, it soon becomes apparent that the chances of stumbling across many of these shy animals by chance are pretty remote. I live a short distance from the edge of Exmoor and for the past ten years or so finding the deer and making a photographic record of their way of life has accounted for much of my spare time.

Male red deer are known as stags, females hinds and youngsters calves. The stag has been described as noble, regal and indeed as a monarch. It may come as a surprise to some to learn that for a part of each and every year a full grown stag is by no means either of these, for sometimes between mid-March and mid-April he must shed the antlers which give him his kingly

Red deer stag

appearance. For a few days after shedding or casting, as it is called locally, he presents a sorry sight.

The process of renewal or growing a new set of antlers is strange indeed. The new growth which commences a matter of days after shedding the old is made under cover of living tissue remarkably velvet like in appearance and at which time the stag is said to be 'in velvet'. During the summer months the new antlers grow rapidly until about mid-August when they are complete. The blood supply to the antlers having dried up, the velvet also dries and commences to peel off, the process being speeded up by the animals themselves thrashing or rubbing their new adornments on whatever bush or sapling takes their fancy. By the end of September most of the Exmoor stags have a new set of antlers entirely free from velvet and are then said to be clean.

At birth both sexes are alike, with big dark eyes and creamy spotted russet red coats—a red deer calf is appealingly attractive. During the male calf's second year the first signs of antler growth appear. It can be very little or might be as much as a foot at which time he becomes known as a pricket. In each successive year as the antlers are shed and renewed, branches or points are added from the main stem or beam until the stag reaches his prime. These additional points are all named. The lower two jut forwards above the brow and not unreasonably are known as the 'brow' points. These are closely followed by the 'bay' points and then some distance further up the beam come the 'tray' points. These six points are known as the animal's 'rights'. Those points above the rights which form in a cluster like the fingers on your hand are merely counted, two, three, four and rarely five or more. Thus a stag can be described as having all his rights and three a' top each side or, in the case of odd numbers, two and three, three and four and so on. This is much more difficult to explain in print than it is to use. Confusingly stags often fail to produce perfect sets of antlers, sometimes lacking one or both bay points and less frequently a tray point. On the other hand it is extremely rare for a mature stag to be without his brow points and to the best of my knowledge my photograph of such an animal is unique as far as Exmoor deer are concerned.

High point of the deer watchers' year is the 'rut' or mating time which occurs during October and November when the stags are in peak condition. Normally silent, retiring and tolerant towards one another, they become vociferous and belligerent. The woods echo to their roaring whilst out on the forest I have heard the clashing of antlers before I've seen the combatants tussling fully a half mile distant. Each stag's aim is to attract as large a group of hinds as possible and thereafter keep all rivals at bay by force if necessary. The rut is possibly the best time of year for watching the deer at close quarters since the stags not only advertise their presence by their roaring but additionally are much pre-occupied by the business in hand. At any other time of year the deers' highly developed senses will defeat all but the most carefully planned and executed approach.

Crawling through rain-soaked heather or peat bog, perhaps lying still for an hour to avoid detection may not be everyone's ideal leisure-time pursuit. I'm often asked why I do it, and one reason must be curiosity but that's not all. I've shown all my four daughters the deer at longish distances and last year I judged my sixteen year old ready to take on a serious stalking 'day out'. Her reaction upon seeing the animals at close quarters for the first time suggests another reason. She remarked 'aren't they beautiful?' They are.

David Doble, 'Finding and Photographing the Red Deer', reprinted by permission of the author.

Notes on the article about the red deer:
1 Largest indigenous wild mammal found mainly on Exmoor

2 Stags, hinds, calves

3 Renewal of stags' antlers:
  (a) shed (cast) March–April
  (b) new growth begins almost immediately
  (c) 'in velvet'
  (d) complete by mid-Aug
  (e) removal of velvet

4 Growth of antlers in male calves:
  (a) first signs in 2nd year – up to 12″ – calf = pricket
  (b) each year, after shedding, branches (points) added to main stem
  (c) points all named:
    (i) brow
    (ii) bay   } rights
    (iii) tray

(d) points above rights in a cluster

(e) antlers often imperfect when fully grown

5 Mating

(a) occurs Oct–Nov

(b) stags in peak condition

(c) stags normally quiet now noisy and aggressive

(d) stag aims to attract and keep large group of hinds – fights off other stags

(e) n.b. best time for deer-watching

It is now obvious that most of the information in this article is about antlers. If you want to know about hinds and calves you will have to look elsewhere.

The notes follow the article with one exception: In Note 1, 'Largest . . . wild mammal' comes from paragraph 2 and has been combined with just the one adjective 'indigenous' from paragraph 1. There is also one omission: at the beginning of paragraph 5 is a description of the red deer calf, but this was omitted in order not to interrupt the information about antlers. Where could it best be included?

3.4 FURTHER PRACTICE

For further practice in extracting bits of information for a particular purpose, read again the piece on the household water supply (p. 80). Imagine either (a) that you have to explain to someone how to turn the water off because you are going away for Christmas, or (b) that you have to explain to plumbing apprentices: rising main, stop-cock and storage tank. Make notes accordingly. (See also Self-test units 16–20.)

Six more passages

Six more passages follow, on a variety of topics. In most cases we have provided an answer, or suggestions for doing one, later in the book (pp. 193–197). It is better to do your own version before referring to ours. *Always time your work,* and try to keep within the time-limits suggested.

Passage 1

Renaissance Italian frescoes

This passage is from an essay describing the recently discovered method of removing frescoes (i.e. wall-paintings) intact, without destroying either the painting or the plaster surface.

> Let us now describe the stages by which frescoes were executed. Since artists in the fourteenth and fifteenth centuries did not feel humiliated by the task of preparing personally every detail of their work, they themselves spread on the wall the *arriccio,* a rough layer of coarse plaster whose surface was uneven so that the upper layer of plaster (or *intonaco*) could adhere to it. It was on this second layer that the painting was executed. A fine cord, soaked in red paint, fastened at each end and pulled taut, was pressed or 'beaten' against the wall, so that it left a mark on the *arriccio.* This established the centre of the space to be painted. When the space was large, the cord was used more than once to make a number of vertical and horizontal divisions in it. The artist then drew in charcoal, directly on to the *arriccio,* the design of the painting he was to make, correcting it if necessary until he was completely

satisfied. With a small pointed brush dipped in a thin solution of ochre which left only a light imprint, he went over the charcoal drawing, which was then erased with a bunch of feathers. The faint ochre was then retraced and reinforced with *sinopia* red, and when this was done the preparatory drawing for the painting was complete. These large mural drawings (which are now called *sinopie* after the special red earth in which they were carried out) disappeared from sight under the wet *intonaco*, and only come to light again when the paint surface of a fresco is detached. No matter whether they are finished with great precision or show traces of rapid, summary execution—this varies from artist to artist according to the importance each attached to this preparatory work—*sinopie* are always of the greatest interest, not only because they are often very beautiful (they were always executed by the master himself, unlike the fresco where pupils and assistants intervened) but also because they are almost the only drawings that survive from early times, when it was not a common practice to draw on paper or parchment. *Sinopie* could also serve to give the donor who commissioned the work a clear idea of how it would look when it was finished, and there are numerous cases in which one can infer that the patron insisted on changes in the composition. They were not, however, intended to be permanently visible or to be exposed to public view. Consequently the *sinopia* constitutes the purest expression of the artist's personality, one in which he is not compelled to follow the conventions of his period. Because they are a free expression of the painter's consciousness, *sinopie* sometimes seem altogether alien to the time in which they were produced.

When the *sinopia* was complete, the artist began his fresco by spreading the smooth *intonaco* on the *arriccio*. In true fresco technique he applied only as much *intonaco* as he could paint and finish between the morning and evening of one day. Although the *sinopia* disappeared under the new plaster, the essential lines of the hidden drawing were rapidly retraced on the *intonaco*. So the fresco came into being.

Ugo Procacci, from 'The technique of mural paintings and their detachment' in Arts Council catalogue to exhibition of *Frescoes in Florence*, 1969.

Question   *Time: 50 minutes*

Briefly describe the way frescoes were made in Italy in the 14th and 15th centuries (80–100 words), and explain the value to art lovers and art historians of the new technique of removing the painted surface (60–70 words). (Our answers pp. 194–195.)

Alternative question

You have to write a long essay on Italian painting in the Renaissance. Prepare notes from this passage for the section of your essay dealing with frescoes.

Passage 2

Children and stability

What is the normal child like? Does he just eat and grow and smile sweetly? No, that is not what he is like. A normal child, if he has confidence in father and mother, pulls out all the stops. In the course of time he tries out his power to disrupt, to destroy, to frighten, to wear down, to waste, to wangle, and to appropriate. Everything that takes people to the courts (or to the asylums, for that matter) has its normal equivalent in infancy and early childhood, in the relation of the child to his own home. If the home can stand up to all the child can do to disrupt it, he settles down to play; but business first, the tests must be made, and especially so if there is some doubt as to the stability of the parental set-up and the home (by which I mean so much more than house). At first the child needs to be conscious of a framework if he is to feel free, and if he is to be able to play, to draw his own pictures, to be an irresponsible child.

Why should this be? The fact is that the early stages of emotional development are full of potential conflict and disruption. The relation to external reality is not yet firmly rooted; the personality is not yet well integrated—primitive love has a destructive aim, and the small child has not yet learned to tolerate and cope with instincts. He can come to manage these things, and more, if his surroundings are stable and personal. At the start he absolutely needs to live in a circle of love and strength (with consequent tolerance) if he is not to be too fearful of his own thoughts and of his imaginings to make progress in his emotional development.

Now what happens if the home fails a child before he has got the idea of a framework as part of his own nature? The popular idea is that, finding himself 'free' he proceeds to enjoy himself. This is far from the truth. Finding the framework of his life broken, he no longer feels free. He becomes anxious, and if he has hope he proceeds to look for a framework elsewhere than at home. The child whose home fails to give a feeling of security looks outside his home for the four walls; he still has hope, and he looks to grandparents, uncles and aunts, friends of the family, school. He seeks an external stability without which he may go mad. Provided at the proper time, this stability might have grown into the child like the bones of his body, so that gradually in the course of the first months and years of his life he would have passed on to independence from dependence and a need to be managed. Often a child gets from relations and school what he missed in his own actual home.

D. W. Winnicott, from *The Child and the Outside World*, reprinted by permission of Tavistock Publications Ltd.

Question   *Time: 45 minutes*

Read the above passage carefully, and then say why young children need stability. Your answer should not contain more than about 100 words. The passage itself has about 500. (Our answer on p. 195.)

Passage 3

Writing detective stories

What about this business of throwing dust in the reader's eye? First, there is one rule the conscientious writer never breaks: he is not required to tell you everything that goes on in his detective's or murderer's mind, but he must not conceal any material clue found by the detective. Apart from this, pretty well anything goes in the great game of reader-baffling. If he is an artist as well as a craftsman, the writer will try to avoid irrelevant red herrings. This sounds like a contradiction in terms: but what I mean is that the false trails and misleading clues should all stem naturally from the story itself, not be superimposed upon it merely for the sake of deception. Whether they are material or psychological, these false clues and trails should be the result of the murderer's trying to shake off the detective, or of other suspects trying to conceal skeletons in their own cupboards, or of some apparently accidental turn of events which is nevertheless brought about by the main action.

Technically, the placing of genuine and false clues is perhaps the most fascinating part of a detective writer's work. A genuine clue—one, that is, pointing to the murderer—may be slipped in unobtrusively in a passage of dialogue or description: on the other hand, it may be positively hurled at the reader (this is double bluff) so that he is convinced it must be a false one, intended to mislead. Similarly a false clue is sometimes made to loom large, sometimes played down so that the warier type of reader may be induced to take the bait. There is always a danger of the detective novelist's being too clever: not too clever for his readers—this he should always aim to be—but too clever for his characters. It is absurd, for instance, if a suspect who has previously been shown as of only average intelligence should turn into a brilliant, audacious liar under police examination.

As with clues, so with the murderer himself. It is an unwritten law of detection-writing that he should be one of the more prominent characters in the story: you musn't smuggle him in, halfway through, as an apparent supernumerary. But here again you can use bluff or double bluff on your reader: you can do everything to persuade him that X is innocent; or you can call attention to X, subtly yet persistently, so as to make the wary reader believe you *want* him to believe X is the murderer. On the whole, though, it is unwise to think a great deal about foxing the reader. Let X do his best to fox the police, and the reader will find himself perplexed enough.

The classic qualities of the detective novel proper are bafflement and suspense. If, when he gets to the end of the penultimate chapter, the reader is unable to pick out the murderer, or has been led to pick out the wrong suspect; and if, when he closes the book, he exclaims 'What a fool I am! Of course it was X. I should have seen it long ago'—then the writer has done a good job. But if, though baffled, the reader is also past caring *who* committed the crime, there has been a failure of suspense. The most effective method of maintaining suspense is to toss suspicion like a ball from one character to another, never allowing anyone to hold it too long: this game can only be played if each character has a practical motive, and/or appears at first not to be disqualified psychologically, for the given murder.

The pattern of a detective novel, which is something more than a mere puzzle, may resemble that of an inverted family tree: at first, a whole line of suspects; then a gradual elimination, until only two are left—the elimination being worked not only through factual evidence (Y couldn't have done it, because three independent witnesses saw him fifty miles away at the time of the murder), but also through psychological evidence (the reader arriving at the legitimate conclusion, 'However much appearances may be against him, I am now convinced that Z simply is not the sort of person who could have committed this particular crime'). In one of my books I made the experiment of eliminating all but two of my suspects some way before the end, and of throwing suspicion back and forth between these two for the rest of the story.

In real life, police investigation is a long-drawn, cumulative and un-dramatic affair, which would make tedious reading for any but a professional criminologist. In our novels, the detection process must be fore-shortened and dramatised. For this purpose, certain conventions have become established—the multiple-killing convention, for instance.

It is uncommon for a real murderer to cover up his initial crime with further killings: multiple murders are nearly always the work of a homicidal maniac. Homicidal maniacs are barred from detective fiction, however, because its very existence depends upon a logic of cause and effect inconsistent with the schizophrenic personality. So detective writers lean—often, I think, too heavily—on the convention that a murderer will attempt further killings, in self-preservation.

On the credit side, this convention creates suspense, since the reader is always wondering which of the characters will be knocked off next; and it contributes to the essential element of fantasy. On the other hand, multiple killing may over-complicate the plot, is sometimes no more than a facile method of eliminating some of the suspects, and too often seems a con-fession of failure—failure to maintain excitement without infusions, so to say, of fresh blood.

This convention, however, was given an original twist in Agatha Christie's *The ABC Murders*. Here, a succession of apparently motiveless murders was committed, the victims being killed off in alphabetical order, the locale of each crime being announced beforehand by the murderer, and a copy of the railway ABC left beside each body. Since no connection could be established between any of them, the choice of victims appeared to be quite arbitrary and the murders were therefore assumed to be the work of a homicidal maniac with a bizarre sense of humour. The murderer got some way down the alphabet before he was stopped. But, in the final solution, it came out that the murderer had committed a number of motiveless murders in order to cover up the fact that, for one of the crimes, he had a perfectly good motive. *The ABC Murders* is a classic example of the pure detective novel—the novel, that is, in which an unbroken and absolutely reasonable thread of consequence has been spun from a wildly fantastic premise: it gives us make-believe carried to its logical conclusion.

Nicholas Blake, from 'School of Red Herrings' in *Diversion,* edited by John Sutro, reprinted by permission of Macdonald and Jane's Publishers Ltd.

Question   *Time: 60 to 75 minutes*

'Writing Detective Stories—Advice from an Expert'. Write 200 words on this subject, using the Nicholas Blake extract (above) as your source of information and advice. (Our answer is on p. 195.)

Alternative question

You are collecting first-hand accounts of writing methods for a project on the subject of *How writers work*. Prepare a set of notes on detective-story writing from the above passage that will help you when you write up the project. (See our answer on p. 195.)

Passage 4

The use of chemicals in agriculture

In many countries there is now concern that mainstream agriculture has taken the wrong course. Researches at the end of the last century led to the belief that the soil can be virtually by-passed, except as a supporting medium, and the plants fed directly with soluble, often synthetic, chemicals. From this sprang the development of further artificial products —insecticides, herbicides and fungicides. Modern agriculture has become a capitalised industry, supported by feed, machinery, packaging, chemical and pharmaceutical firms and research institutions—a giant network concerned more with production of money than with food. Farms have become factories where plants and animals are injected with every sort of industrial product in order to achieve maximum yields—and maximum return on capital.

The excessive use of chemical fertilisers not only pollutes rivers and lakes, but it also destroys the fertility of the soil itself, and may lock up essential minerals necessary for the health of plants and livestock. One example is that potash will go into insoluble compound with magnesium, thereby denying magnesium to the plant and to the animal which eats the plant; this is one of the causes of hypomagnesaemia in cattle. The farmer is compelled to resort to an arsenal of poisons against pests and diseases which are not fully effective as controls, and the long-term results of which are unseen.

Also unseen is the waste of energy. To produce one ton of nitrogen fertiliser, between three and five tons of fossil fuels are needed—50 per cent of which is absorbed by the plant, the rest being lost in run-off or seepage, during which it can turn to poisonous nitrate. A number of recent publications have analysed various aspects of energy use, particularly in United States agriculture. Approximately five times as much energy goes into the production of food as is actually contained in the food itself. Furthermore, as far as scientific research has gone in the past, all work has been directed to improving *quantity* of yield, not quality, and value is assessed by bulk, not nutritive content.

Health, quality and rejection of dangerous practices are the priorities of the alternative movement in organic or biological agriculture, which is supported by several organisations. (The Soil Association, The Henry Doubleday Research Association and The Organic Farmers and Growers are just three.) These practical people have little time for woolly romanticism, hippies, food faddists and cranks. They have evolved a positive scientific system of agriculture based on a more complete biological view – growing food from the land, rather than transmuting imported chemicals and proteins into eatables using the land as a factory floor.

The central idea is to build up soil fertility (and the population of micro-organisms which create humus and produce natural plant foods to maintain all plants' health and resistance to disease) by returning all organic waste to the land in a cycle of renewal. Feed the soil to feed the plant to feed the animal/human. Animal residues are vital for the health and nutrition of plants – if all animal and human excreta were harnessed, chemical fertilisers could become virtually redundant.

Recent surveys in France and the United States corn belt, together with a preliminary report from the Agriculture Economics Unit at Cambridge University (currently working on British organic farm costings) show that organic farmers can obtain yields as high as those of industrial farming with sometimes greater profits. Moreover these results are achieved without the aid that conventional agriculturalists receive from chemical and governmental advisory services into which millions of pounds are poured – the British spend £50m on research and development in agriculture, 80 per cent in research. What might these farmers achieve with the backing of scientific research? It is not a question of regression, but of how to go forward.

Philippa Pullar, from 'Are we feeding ourselves to death?', reproduced from *The Times* by permission.

Question   *Time: 45 minutes*

Summarise the evidence given by the writer (above) to support the view that 'mainstream agriculture has taken the wrong course' and state what alternative she describes. The first part of your answer should not be more than about 80 words, and the second not more than about 40 words. (See our answers, p. 196.)

Passage 5

Vole plagues

There was another plague, this time of water voles, on the Humber in 1896. This was on a particularly valuable tract of land that had been reclaimed from the sea, but conditions became so bad that it was eventually decided that the only cure would be to flood the land again. It was hoped that the troublesome visitors, mistakenly thought to be ordinary rats, would be drowned. It must have been a sad disappointment to everyone when the 'rats' swam to safety.

The Humber plague was unusual because such plagues as we do get are normally caused by the field vole *(Microtus agrestis)*, and are a particular nuisance to foresters. When the population has built up to such a level that the usually plentiful supply of grass runs short, the voles start nibbling at the young trees, pulling away patches of bark to get at the bast. Many of the saplings are killed by having a complete ring of bark removed, and a vastly greater number are checked and distorted in their growth.

The defence of a young forest against this sort of attack is very difficult. It is true that the voles are easily trapped and killed, but the numbers involved are so enormous that such measures cannot hope for much success. Short of surrounding each tree with a close-meshed screen there would appear to be no complete answer. It is easy to understand the hopeless feeling of the seventeenth-century writer who, faced by such an attack of voles, gloomily forecast that in future all young trees would have to be raised in special nurseries, heavily guarded by traps.

He apparently thought that vast numbers of voles were in future to be a regular feature of the countryside, but he was being unduly pessimistic. The vole plagues, severe as they undoubtedly are whilst they last, are local in their effect and, as had been previously remarked upon by Aristotle, comparatively short-lived. Nor, fortunately, do we get very many of them. In the present century the major outbreaks have been in forests in Argyll in 1929, in Wales in 1933 and in Scotland again, in the Carron Valley Forest in 1953.

It is sometimes suggested that the afforestation of previously barren areas is the cause of the sudden increases in the vole population. The argument is that grazing animals are excluded from the forests, and therefore the grass grows long, providing both food and cover for the voles, who can thereupon multiply unchecked. Before the forester put in an appearance, the sheep not only competed with the voles for the available food supply but, by cropping the grass short, exposed them to their many enemies among the predatory birds and beasts.

There is undoubtedly a lot in this, but it can only be a part of the story, for the two most severe outbreaks of recent times have both been in the sheep-rearing areas of the southern uplands of Scotland. In the years 1875 and 1876, and again in 1890-92, the grass was destroyed by the millions of voles that suddenly appeared, and the ground was riddled with their burrows.

An enormous amount of damage was done and the farmers suffered appalling losses. As a vole eats about his own weight in dry food in ten days, a plague of them soon literally eats up the countryside. It was estimated that 1,000 square miles were affected in these Scottish outbreaks and fodder had to be imported in order to keep the sheep alive. Even then a great many of the ewes died, and there were smaller crops of lambs than was usual.

There was such an outcry raised over all this that the Government had to set up a special Commission of Investigation, but this was unable to suggest any really effective remedy or measure of control. One Commissioner even went as far afield as Turkish Epirus, where there was a similar plague, to see what course of action was adopted in those parts. It proved a wasted journey, for he found that the Turks were putting their faith in holy water imported from Mecca and sprinkled on the affected fields.

There is still a great deal that is not fully understood about the cause and cure of these vole plagues. It is thought, though, that the Scottish outbreaks were at least partly the result of the intensive game preservation of the times, which led to the widespread slaughter of foxes and weasels and birds of prey. When the vole population increased so spectacularly, these predators made a reappearance, but it is unlikely that this form of natural control was solely responsible for bringing the plagues to an end. The eventual disappearance of the voles was much too sudden and catastrophic for that and was more probably the result of some form of epidemic. Biologists think it possible that the increased competition for food could set up a condition known as 'shock disease', which might be the reason why such outbreaks come to such a sudden end.

R. A. Marchant, from *Nature on the Move,* reprinted by permission of Bell and Hyman Publishers Ltd.

Question   *Time: one hour*

Summarise, in about 250 words, the cause, effect and cure of vole plagues described above. (See our answer on p. 197.)

Passage 6

The art of the cave-dwellers

The culture of man that we recognise best began to form in the most recent Ice Age, within the last hundred or even fifty thousand years. That is when we find the elaborate tools that point to sophisticated forms of hunting: the spear-thrower, for example, and the baton that may be a straightening tool; the fully barbed harpoon; and, of course, the flint master tools that were needed to make the hunting tools...

The author goes on to describe how man survived the Ice Age by means of 'the master invention of all — fire'.

Fire is the symbol of the hearth, and from the time *Homo sapiens* began to leave the mark of his hand thirty thousand years ago, the hearth was the cave. For at least a million years man, in some recognisable form, lived as a forager and a hunter. We have almost no monuments of that immense period of prehistory, so much longer than any history that we record. Only at the end of that time, on the edge of the European ice-sheet, we find in caves like Altamira (and elsewhere in Spain and southern France) the record of what dominated the mind of man the hunter. There we see what made his world and preoccupied him. The cave paintings, which are about twenty thousand years old, fix for ever the universal base of his culture then, the hunter's knowledge of the animal that he lived by and stalked.

One begins by thinking it odd that an art as vivid as the cave paintings should be, comparatively, so young and so rare. Why are there not more monuments to man's visual imagination, as there are to his invention? And yet when we reflect, what is remarkable is not that there are so few monuments, but that there are any at all. Man is a puny, slow, awkward, unarmed animal — he had to invent a pebble, a flint, a knife, a spear. But why to these scientific inventions, which were essential to his survival, did he from an early time add those arts that now astonish us: decorations with animal shapes? Why, above all, did he come to caves like this, live in them, and then make paintings of animals not where he lived but in places that were dark, secret, remote, hidden, inaccessible?

The obvious thing to say is that in these places the animal was magical. No doubt that is right; but magic is only a word, not an answer. In itself, magic is a word which explains nothing. It says that man believed he had power, but what power? We still want to know what the power was that the hunters believed they got from the paintings.

Here I can only give you my personal view. I think that the power that we see expressed here for the first time is the power of anticipation: the forward-looking imagination. In these paintings the hunter was made familiar with dangers which he knew he had to face but to which he had not yet come. When the hunter was brought here into the secret dark and the light was suddenly flashed on the pictures, he saw the bison as he would have to face him, he saw the running deer, he saw the turning boar. And he felt alone with them as he would in the hunt. The moment of fear was made present to him; his spear-arm flexed with an experience which he would have and which he needed not to be afraid of. The painter had frozen the moment of fear, and the hunter entered it through the painting as if through an air-lock.

For us, the cave paintings re-create the hunter's way of life as a glimpse of history; we look through them into the past. But for the hunter, I suggest, they were a peep-hole into the future; he looked ahead. In either direction, the cave paintings act as a kind of telescope tube of the imagination: they direct the mind from what is seen to what can be inferred or conjectured. Indeed, this is so in the very action of painting; for all its superb observation, the flat picture only means something to the eye because the mind fills it out with roundness and movement, a reality by inference, which is not actually seen but is imagined.

Art and science are both uniquely human actions, outside the range of anything that an animal can do. And here we see that they derive from the same human faculty: the ability to visualise the future, to foresee what may happen and plan to anticipate it, and to represent it to ourselves in images that we project and move about inside our head, or in a square of light on the dark wall of a cave or a television screen.

We also look here through the telescope of the imagination; the imagination is a telescope in time, we are looking back at the experience of the past. The men who made these paintings, the men who were present, looked through that telescope forward. They looked along the ascent of man because what we call cultural evolution is essentially a constant growing and widening of the human imagination.

The men who made the weapons and the men who made the paintings were doing the same thing—anticipating a future as only man can do, inferring what is to come from what is here. There are many gifts that are unique in man; but at the centre of them all, the root from which all knowledge grows, lies the ability to draw conclusions from what we see to what we do not see, to move our minds through space and time, and to recognise ourselves in the past on the steps to the present. All over these caves the print of the hand says: 'This is my mark. This is man.'

Jacob Bronowski, from *The Ascent of Man*, reprinted by permission of the British Broadcasting Corporation.

Spanish cave paintings

Question   *Time: 45 minutes*

'Art and science...derive from the same human faculty: the ability to visualise the future, to foresee what may happen and plan to anticipate it...'/'...the imagination is a telescope in time...'. In 80 to 90 words state the substance of the writer's argument leading to these conclusions.

Note This is intentionally more difficult than some of the other exercises. If you need help with it, turn to page 197 and read the preliminary notes, but don't read our finished summary until you have tried writing your own.

3.5   CHECK-LIST OF SUMMARY PASSAGES

A	Wolves and people	factual	(with worked answer)
B	Domestic water supply	factual	(for practice)
C	The Ik—a dying race	factual	(with worked answer)
D	Pollution in the Mediterranean	factual	(for practice)
E	Weeds	factual	(with worked answer)
F	The red deer	factual	(with worked answer)

Further practice, with comments and answers on pp. 193-198

1	Rennaissance Italian frescoes	(the arts)
2	Children and stability	(sociology)
3	Writing detective stories	(writing)
4	The use of chemicals in agriculture	(science)
5	Vole plagues	(natural history)
6	The art of the cave-dwellers	(art/prehistory)

4 Letters, reports, practical writing; books and poetry; oral English

4.1   WRITING LETTERS

Writing a good letter may help to get you an interview, a job, an 'O' level pass, a chance to air your views or present your ideas in a newspaper or magazine. A good secretary writes letters for the manager to sign as his or her own; many secretaries write better letters than their employers. Most important of all, letters are still one of the best ways of keeping in touch for people who are separated. Nearly everyone writes a love letter at some time; many older people live for letters from their grown-up family.

Layout (formal letter)

Here is a letter one of us wrote to his insurance company. It is a formal letter, of course, because he did not know who exactly might read it, and simply needed to carry out a business matter.

---

4 The Square
Clun
CRAVEN ARMS
Shropshire SY7 8JA
22nd January 1983

Commercial Union Assurance Co Ltd
1 Merridale Road
Chapel Ash
WOLVERHAMPTON WV3 9RT

Dear Sir,

<u>Key Household Policy no. HA 170733113</u>

I wish to add two more named items to those already listed in this policy, so that the two additional items can be covered against loss, fire and theft under the terms of the policy. The two items are:

(1) Cello bow by Cuniot-Hury (named on stick)   value £1,000
(2) Camera: Ricoh 500G, body no. 27315956   value £80

Can you please let me know what additional premium you will require?

Yours faithfully,
[signature]
Mr S. Tunnicliffe

Points to notice

The date is given in full.
The tendency nowadays is for the address to be unpunctuated. As long as it is clearly spaced and properly aligned this is quite acceptable. If you do punctuate

the address – and some examiners still prefer it – use a full stop after any abbreviation (e.g. St., Lancs.), and a comma at the end of each line except the last, which has a full-stop.

If you are replying to a letter that has a reference number it is sensible to quote it, so as to get your letter to the right person and department quickly. In a large office hundreds of people may be dealing with letters.

The whole letter should be well set out on the page; notice how the spacing makes our sample letter easier to read.

Use capital letters for both opening words (Dear Sir, Dear Madam), but for the first word only of the closing phrase (Yours faithfully).

Use your normal signature. If possible it should be easily read and roughly parallel with the rest of the letter. If you can't write your name legibly, type or write it in script or capitals below the signature. It may help your correspondent to put (Mr), (Ms), (Mrs) or (Miss) in brackets before or after your signature.

The envelope

There should be a space of at least $1\frac{1}{2}$ inches (5 cm) above the address on the envelope so that it is clear of the postmark. For a formal letter write or type the address exactly as it appears at the head of your letter. When writing to a private address use the number of the house if it has one, whether or not you also give its name. Use capital letters for the name of the postal town, and put the postcode on the last line of the address.

Beginning and ending

There are three methods, according to the type of letter:

1 Business and official or formal letters, to firms or to individuals whom you may not know, start: Dear Sir   Dear Sirs   Dear Madam and end: Yours faithfully (note the two '*l*'s   or Yours truly (note no *–e–*).

2 Less formal letters to people you know fairly well or have met recently, for example to a teacher in your school or to someone who has employed you, start: Dear Mr Jones   Dear Mrs Roberts   Dear Dr Graham and end: Yours sincerely (note the two '*e*'s). Never use the formal 'Dear Sir' for someone you have met personally or know well.

3 Informal letters between relatives and close friends start 'Dear Jane' or in any way you think suits the person you're writing to. Endings can also be as varied as you like: Yours ever   Love to you both   Regards and best wishes   etc.

Nowadays firms and government departments sometimes use style **2** instead of style **1**. The practice came from America, where an appearance of friendliness is thought to be appropriate even in business matters. It can certainly make a letter from an official such as a tax inspector, for example, less intimidating.

Content, tone and style

Before writing anything in the actual letter think out what you want or need to say, and the best order to say it in. If the letter is an important one make rough notes first. Try to state clearly at the beginning why the letter has been written. Use a fresh paragraph for each division of the subject. The content of the letter requires the best words for the job and the right tone of voice. The tone is sometimes more difficult to gauge than the words.

If you are writing about something for which you are going to pay, e.g. answering an advertisement about a holiday, booking theatre tickets, or sending for a special offer of a shirt, you need a different tone from the one in a letter which is asking for a reference, applying for a job, or suggesting an exchange holiday with a member of a French family.

The first tone should be polite but not too polite. You are paying, therefore: 'Please send me ...' or 'Kindly send ...' is enough, with the ending 'I shall be glad to hear from you as soon as possible.' It is too polite to say 'I shall be very grateful ...'. You are the buyer; your money expresses your gratitude; let the seller be grateful to you. Your tone should be warmer and more polite when you are asking for – not buying – someone's time or services.

If you write to invite someone to speak at your school or college, if you ask an individual or organisation to sponsor a charity appeal, then you must choose words which show that you appreciate the time and effort involved. 'Very grateful', 'much appreciate', 'generosity', would all be in place.

The tone of a letter containing or supporting an application for a job needs very careful thought. It can reveal your personality more clearly than any facts you state about yourself, and it will be closely read by someone who may later be working with you. What do you think are the relative chances of these two applicants for a post as receptionist in a business firm?

1 ... because I like lots of people, and often go to parties. They say I'm a good mixer ...

2 ... understand that the successful applicant will often need to put people at their ease. My experience at Smith and Hardy is relevant here ...

The best words for a formal letter are often the fewest needed to state your purpose clearly. You may not write many formal letters but the chances are that the person you are writing to will receive a great many. So keep it as short as politeness and clarity will allow. This should prevent the too chatty approach:

'I know you're terribly busy but it's better to be busy than bored isn't it?' or the irrelevant information:

'The reason I'm writing is because my handwriting is the best although I'm not so good at English as Jane. I do hope you can come because if you do I can have a new outfit.' Or the afterthought which should have come earlier:

'P.S. We hope you will be able to stay for a cup of tea afterwards.'

If you receive a rude letter do not reply rudely, however provocative and insulting your correspondent may be. In conversation it is easy to withdraw or tone down rude remarks; it is much more difficult once they are in writing. If you have to complain about something, state the facts calmly; don't get worked up or abusive. Normally a polite complaint is effective, because it is in a firm's interest to satisfy its customers. Whatever letter you write will be read by someone who is as human as you are, someone who will attend to difficulties and give help more willingly if you ask rather than demand, explain rather than complain.

Avoid 'business' English; although outlawed by most good firms and departments for many years it is still about. In the following examples the right-hand column gives the preferred version:

In connection with your inquiry, we have to acquaint you that our practice is to prefer payment by cheque.	We prefer to be paid by cheque.
Such employment does not involve the necessity of obtaining a certificate of fitness.	A fitness certificate is not needed for such employment.
be good enough to advise us	tell us
the attention of your good selves	your attention
have delivered same	have delivered it
acquaint with	tell
alternative	other, another, different
anticipate	expect
commence	begin
consider	think
inform	tell
proceed	go
a proportion of	some
purchase	buy
residence	home
to state	to say
terminate	end
utilise	use

PRACTICE

You have to write to a local celebrity to invite her to plant a tree for which you have helped to raise the money. What do you need to say? Jot down your ideas and then check with the list below; you may think of something we haven't included:

1 Reason for writing.
2 Date, time, place.
3 Exactly what are you inviting her to do? Shovel soil? Make a speech? Meet any particular people?
4 Estimated length of ceremony.
5 Who and how many present.
6 Gratitude and appreciation.
7 Offer to provide any other information required.

The last point is a precaution; you hope the letter has included everything necessary. (You can compare your letter with the one we wrote if you turn to page 198.)

Finally, here are three letters which were sent to an engineering firm that manufactures motor-cycle sprockets (toothed wheels driven by chain). Which do you think is the most efficient for its purpose? Make up your mind, then turn to page 199 to find out the manufacturer's reactions. It would be a worthwhile exercise to re-write those that were not satisfactory. Names and addresses have been changed to spare the writers' blushes.

I

22 FAIRFIELD DRIVE,
FADESLEY
LANCS

Dear Sir

Can you make me a rear sprocket for a 1958 Ariel Huntmaster but not cast as the original but in steel same size as standard How much.
Arielly,
Alan Becking

II

98, Steep St
Burton-on-Hill
Staffs
March 3rd

Dear Sir,

Have you a sprocket suitable for a AJW Greyhound moped, sizes 25 teeth by 3/16. The holes to fit the sprocket to the wheel can be drilled from the old sprocket which I am quite willing to do myself. If you have same would you please send me price etc so I can forward my money on to you as I'm waiting for the sprocket as I need my bike to go to collage on.

Yours faithfully,
[signature]
Mr B Rider

III

21, Spring bank Rd.
Farnsworth,
LANCS.

Dear Sir,

I am writing to enquire exactly what information you require when asked to make a gearbox and rear wheel sprocket to suit a particular bike.

I am in a position to acquire Reynold chain for no cost but the pitch is slightly larger than my standard chain which is fitted to a Suzuki 'GT.750A' motorcycle.

Obviously I cannot supply a pattern of either sprocket as it is going to be different to the standard ones due to the pitch difference.

Hope you can help me,

yours faithfully,
[signature]
Mr F. Wheeler

4.2 REPORTS, PRACTICAL WRITING

Most English Language examinations inclùde questions to test your ability to write clearly on factual or practical matters, or for a definite purpose, like reporting an accident. One kind of 'practical English' is the one we have already discussed in this chapter, letter-writing. Others may involve skills similar to those used in *comprehension*, or in the writing of *notes* and *summaries*. (See, in particular, 2.5, 2.6 (p. 58), 3.2 Practice (p. 84), 3.3 (p. 87)).

Here are a few more examples of the kind of questions that are set to test your ability in practical writing:

1 The average house is often described as a very dangerous place, especially for old people and small children. Electricity and gas, staircases and slippery floors can all be sources of accidents. Write a short 'Guide' as though for the purpose of being printed on a single sheet circular for distribution by your Local Authority, entitled *Safety in the home*. (CSE)

2 Write a report of an accident which you witnessed when a motor-cyclist ran into a stationary car near a school entrance. No-one was hurt. (CSE)

3 A group of 5th-formers is organising a campaign to reduce litter in the school buildings and ground. Write the speech in which the campaign is explained to the school in an Assembly. (GCE)

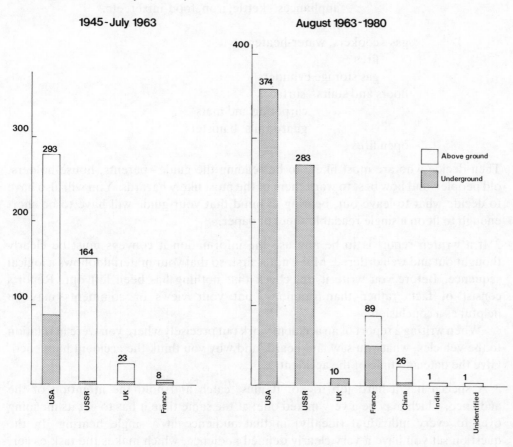

4 Study the accompanying diagram (page 109). Write one paragraph to explain the information given in the chart, and a second paragraph about the effectiveness of the Limited Test Ban Treaty in reducing the danger from nuclear weapons. (16+)

Questions like these often do not include any guidance as to the length of your answer. As they are usually set in addition to the main essay or composition question(s) you can assume they do not need very long answers – perhaps a maximum length of 200 to 250 words, and often a good deal shorter. The important points to remember are not to waste words by 'padding' or repetition, and to shape your answer according to the particular purpose of the piece of writing, whether report, speech, information leaflet or explanation. Use the four examples for practice. We have given you some hints on how to set about each one, and answers are given in full on pp. 199-201. Each question should take you about twenty minutes.

Hints on answering

1 Before you start writing your 'Guide' make some rough notes. List the hazards you want to cover, e.g.:

> electricity – power-points and wires
> > appliances – kettle, iron, food-mixer, etc.
> > fires
> gas – cookers, water-heaters
> > fires
> > gas storage cylinders
> floors and stairs – surfaces
> > carpeting and mats
> > guard rails, banisters
> open fires

Then decide who are most likely to be reading the guide – parents, house-holders, old people – and how best to warn them of the most likely hazards. You will also have to decide what to leave out, bearing in mind that your guide will have to be short enough to fit on a single readable sheet of paper.

2 If a written report is to be any use the information it conveys must be clearly thought out and well ordered. Make notes first, so that your material follows a logical sequence. Before you write it up, check that nothing has been left out. Reports consist of facts rather than opinions, but your views or comments may be helpful as a conclusion.

When writing a report of an accident work out precisely where you were in relation to the vehicles, what you saw and heard, and why you think the accident happened. Give the date and time of the accident.

3 A speech has a hard job to do: it must catch and hold the attention of the audience, which may be a very mixed one; at the same time it has to get its meaning over to every individual (ideally) in that audience at a single hearing. In the question set you have a very clearly defined audience, which makes the task easier, but there is also a special problem, because what you say has to interest a wide age-range. Keep the sentences simple in structure. Try to use humour – people listen better if they can smile – but show also that you are convinced of the importance of your subject. Be courteous to your audience; they did not ask to hear you. If you leave them with a good opinion of you they are more likely to remember what you say.

4 This kind of exercise is set more frequently nowadays. It really involves a similar skill to that dealt with in chapter 3 (summarising), but your first task is to *interpret* the chart or diagram. You will find some guidance on this in paragraph 2.5.(p. 58). The second paragraph involves drawing *inferences* from the information you have gleaned (see 2.3, p. 54).

4.3   WRITING ABOUT BOOKS

There are questions in some English examinations (particularly in CSE papers and in the SCE Paper 1) which ask you to write about books you have read. They ask you to write about topics like the following:

1   An important incident in the story.
2   Relationships between the characters.
3   The setting of the story.
4   A child character and his relation to adults, or animals, or strangers, or old people.
5   An important conversation.
6   Minor characters in the book.
7   A book's suitability for television or radio serialisation.

In some form or another all of these have been set in recent examinations. You will easily recognise them, even if the wording is not quite the same as ours. Try it! Here are four questions on books. Beside each one put the number of the topic (1 to 7) you think it is asking about (answers at the foot of the next page):

(a) Think of two people in the story who are not in the centre of the action, but still stick in your mind. Write about their contribution to the story as a whole.
(b) Describe one person in the book who is younger than you, and tell of his or her behaviour with a pet or other animal(s).
(c) Many television plays or serials are based on books. Think of *one* book you have read that has been adapted for TV or would be suitable for it, and explain what came (or would come) over best in the screened version, and what came (or would come) over least well or not at all.
(d) Think of a book you have read in which the place or places where the story was set makes an important contribution to the effect. Explain how and why this is so.

It is a good plan to read one really interesting book just before your examination —say, within six weeks of exam day. If it has really gripped your attention you will have no difficulty in remembering details, though after six months they will have faded in your memory. Choosing the right book is half the battle. It needs to be worth-while in its own right—a librarian, or an older friend keen on reading, or one of your teachers will help you on this if you're not sure. Don't choose too long a book—150 to 200 pages should be plenty for you so soon before the examination. If the book is in paperback get your own copy. But don't choose one that everybody is reading; the examiner will hear plenty about that one without your help! If you possibly can, choose a book that you know you will enjoy. Maybe you have read others by the same author, or in the same series. Maybe it is about a place, or a sport, or a job, or a hobby that you are very interested in or know a lot about.

Places to look for ideas about what to read:

BOOK-LISTS in your English class book, or given to you by your English teacher or school librarian.

'FURTHER READING' suggestions at the end of a book you have enjoyed, or that is about a subject you are interested in.

BOOK CLUBS These are often formed in school nowadays, and usually have a newsletter with information about the club's choices.

MAGAZINES often have a 'Books' section listing new books and saying a bit about them.

NEWSPAPERS Some of them have a special review page once or twice a week. Sunday papers usually have more space for book reviews.

Once you have chosen your book do make time to read it. Go to bed earlier—take a drink, some biscuits, make yourself comfortable. Leave the others watching TV—you won't miss much!

Let's now look at one book and see what might be expected of us. We have chosen a fast-moving adventure story of events taking place about a hundred and fifty years ago—*A High Wind in Jamaica*, by Richard Hughes. We hope to convince you that it is a good choice; it has, in fact, often been set for close study in English Literature examinations—but don't let this put you off!

The opening chapter gives a wonderful description of an old house on a ruined sugar plantation in the West Indies—its slave quarters, sugar grinding and boiling houses. We read of the devastation caused by earthquakes, fires and floods, and of the abundant, luxuriant tropical vegetation that took over when the place became derelict.

Next the book describes some English children who lived there. We hear plenty of detail about their clothes, their games, their cat and what he used to do (swim round the bathing pool, and fight with snakes). The children's daily life and activities were very different from those of any child living in this country nowadays.

After this comes a vivid and frightening description of a tropical hurricane: fierce lightning all over the sky, cracking thunder, torrents of rain, devastating wind. The children's poor cat was chased through the house and out again by a pack of maddened wild cats. The roof collapsed, and the family had to take refuge along with the negroes and the goats in the cellar. The father handed wine round and all the children went to sleep drunk.

Following this disaster the parents decide to send their children to school in England. The rest of the book is about their adventures—equally hair-raising and unusual—at sea. The children find themselves on a pirate schooner, and have many an excitement, and experiences both funny and terrifying, before they finally disembark in England.

What we have done here is to **review** the book—to go over it in our mind after reading and enjoying it as a whole, in order to see more clearly what made it enjoyable and therefore memorable to us. Professional reviewers, whose job it is to do this for the 'books' columns of newspapers and magazines, know well enough that if they tell the whole story, or go into too much detail about the setting or the characters, they may be spoiling the book for other readers. Their job, after classifying the book (adventure story, thriller, autobiography etc.), is to whet appetites. If you haven't read *A High Wind in Jamaica* we hope we have whetted yours.

Types of question: answers (a) 6; (b) 4; (c) 7; (d) 3.

However, in an examination your job isn't quite so straight-forward, even if you are asked simply to 'write a review of a book you have enjoyed'. Your job is to prove to the examiner that you have read and responded to the book. Most people who will read a review have not read the book; they are looking for guidance as to whether it is worth buying or asking for at the library. But when you write a review, keep in mind that you will have one critical reader rather than many who haven't read the book.

We have shown you that *A High Wind in Jamaica* is easy to use as the subject of a review. It is so full of detail and variety that it would be easy to answer the sort of questions we looked at earlier, on different aspects of the story.

● A question on **the setting** (type 3 in the list of seven likely topics given on p. 111) would be easy; the details Richard Hughes gives of the island, the houses on it, the pirate ship, are all so vivid and memorable.

● A question about **children** (type 4) would be a gift; the novel is all about children, and they are very different from one another.

● A question that asks you to describe **an important incident** (type 1) would be a walk-over. The tropical hurricane comes near the beginning, and is so well described that you can almost feel you are in it. If you want other incidents to choose from there are many memorable scenes later in the book: two unexpected and bizarre deaths, for instance, or a hilarious episode where the sailors are trying to catch a drunken monkey who has escaped up the rigging.

When such a book is fresh in your mind, it is like having someone by your side in the exam room telling you what to write; memorable details come into your mind which will give interest and life to anything you write about the book.

It is essential that you convince the examiner you have really read the book you are talking about, not just skimmed through it, or—worse still—seen it on film or television without having read it at all. (**Warning** Nothing is easier for an experienced examiner to recognise than second-hand knowledge of a book as derived from TV adaptations.) A very good way to show that you know the book well is to **quote** some of the actual words you have been reading. Let the book grip you, enter into its world, see it through the eyes of its author, and before you know where you are the words and sentences of more interesting parts will be fixed in your memory. Here are three bits we found no difficulty in remembering after putting down *A High Wind in Jamaica*:

When Lame Foot Sam the negro is tempted to steal a handkerchief someone has dropped, he suddenly remembers it is Sunday. He drops it hastily and starts covering it with sand—*'Please God, I thieve you tomorrow,' he exclaimed hopefully. 'Please God, you still there.'*

After the storm which destroys the children's house—*'The furniture was splintered into matchwood. Even the heavy mahogany dining table, which they loved, and had always kept with its legs in little glass baths of oil to defeat the ants, was spirited right away.'*

On board ship the children make friends with a black pig. They like to sit on him—*'If I was the queen,' said Emily, 'I should most certainly have a pig for a throne.'*

Quoting details like these often gives the flavour of the book better than describing it in general terms. Quoting them *accurately* — even just a few words like 'have a pig for a throne' — also proves you are a careful and observant reader.

Remember what we said at the beginning of this book about reading?
When an English examination includes a question on books the examiner is playing into your hands because reading a really good and absorbing book is just about the most pleasant and easy way of preparing yourself for an examination.

POETRY

So far in our discussion of written English we have been concerned mainly with prose. This is because English Language as a school or examination subject generally concentrates on this form of writing. We need to remember, however, that poetry has always been and still remains the language form capable of containing the greatest intensity of feeling, as well as the greatest precision. Some examining bodies recognise this — more CSE than GCE — and ask candidates to read and respond to poems, either in connection with compositions or in comprehension and appreciation questions. Poetry written in our own times is usually chosen.

Here is a recently written poem that might well form the basis of an examination question.

Cathedral builders

They climbed on sketchy ladders towards God,
With winch and pulley hoisted hewn rock into heaven,
Inhabited sky with hammers, defied gravity,
Deified stone, took up God's house to meet Him,

And came down to their suppers and small beer;
Every night slept, lay with their smelly wives,
Quarrelled and cuffed the children, lied,
Spat, sang, were happy or unhappy,

And every day took to the ladders again;
Impeded the rights of way of another summer's
Swallows, grew greyer, shakier, became less inclined
To fix a neighbour's roof of a fine evening,

Saw naves sprout arches, clerestories soar,
Cursed the loud fancy glaziers for their luck,
Somehow escaped the plague, got rheumatism,
Decided it was time to give it up,

To leave the spire to others; stood in the crowd
Well back from the vestments at the consecration,
Envied the fat bishop his warm boots,
Cocked up a squint eye and said, 'I bloody did that.'

John Ormond, from *Requiem and Celebration,* reprinted by permission of Christopher Davies Ltd.

We have printed the poem first, before saying anything about it, because a good poem makes its own impact best for itself. Perhaps this one has caught your interest, amused you, made you think. If so it has already started doing its job. Sometimes, however, readers feel baffled or even cheated when they encounter a poem. What is it *for?* Why is it printed like that instead of in the 'normal' way, i.e. like prose? Some even let their prejudices prevent them from enjoying or understanding poetry at all, and 'switch off' as soon as they see the way it is set out on the page. We can't help such people until they help themselves. What we can do is to suggest to more open-minded readers a few ways of approaching poetry, whether in an examination, in school, or in reading for their own enjoyment.

Title

If the poem has one it usually plays an important part. In *Cathedral builders* it is like a label or a headline, defining the subject clearly. As we start reading, the first word — 'They' — simply continues the idea, so that we are prepared for what follows.

Subject-matter

With most of the things we read we have some idea what to expect, because of the setting or form — newspaper, travel brochure, driving licence application, instruction manual or recipe book, letters . . . they all set up particular expectations in the reader and aim to satisfy them.

A brochure describing a package holiday in Benidorm is *not* likely to include things like this, for obvious reasons:

There are so many hotel tower blocks that the Mediterranean is invisible to most visitors for much of the time, and its waters are often polluted by sewage.

Poems are not so predictable. Instead, they often please by surprising you, by presenting things in a new light, or by using words in new ways. Most of us have seen cathedrals. The older ones in particular may be connected in our minds with feelings of awe, or solemn thoughts. It is startling to put our ideas next to the ones in the poem about the men who actually built them; yet as we read of their daily lives — supper, beer, having children, growing old — we are convinced that this is how real labourers would have been, even centuries ago. By the time we reach the last verse we are sympathetic to these anonymous craftsmen, and the poet can count on our support when he contrasts them with 'the fat bishop' in his boots (a rare luxury!). The last line, with its irreverent but genuine exclamation 'I bloody did that', brings the man who says it into sharp focus. We may laugh at the comment, but we now have a vivid idea of the true 'cathedral builders'.

Tone

When we talk, our tone of voice is often as important as what we say. Sometimes it is much more important: small children learn to recognise and respond to it long before they grasp actual meanings of words. Good writers also convey their feelings and attitudes through tone, and for poets it can be one of the most valuable ways of getting their full meaning across. We can tell from John Ormond's tone that he feels warmly towards the thousands of humble workmen who made cathedrals possible, who, as they grow older

> . . . greyer, shakier, become less inclined
> To fix a neighbour's roof of a fine evening.

It is our response to this tone of friendly sympathy that makes the last verse so effective.

Shape and language

Poems have one great advantage over prose, in that their actual shape on the page, their arrangement into stanzas (verses), sometimes with a particular pattern of line length, or rhythm, or rhyming words, can be made to contribute to their total effect. Here the five four-line stanzas, with a basic five stresses to the line

> They climbed on sketchy ladders towards God,

give the poem a progress: first the work routine—'They climbed...', 'And came down...', 'And...took to the ladders again'; then they watch the cathedral grow without them (notice the dynamic words 'sprout', 'soar' in the fourth stanza); and finally see the finished building.

We said just now that the language of poetry is capable of the greatest precision. This may seem surprising; perhaps you connect precision more with science or engineering than with poetry. If you do, look again at Passage 6 (p. 71) and decide which uses language more *precisely*, that or the poem we have just read. Poetry has a great advantage over other language forms, in that the poet, if he knows his job, can include as much of the total meaning of a word or expression as he wants. His words are not merely restricted to one sense like scientific terms or public notices. They can set off chain reactions in your mind, can explode in your imagination; and the poet's skill can control the direction in which his words 'take wing'.

Look at the word 'sketchy' in the first stanza. A dictionary tells us this means 'giving only a slight or rough outline of the main features, facts or circumstances without going into details'. One would not normally expect ladders to be described like this. But the very unexpectedness of the adjective makes us alert to other possibilities in the word. A sketch is an outline drawing; thin ladders scaling a vast cathedral structure can be seen in just this way. Even the sound of the words '*sk*etchy la*dd*er*s*' seems to be describing the precarious climbing of the builders, making it seem more real. If we think more about it we realise that the ladders do 'sketch out' the lines of the great cathédral by enabling the builders to do their work.

Now think about 'defied' and its deliberate half-echo 'deified' (i.e. made a god of), or the word 'inhabited', or the alliterative phrase '*h*oisted *h*ewn rock into *h*eaven'—all in this same first stanza—and you can get some idea of the rich resources of poetic language.

Conclusions

When we have looked at the details like this, it is a good idea to stand back, like the cathedral builders, and survey the poem as a whole. We cannot claim that we 'bloody did that', but we can, if we have responded to its tone and language, see something of its shape, and understand more fully the poet's intention. Ormond is not just mocking 'fat bishops', nor is he merely writing social history, though both these contribute to the poem. The freshness and modernity of his vision show us the discomforts, the pettinesses and drudgery involved in building a medieval cathedral; but he also conveys the shared sense of achievement in 'taking up God's house to meet Him', and the way in which a cathedral represents in a solid and permanent form the lives and faith of its human creators.

Poetry and the English examination

Most CSE boards include some poetry in written examinations, and poems form part of the GCE English Language papers of at least two examining bodies (the Oxford and Cambridge Schools Examination Board and the Joint Matriculation Board). The SCE Paper 1, Section B, always includes general questions on poetry.

PRACTICE

Here are some questions that might have been set in a CSE or GCE paper on *Cathedral builders*. If you have followed our comments carefully, you should have no difficulty in answering most of them. (For further practice in poetry appreciation and comprehension try the questions on Passage 9, pp. 75–76).

1 (a) How is the routine, hum-drum nature of the builders' lives emphasised in the poem?
(b) What details help to make the builders seem real people like ourselves? Quote two of them.
(c) Why does the poet say '. . . into heaven' in stanza 1?
(d) Explain what is meant by

> 'Impeded the rights of way of another summer's
> Swallows . . .'

2 Imagine you are one of the builders. Describe the scene, and your feelings, on the day the cathedral is consecrated. (Answers on pp. 192-193)

4.4 SPEAKING AND LISTENING

(Oral and Aural English)

All language starts as sounds rather than signs. A slow reader can often be seen silently mouthing the words he reads, converting them back into their original form to make them easier to grasp. We learnt most of our normal speech patterns and habits in our first five or six years of life. Only rarely were we aware that we were *learning*; this is why we find it hard to realise, and difficult to put right, when our way of speaking does not match the demands we make on it, or the expectations of the people we live amongst.

You can get some idea of how good you are at oral English by noticing how people respond to what you say. If they often say 'I beg your pardon' or 'Speak up!' you probably talk too quietly, mumble, or pronounce the words indistinctly. If people often seem to be hurt or offended by what you say you probably make mistakes in *tone*.

Use a tape-recorder

Most people can have the use of a tape-recorder now they are so readily available. If you feel you need to improve your spoken English, and particularly if your English examination includes oral English it is a good idea to have a tape-recorder of your own if possible. Get one with a counter if you can.

You can find out how you speak, and pin-point just where you need to improve, by talking and reading into a tape-recorder, then listening carefully to what you have recorded. The points we draw attention to later in this section will guide you to what you should listen for. You can also compare what you hear with other spoken English — radio talks, news bulletins, discussions; teachers and lecturers, even parents and friends. Tape some of these as well, and develop a critical ear. As you play back your own recordings and listen to them, ask yourself such questions as these:

What is this particular bit of speech aiming to do?

Who is it addressed to?

Can every word be heard clearly? If not, which words, or kinds of words, are indistinct? Is it the vowels or the consonants that are not clear?

Does your choice of words do justice to the subject? Will it be understood by the intended listeners?

Is the *pace* right — neither too fast nor too slow, neither hurried nor long-drawn-out? Is it *varied* according to the needs of the subject-matter?

Is the *tone* right — friendly, courteous, deferential, respectful, casual, authoritative, intimate or cool — which of these is likely to match best the purpose of the talk and the people listening to it?

Warning

Don't expect to get all the help you need for oral English from this, or from any *book*. The best help will always be 'oral' itself, and will come to you through your ears rather than your eyes. Here we can tell you what to listen for and how to practise; we can't demonstrate or give you samples. If your English examination includes oral and aural tests, records or tapes and other practice material should be available to you. Ask for them.

THREE KINDS OF SPOKEN ENGLISH

Because the spoken word is so important today, many English examinations, whose job is to measure your competence in using your language in all its forms, include an assessment of candidates' oral and aural competence. For some examining bodies — particularly in CSE examinations — the marks include an assessment of your ability as shown during the months before the final examination. Check what will be expected of you (see list of syllabus requirements, Section I). Most examinations will include one or more of the three main kinds of spoken English; some include all three. Here they are:

I Reading aloud

What reading aloud have you heard — a friend or parent, a teacher, an actor or a newscaster? Think about them, and decide which held your attention most. Was it the subject-matter alone, or was it also the reader who engaged your interest, kept you listening? Even if you are not used to doing so, try to listen often to reading, particularly of stories. (They are often read on the radio.) Listen to *the way they are read* as well as to what is read. Here are some points to note:

(a) Audibility — can you hear it?

(b) Clarity — can you hear it clearly?

(c) Articulation — can you hear all parts of the words, even unfamiliar words? Try writing them down, then checking, with the help of a dictionary, whether you heard correctly. Was the reader clear enough for you to tell the difference between 'rabbit' and 'rabid', or between 'Malta' and 'mortar'?

(d) Fluency — do the words flow naturally, or are there stumbles and hesitations?

(e) Variety—does the reader respond to his material by changing his tone and his expression, or by altering the pace he reads at?

(f) Sense—is it easy to follow the sense of what is being read, or are there things about the way it is read that make it difficult to understand? This is often a question of putting pauses in the right place, and of emphasising words or syllables sensibly, e.g.

(i) There *will* be sleet *or* snow on high *ground* tonight.

(ii) There will be *sleet* or *snow* on *high* ground tonight.

Which of these would make better sense in a weather report?

Put what you have learnt from listening like this into practice by doing some reading of your own, regularly. In the examination you may be allowed to choose your own passage to read. In choosing it, concentrate on interest. It should interest you, and the examiner. He or she is much more likely to be interested if it is obvious that you are interested in what you are reading.

Some examinations supply a passage to read. You always have time to read it through to yourself before reading it aloud. Make good use of this time. Here are some ways of doing so:

● Get the gist of the passage (what it is about) as quickly as possible.

● Look for unfamiliar words and try saying them to yourself—mouthing the words if you can. Remember! A confident mispronunciation of an unknown word is better than a gap, which could destroy the whole sense of the passage.

● Notice where the sentences end (marked by stops, question marks, or exclamation marks) so that you can indicate these and other pauses in your reading.

● If there is time, skim through it all again. You may be able to decide on one or two places for special emphasis this time.

II Conversation/discussion

Sometimes this involves you with a group—probably others taking the examination; sometimes you are expected to keep up a conversation with one other person (the examiner, or moderator). Whichever it is, you need to be interested in the topic *and* in the person/people you are talking to. Follow a lead if you can, but be prepared also to lead the conversation back if you think it is going astray or getting dull. Be prepared to listen as well as to talk. Here are two examples:

(a) *Examiner*   What have you chosen to talk about?
    Candidate   My dog.
               Pause
    Examiner   Tell us about him.
    Candidate   Well—er—as a matter of fact, I haven't got a dog now.
    Examiner   No?
    Candidate   No.
               Pause
    Examiner   Can you tell us what happened?
    Candidate   My married sister's got him.

(b) *Examiner*   What have you chosen to talk about?
    Candidate   My dog—at least he used to be my dog but he's gone to my married sister now.

Examiner   Oh. How do you feel about that?
Candidate   I was upset at first, and I still miss him but I can see why my sister
has to have him.

It is not difficult to see which of these conversations is likely to last longer and develop more interestingly. Notice how in the second example the candidate volunteers information in her first reply. This gives the examiner an opportunity to respond with another lead, making the candidate's task easier.

III Aural tests

All talk involves listening, or there would be no point in it. In tests of listening you may be asked to listen to a recording, or to a passage read aloud, then to answer questions on it. Often your answers have to be written rather than spoken. This is a fair and sensible test. Think how often you need to be able to listen carefully, and to act on what you hear — from a teacher, or a friend; your boss at work, a customer in a shop or garage. You may be expected to remember details of the instructions, perhaps with the help of notes made while you were listening. Think of the example we gave on p. 77 of the boy and the weather report.

In the examination you can almost always hear the test piece at least twice. Use the first hearing to sort out what is happening, and who is involved. How many? How are they distinguished from each other? Before the second hearing look carefully at the questions. They will direct your attention to particular points, so that your second hearing allows you to concentrate on those details.

You have a chance to do aural practice every day. Many news bulletins on TV or radio start with headlines. At the end of the bulletin the newscaster says 'Here are the main points again.' Before he gives them, try to jot down notes on all of them.

5 Essential skills

5.1 SPELLING

There are almost 500,000 words in a standard English dictionary. Shakespeare used about 25,000 of them; most adults limit themselves, or are limited by their education and environment, to about 4,000 words. But when Shakespeare lived, writers and readers accepted variations in spelling as a matter of course. Milton, in *Paradise Lost*, wrote 'me' with one 'e' normally, with two ('mee') when he wanted to emphasise it. Shakespeare wrote his own name in two or three different ways. At that time spelling could reflect the writer's mood and personality.

The development of mass print technology has changed all this. We now accept only one spelling, or at most two, as 'correct' for each word. It's not surprising that out of the half million words most writers find some they 'can't spell', i.e. can't *remember* the accepted spelling. It is a remarkable **feat of memory** to be able to use the accepted spellings for all the 8,000 or so words in an educated person's vocabulary.

Your memory will help you in two ways:

1 Visual

If you see a word frequently in its normal spelling you remember *what it looks like*. (Plenty of reading helps!) So if you're unsure that you know a particular word, try writing it on scrap paper to see its shape. If that doesn't work, try using your memory another way:

2 Intellectual

— There are some useful rules.
— Some words spelt alike can be learnt as groups.
— Some related words form families.
All these can be learnt and remembered. Some kinds of mistake can be seen to happen with many words spelt in similar ways. (Words with double letters form one of the commonest traps.) These can be learnt too.

Reasons for faulty spelling

Letters are sometimes omitted (begining instead of begin*n*ing, occured instead of occur*r*ed). Sometimes they are added (al*l*ready instead of already, am*m*ount instead of amount). They are also changed around (bu*is*ness instead of bu*si*ness, fr*ei*ndly instead of fr*ie*ndly). Many words are not spelt as they are pronounced (biscuit is pronounced 'biskit' and minute pronounced 'minnit'—when it refers to time). Slovenly pronunciation can also cause spelling mistakes (recognise is sometimes wrongly pronounced 'reconise' and arctic pronounced 'artic').

Do you make mistakes like these? Now's the time to put them right. Three of the most useful rules to remember are given below. But first of all, here are two pairs of terms we need to use when dealing with spelling:

(i) Letters of the alphabet are either called **vowels** (a, e, i, o, u) or **consonants** (all the others). Exception: 'y' can act as either a vowel or a consonant.

(ii) Vowels, when they are spoken, have **long** and **short** forms:

	long			short		
a	m*a*te	er*a*se	inh*a*ling	r*a*t	ex*a*ct	unh*a*ppily
e	sc*e*ne	*e*ven	rem*e*dial	p*e*n	*e*xtent	inv*e*ntive
i	m*i*ce	arr*i*ve	accl*i*mat*i*se	s*i*t	cred*i*t	pen*i*nsula
o	p*o*le	al*o*ne	potat*o*	g*o*t	al*o*ng	forg*o*tten
u	d*u*ne	s*u*per	ill*u*minate	f*u*n	tri*u*mph	pres*u*mption

RULES

I A stressed syllable with a short vowel, which ends in a single consonant, needs to double the consonant before adding an ending:

$$\text{begin} \quad \text{begin} + \text{n} + \text{ing} = \text{beginning}$$

(The effect of a vowel following a single consonant is to lengthen the vowel *before* the consonant; doubling the consonant makes a 'buffer' which prevents this effect.)

Examples: rat   ratting (=hunting for rats)
          rate   rating (=deciding a suitable rate)

          transmit   transmitter
          bite   biter (=one who bites)
                     (compare 'bitter')

II Prefixes (additions to the beginnings of words) are generally added without alterations either to prefix or word:

dis + appear = disappear   mis + spell = misspell
re + commend = recommend   ex + terminate = exterminate

This often leads to double letters; remember *why* they are doubled and it will be easier to spell the words accurately.

Examples: *dis*satisfy *in*nocent *un*natural *con*nivance

Note Sometimes, if the last letter of the prefix and the first letter of the root word are awkward to say together or similar in sound, the sounds are merged and the initial letter of the root word is doubled.

Examples: prefix *ad-*   accept account attract allude
          prefix *con-*   collapse command correct
          prefix *in-*   immoral irresponsible illegal

Advice If you often make mistakes over words like these, find out and learn the commonest prefixes and their meanings. A dictionary will usually include them.

III The *-ie- -ei-* rule
There are very few exceptions to this rule if you learn it fully:
When the syllable is pronounced 'ee', place -i- before -e- except after -c-.

Examples: rec*ei*ve (after c) bel*ie*ve conc*ei*t (after c) w*ei*ght (not pronounced 'ee')
Exception: seize.

Groups

Hundreds of words can be grouped according to similarities in spelling. It is often easier to remember the group than all its member words separately. The examples here will show you how to find groups of your own. If you often misspell a particular word, collect a group it can belong to and remember it that way.

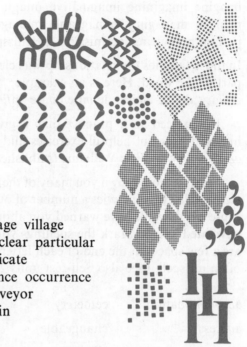

Words with the same ending

–age   average courage damage sausage village
–ar   calendar circular grammar nuclear particular
–ate   accurate delicate separate intricate
–ence   convenience difference experience occurrence
–or   author councillor radiator surveyor
–ain   captain certain curtain fountain
–tion   invention dictation

Words with silent letters

–c– (with *–s–*) ascent discipline scene scientist scissors
–i– (with *–u–*) cruise juice fruit nuisance pursuit
–p– (with *–s–*) psychology psalm
–h– (with *–c–*) character choir scheme stomach technical ache

Plural forms

–y to –i–   babies territories
–y kept   alloys chimneys donkeys valleys
The letter before the –y determines the plural: vowel=no change; consonant =change to –i–.

–f to –ves   calves knives lives shelves wives
–fs   chiefs proofs reliefs roofs

–oes   potatoes tomatoes mosquitoes cargoes volcanoes
–os   commandos curios dynamos photos radios solos

Some other groups

–c– pronounced –s– concern criticise deceit defence recent
all– to al– almighty almost already although altogether
But 'all right' stays as two words.
–ise (verb) to *–ice* (noun)
(verbs)   advise devise license practise prophesy
(nouns)   advice device licence practice prophecy

Families

Related words are as common as related people. The 'blood link' usually has to do with the words' origins as well as with their function. A few examples will show you how to recognise and collect them:

imagine imagining imaginative imaginary imagination
manage managing manageable management manager
permit permitting permissible permission

In those families the relationship was clear. In others it may be shown by only one part of the word, Here is an example:
af*fin*ity de*fine fin*ish de*finite *fin*ite inf*in*ity

If you need more practice than is given here, the following book has over one hundred pages of helpful exercises and information: *Assignments in Punctuation and Spelling* by Eric Williams (published by Edward Arnold).

We have now shown you many of the spellings people find difficult to remember. Here is a list that includes a number of others. The letters in italics are the ones that cause trouble. We have warned you about the most usual misspellings, like adding unwanted letters. Mark the spellings you know you have had trouble with. There are a few spaces at the end of each letter of the alphabet for you to add words you often misspell. (See also Self-test units 2 and 3.)

ac*comm*odation	cemet*e*ry	everyone	he*i*ght
add*r*ess	chang*e*able	except	hurriedly
advertis*e*ment	clim*b*ed	ex*ci*tement	_____
ag*ree*able	com*mitt*ee	experience	_____
a*pp*roach	cu*p*board	_____	_____
attem*p*t	_____	_____	_____
_____	_____	_____	i*mm*ediate
_____	_____	_____	implement
_____	_____	_____	independ*e*nt
_____	_____	Feb*r*uary	interrupt
_____	_____	for*eig*n	_____
_____	defin*i*te	_____	_____
beautifu*l*	d*e*scribe	_____	_____
begin*n*ing	des*pe*rately	_____	_____
bel*ie*ve	disa*pp*ointed	*gau*ge	_____
bur*i*ed	draw*e*rs	glim*p*se	_____
_____	_____	govern*n*ment	_____
_____	_____	_____	knowle*dg*e
_____	_____	_____	_____
_____	_____	_____	_____
_____	em*b*ar*r*assing	han*dk*erchief	_____
_____	equi*pp*ed	happe*n*ed	_____

lamp*p*ost _____   _____ usua*ll*y

*lei*surely _____   _____

lib*r*ary _____ sentence _____

lone*li*ness _____ sep*arate* _____

*lo*se _____ sever*e*ly _____

_____ pa*ss*en*g*er sincer*e*ly

_____ p*eo*ple sto*pp*ed valu*a*ble

_____ po*ss*e*ss*ion succ*ee*d veg*e*table

_____ _____ veter*i*nary

mach*i*ne _____ _____

man*n*er _____ _____

ma*n*or _____ _____

med*i*cine _____ _____

mere*l*y _____ _____ we*a*ther

mini*a*ture quarre*ll*ing _____ w*h*ether

minu*t*es quie*t*ly temper*a*ture who*ll*y

monas*t*ery _____ th*ei*r woo*ll*en

mu*sc*les _____ tr*ie*s wor*r*ying

m*y*stery rec*ei*ve _____ _____

_____ recogni*s*e _____ _____

_____ _____ _____ _____

_____ _____ _____ _____

obed*i*ent _____ _____ _____

o*cc*ur*r*ed _____ _____ _____

Here are some more words that often give trouble:

across (one –*c*–)   corridor (ending –*dor*)

although (one –*l*–)   damaged (no double letter)

always (one –*l*–)   development (develop+ment)

amount (one –*m*–)   emigrate (no double letter.

argument (no –*e*– after –*u*–)   cf. im*mi*grate)

awful (no –*e*–)   finished (no double letter)

college (no –*d*– before –*g*–)   humorous (–*mor*–. cf. *humour*)

completely (ending –*ly*)   imitate (no double letters)

necessary (one –c–)

noisy (no –e–)

occasionally (one –s–)

omitting (one –m–, as in omit)

parallel (one –r–. Think of two *ll*'s as being parallel)

personally (one –n–)

pigeon (no –d– before the –g–)

pity (one –t–)

preferring (one –f–)

professional (one –f–)

reference (no double letters)

safety (ending –ty)

shining (see Rule I)

skilful (no double letters)

souvenirs (ending –ir, French)

telephone (one –l–)

tragedy (no –d– before –g–)

truly (no –e–. cf. *true*)

umbrella (no –e– after –b–)

unnecessary (one –c–. NB *un*– prefix has effect of doubling –n–)

until (one –l–)

writing (one –t–)

5.2   PUNCTUATION

Here, in writing, are some words spoken casually to a friend:

> *'I went into the town to do some shopping, and met Jean coming back—she'd gone early to avoid the crush.'*

In the process of converting the sounds into signs on the paper we have had to use three marks of punctuation:

. a **full stop**	at the end of the utterance, to show it had finished;
, a **comma**	to indicate that the speaker paused between the two connected statements

'I went into the town...'

and

'(I) met Jean coming back';

— a **dash**	because the speaker wanted to explain the second statement straight away, interrupting the natural flow to do so.

Once writing looked like this:

thefirstwritinghadnopausespunctuationorcapitallettersbutranstraightonlikethis

It was soon realised how helpful it would be to separate out the groups of letters (signs for sounds) into words, so that they could be converted back into speech more easily. Most readers did this; silent readers were rare, and in one case a man who could read without mouthing the words was something of a tourist attraction: people came from miles away to see St Ambrose reading in silence. The next logical step after separating the words was to punctuate them.

We use letters of the alphabet in groups to represent the actual words spoken. We use marks of punctuation between the words to show how the *parts* of a sentence relate to the *whole* of the sentence, how the words were spoken, or how the speaker paused. If the writing has never been heard, these marks tell a reader how to make it sound—either aloud or in his head.

pauses , – ;

sound of surprise !

a questioning tone ?

These are the kinds of things punctuation was invented to deal with. Now that writing is no longer restricted to a few specialists, but is used by everyone, punctuation is indispensable. It helps *the reader* to understand more exactly what is written. It helps *the writer* to tidy up and put in order his thoughts and ideas.

Most people, once they have had a reasonable amount of practice in reading and writing, punctuate almost automatically. If you feel uncertain about where to use punctuation, try first saying aloud what you want to write (or with the 'voice' inside your head if you are in the examination room), and notice where you pause and why.

PRACTICE

Use a tape-recorder. Describe something straightforward — the cat settling down to sleep, sounds of the central heating or the wind, the clothes you are wearing — for *not more than a minute*. Then transcribe what you said, putting punctuation wherever you paused and to represent

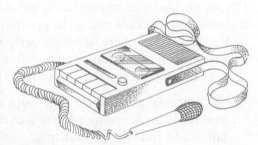

changes of voice, pace or tone. Check your written version by following it closely during a second playback of your recording. Another way of checking is to give your 'script' to a friend who can be persuaded to read it into the tape-recorder, then compare the two recorded versions.

MARKS OF PUNCTUATION

We list the stops roughly in the order of their importance.

Full stops come after any complete unit of expression: a sentence, a group of sentences, even a phrase or single word e.g. 'What's the time?' 'Two o'clock.' They are also sometimes used after abbreviations: Rev., C.S.E. (Because print is clearer than hand-writing this rule is sometimes not followed for abbreviations in books. In this book, for instance, you will see GCE and CSE without the full stops.) When the abbreviation ends with the same letter as the complete word, as in Dr, Mr, Wm etc., there is no need to insert a stop.

Commas are used:

1 To divide a sentence into its component parts so as to make it easier to take in and understand. There are plenty of examples in this book.

2 To separate the items in a list: 'Shoes, socks, shirts, jeans and an anorak.' Note that *and* replaces the comma between the last two items.

3 Often in pairs to mark off words or phrases or quoted words: 'Stamford, formerly on the Great North Road, has become much quieter since the by-pass was built.'

N.B. Commas must not be used between two separate statements, unless they are linked by a conjunction. (The conjunctions in the sentences below are *so* and *but*.)

(i) RIGHT: Mum had a filthy cold, so she spent the day in bed.
(ii) WRONG: Mum had a filthy cold, she spent the day in bed.
(iii) RIGHT: We went to Spain for a holiday, but we found it on the warm side.
(iv) WRONG: We went to Spain for a holiday, we found it on the warm side.

Semi-colons are used between statements which are complete in themselves, but deal with the same idea or subject. We could have used them instead of the commas in sentences (ii) and (iv). Here is another example, taken from a SF story:

Above her, beneath her, and around her, the Machine hummed eternally; she did not notice the noise, for she had been born with it in her ears.

Colons are often placed before lists, quotations and examples:

If you're taking the Pennine Way, you'll need at least: a really good map, a compass, a sleeping-bag, a torch and an emergency ration quite separate from your food for the day.

Colons are also used to emphasise a close connection (but not close enough to use a semi-colon) between two word groups of which each forms a complete sentence, and which might otherwise be properly separated by a full stop. Often a colon is followed by an expansion or elaboration of the statement which precedes it. Here is an example [and see also question 5 (3) on p. 175]:

An old 'rule' about these four stops is still worth remembering as a rough and ready guide: count one for a comma, two for a semi-colon, three for a colon and four for a full stop.

We have given you the standard rules for these marks of punctuation because examiners expect students of English to follow them. *Some* professional writers may ignore or over-ride them for special effects, but we advise you to play safe and stick to them.

Question marks are placed after direct questions. Consider this example:

I asked him whether he was coming to the sale.
'I don't know yet,' he replied. 'Will you be there?'

There are two questions here, but only one of them is direct, so only one question mark is needed. In the following piece there are three questions. One of them requires a question mark. Which one? (Answer on p. 199)

It was difficult to decide what to wear. Would I look out of place in a long dress. I asked Jean what she would be wearing, but she had no more idea than I had.

Exclamation marks (a nickname for them is 'shriek marks') indicate tone, and are effective if they are used rarely, and *one at a time!*

The **Dash** is used:

1 To act like brackets, placed round an extra idea inserted into a statement:

There was no one about—we'd forgotten it was Boxing Day—and we couldn't find a garage open anywhere.

2 To indicate a surprise or abrupt change:

We thought someone was ill in the next room—but it turned out to be an owl, snoring and snuffling on the chimney top.

In the following examples, one is a plain statement, another is a surprising statement, and the third is both surprising and alarming. How do you know from the punctuation which is which? (Answer on p.199)

(a) I opened my brief-case, but the money was not there.
(b) I opened my brief-case—but the money was not there.
(c) I opened my brief-case—but the money was not there!

A **Hyphen** is not a mark of punctuation in the same sense as those we have been discussing. It is a short dash used to link two or more words that are to be thought of as a single word, e.g. a red-hot poker, happy-go-lucky, in-service training. If the words can be united (e.g. wheelbarrow, candlelit, classroom) it is neater to do so. A good dictionary will tell you whether such words need a hyphen or not. The rule is that if they make the same sense without the hyphen(s), do without. The use of hyphens partly depends on the context: compare 'He is writing a short story' with 'He is a short-story writer'.

Quotation marks are also sometimes called 'inverted commas'. Single quotes ('...') are nowadays more commonly used than double quotes ("..."). They are normally placed outside the punctuation—the comma and full stop in these examples:

'It's time we started,' Robert remarked.
One of the most ancient proverbs is: 'Early to bed and early to rise makes
a man healthy, wealthy and wise.'

The mark (') used for closing a quotation is also known as an apostrophe when it:

1 indicates an abbreviation, as in: can't, I've, they're, who've, etc. Think why the repeated word is correct in: It's lost its bone. (Answer on p.201.)

2 indicates possession. With singular words the apostrophe+*s* is added, as in: Jennifer's handbag, the cat's bowl, tomorrow's pudding. With plural words the main method is to put the apostrophe after the *s* that shows the word is plural, as in: five years' steady work, employees' cars only, visitors' entrance. But when, as in a few very old English words, the plural ends with *n* (men, women, children) an apostrophe+*s* is added, so that we get: men's coats, women's shoes, children's books.

PUNCTUATION FOR DIRECT SPEECH

In writing, **direct speech** is the term given to a written version of words actually spoken, for instance in a conversation that is part of a story. The rules already given for quotation marks are the most important things to remember, but there are one or two additional points worth making. Layout and punctuation are fairly standard, the aim being to make the passage easy and unambiguous to read.

The best way to revise speech punctuation methods is to look closely at examples ready to hand, and check your own writing from them. Almost any printed work of fiction will do for this. For our example here we need go no further than the story *Something gets to them* (p. 24):

> 'D'you want to go home?' she asked.
>
> 'We only just got here.'
>
> 'If you didn't want to fish we could bathe. It's hot.'
>
> 'It's too bloody bright; we need a bit of wind. If you hadn't have shouted at me up there — I nearly had a bite —'
>
> 'It's no fun if you can't talk.'
>
> 'You better bloody go home then.'
>
> A bathe, she thought. A lovely cool bathe.
>
> 'Hey, look,' said Peter, 'there's that big 'un again!'
>
> 'He's too wily; you'll never catch him.'
>
> 'Want to bet?'
>
> She clenched her fists and stared at the line . . .

Points to note:

1 Other marks of punctuation *inside* the closing quotation marks at the end of a speech, e.g. . . . *home?'* . . . *a bite —'* . . . *that big 'un again!'*

2 Change of paragraph for each change of speaker, however short the speech.

3 Words indicating who the speaker is — *she asked, said Peter* — only put in when necessary to avoid confusion. When it is obvious who is speaking, leave them out. In this extract the change of paragraph makes it clear most of the time.

4 Notice how the punctuation is placed when a speech is interrupted in order to indicate the speaker: *'Hey, look,' said Peter, 'there's* . . . (Here an exclamation mark could have been placed after *look*, but the writer chose to save it for the end of Peter's remark.) The comma after *look* comes before the quotation marks; *said* has a small letter, because it is within a sentence, not starting a fresh one. Similarly *there's* has a small letter, being a continuation of Peter's remark. Without the interruption it would have read: *' . . . look, there's that big 'un again!'*

With practice, and with constant careful checking of your writing, punctuation, even of speech, soon becomes automatic.

5.3   GRAMMAR AND USAGE

Grammar is the word used for the system of rules that governs the orderly use of a language – especially the parts of speech, the way words change or **inflect** their forms and how these forms are used, and the combination of words into sentences. Here are some examples of **inflexions:**

he him she her they them
do does doing did done
happy happier happiest happily.

Because any living language is constantly in use it is bound to be constantly changing — growing, developing, shedding words and adding new ones, responding to the changing demands made on it by its users. So no account of the grammar of a living language can ever be complete or unchangeable. (For this we need a 'dead' language like Latin.)

Words form sentences — units of meaning. The branch of grammar concerned with sentence structure is called **syntax**. Points of grammar and syntax that affect the way we use English are sometimes grouped together under the general term **usage,** and this word emphasises the value of understanding English grammar: it can help you to **use** words more effectively.

SOME USEFUL GRAMMATICAL TERMS

PARTS OF SPEECH — in traditional grammar this is the term for the eight types of word usage. Here they are, with examples:

noun	chair house idea London
pronoun	I you ourselves
adjective	comfortable (chair) big (house) bright (idea) busy (London)
verb	hear explore agree
adverb	(hear) clearly quite (busy) sometimes (agree)
preposition	at in with
conjunction	and but although if
interjection	hullo ah

These terms relate to *the way words are used* rather than to the words in isolation. Often the same word is used in many different ways, e.g.

If you commit an offence the police may *fine* you. (verb)
I have paid my *fine*. (noun)
London has several theatres. (noun)
He soon acquired a *London* accent. (adjective)

Adjective or adverb?

Adjectives help (or **qualify**) nouns and pronouns. Adverbs help (or **modify**) verbs, adjectives and other adverbs. The *–ly* ending is a common way to form adverbs from adjectives, but look at these: *real* adj./*really* adv.
loud adj. or adv./*loudly* adv.

You look real smart. WRONG
('Smart' is an adjective, and needs the adverb 'really' to modify it.)
'Am I talking too loud?' 'No, I like loud voices.' RIGHT
(The first 'loud' is an adverb, the second an adjective.)

SUBJECT AND PREDICATE — the two parts of a sentence:
The miner, dazed and shaken, (subject) strikes one of his few remaining dry matches with extreme caution. (predicate)

MAIN VERB AND OBJECT — these are parts of the **predicate** of a sentence. There *must* be a main verb for it to be a complete sentence. This verb agrees with the subject, e.g. if the sentence above had *miners* the verb would become *strike*.

NOMINATIVE AND ACCUSATIVE — used with reference to nouns and pronouns.

Pronouns change their form (**inflect**) according to their job in a sentence:
Nominative I he she we I shot the albatross. He/She was making cakes. Are we too soon?
Accusative me him her us He hit me. (etc.)

POSSESSIVE OR GENITIVE—can be regarded as a third inflected form, indicated by *'s* or *s'*.

PRESENT, PAST AND FUTURE TENSE—different forms of **verbs**:

I *make/am making* bread (present)
I *made/was making* bread (past)
I *shall make* bread   (future)

ACTIVE AND PASSIVE—concerns the way **verb** and **subject** are related:

             bites
The dog *bit*   the man. (active)
             will bite

             is bitten
The man *was bitten*   by the dog. (passive)
             has/had been bitten
             will be bitten

TRANSITIVE AND INTRANSITIVE—**Verbs** are said to be transitive when their action or state is transmitted to an **object** (which will be a noun, pronoun or its equivalent):

He *was driving* the car. (transitive, 'the car' being the object)
The great day *has come*. (intransitive)

Some verbs are used both transitively and intransitively, e.g.:

That girl *plays* the trumpet. (transitive)
That girl *plays* happily by herself. (intransitive, the words after the verb being adverbial)

AGREEMENT

1 However extended the sentence may be,
subject and main verb must always agree:

The old fellow, silver-haired and decrepit, and his daughter, well-known locally
for her skill as a tennis player, *was* seen enjoying the morning sunshine. WRONG
(The sentence should read '*were* seen' because there are two subjects, 'fellow'
and 'daughter'.)

Sometimes the subject word refers to a collection or group (e.g. committee, board, team, herd). If they form a single unit the verb is singular:

The team is (*not* are) flying to Moscow for the Olympic Games.

If the context makes it clear that they are a number of individuals the verb is plural:

The committee *were* a long time making up *their minds* about the candidate.
(The plural must then apply throughout.)

2 In any continuous writing tenses of verbs should agree:

When I *arrived* (past) he *greeted* me warmly and *took* my coat.

Every time I *sleep* (present) here I *feel* uneasy, although the proprietor *does*
all he *can* to make me comfortable.

(See *Direct and Indirect Speech*, p. 134)

3 *This/that* (singular) *these/those* (plural)
Make sure that you are consistent:

This thing is   } obvious. RIGHT
These things are }

These kind of things always cause trouble. WRONG

This kind } of thing always } causes trouble. RIGHT
These kinds } { cause trouble.

4 *Anybody anyone everyone nobody no one none nothing*

All these words (and others like them) are singular, and should be followed appropriately:

No one *is* expected to wash up today.
If anybody *makes* a move, I'll shoot.
None of the people here *is* too fat.

(The last example may sound unnatural; the plural word 'people' makes the ear expect a plural verb.)

Everyone in the plane had *his* hands up.

(The problem here is that 'everyone' may include both male and female. If the sentence begins to sound awkward it is best to change the wording, e.g. 'They all had their hands up.')

PRONOUN INFLEXIONS

1 Linked pronouns can sometimes cause confusion:
You and I (=we) *are* invited. RIGHT
('I' is in the nominative because it is the subject.) **But**
They asked you and I to come. WRONG
Here 'you and —' forms the object, so the accusative is needed:
They asked you and me (=us) to come. RIGHT

2 Pronouns following a preposition are in the accusative:
Between *you and me*, I think he is a liar. RIGHT

3 *Who* (nominative)/*whom* (accusative)/*whose* (possessive)
The accusative 'whom' can sound pedantic and is used less often nowadays than it used to be, e.g. *Who did you want?* sounds better than *Whom did you want?* even though as the object it should be in the accusative.

COMPARISON OF ADJECTIVES AND ADVERBS

Many adjectives and adverbs have different forms for *comparing* two people, things or states (**comparative**), and for the *highest* degree (**superlative**):

	comparative	*superlative*
happy	happier	happiest
miserable	more miserable	most miserable
good	better	best

1 It is wrong to double the comparative:
I couldn't be more happier. WRONG

2 Some adjectives and adverbs, because of their meaning, have no comparative or superlative degrees, e.g. *unique* (it is impossible to be more unique than unique).

OTHER DOUBLES

1 Negatives: He never gave me no book. WRONG
(Logically this means he *did* give a book.)

2 Past Tense: I would have loved to have gone. WRONG
           I would have loved to go. RIGHT

3 'The reason is because...' WRONG
The word 'because' itself contains the idea of 'reason'. The correct form is *either*
'the reason is that...' *or* 'because...'.

DIRECT AND INDIRECT (REPORTED) SPEECH

Because any language starts and is sustained by its spoken (oral) forms, we find the
need to record speech in various ways when we write. In stories or narrative essays,
which are often the easiest kinds of continuous writing in examinations, two
chief ways are used.

This short piece comes from a paperback version of a popular television series
(Starsky and Hutch). Jamieson, the detective, has been hiding on board a berthed
ship, listening to a group of criminals:

'Starsky and Hutch'

As he neared the outside vent, he
reminded himself that he ought to be
thankful he had at least overheard the
plotters, even though he couldn't see
them. It was the first break of any
kind he had gotten* in three weeks of
investigation. He emerged from the
shaft without being seen, screwed the
wire mesh cover back in place and
hurried to join his work crew. When
the quitting whistle blew at five-thirty,
there was a general exodus from the
dock area. Jamieson headed for a nearby pay phone. He dialed, then asked
for an extension number.
      'Dobey,' a male voice said.
      The undercover officer said, 'Jamieson here, Captain. Glad I caught you
      before you left.'

Here are alternative ways of writing three parts of the extract:

1 ... he reminded himself that he ought to be thankful he had at least overheard
the plotters, even though he couldn't see them.
Alt. *'I ought to be thankful,' he said to himself, 'I have at least overheard them. Pity
I couldn't see their faces, though.'*

2 He dialed, then asked for an extension number.
Alt. *He dialed. 'Put me through to extension 34, please.'*

3 The undercover officer said, 'Jamieson here, Captain. Glad I caught you before
you left.'
Alt. *After giving his name, Jamieson told the captain he was glad he had caught him
before he left.*

What we have done is to change a report of the words into the actual words
thought or spoken (1 and 2), and vice versa (3). It is useful to have both these
methods at your fingertips. In general, indirect speech is more formal, less lively
than direct speech. Notice how it works. Indirect speech doesn't need the quotation
marks needed for direct speech. Other changes are:

* *Note:* 'gotten' is American for 'got'.

	direct	indirect
(a) Verbs change tense	1 I have	he had
	2 Put me...	he asked
	3 I caught	he had caught
(b) Pronouns change	3 I caught you	he caught him

(**Note** Because both first and second person pronouns change to third person, you need to make sure that no confusion arises, e.g., 'He told him that he thought he was coming with him.' This could mean EITHER 'I thought you were coming with me.' OR 'I thought I was coming with you.' To avoid confusion you may need to use nouns: He told John that he thought he, Peter, was coming with him.)

	direct	indirect
(c) Colloquial turns of phrase are avoided	1 Pity I...	_____
	2 Put me through	asked for

(d) References to time are changed (e.g. today/that day; tomorrow/the next day etc.)

(e) 'this' becomes 'that' etc.

PRACTICE

Try it for yourself on the story *Something gets to them*. Use the part which begins on p. 23 (see p. 201 for the rest of our version):

'You ought to hold it still.'   She said that he ought to hold it still.

'I know what I'm doing...'   He retorted that he knew what he was doing...

REGISTER AND APPROPRIATENESS — does it fit?

We are all used to changing the way we speak according to the person we are talking to or the particular circumstances. We try to choose the most effective **manner** of speaking as well as the best words. This is sometimes called the **register** we employ.

When it comes to English for examination purposes, register is an important matter. If you are writing a story, slang and colloquialisms may be needed in the direct speech, but should be avoided in the background narrative. In *Something gets to them* the girl, holding the tin of bait, says 'Yuk!... ugh, horrible!' but the adjective used to describe the maggots is not 'yukky' but 'nauseating'.

In conversation we may use the expression 'dead nice' to express approval, but it would add less than nothing to a description of a dress, a book or a person in a written essay. 'Moan' is a popular alternative to 'complain'; it might fit into a conversation in a story. But no examiner would like to read that Juliet 'moaned' when Romeo was banished, or that Heathcliff (in *Wuthering Heights*) was 'a bit of a moaner'.

It is not always slang that is inappropriate. An examination candidate once wrote that Macbeth was 'upset' after the murder of King Duncan (which he had in fact committed himself). The word is too feeble; 'appalled' comes nearer to the scale of Macbeth's feelings.

Peter, in *Something gets to them*, is quarrelling with the girl for disturbing the fish by throwing stones. His feelings boil up, and lead to his order: '...keep your hands in your bloody pockets.' The swear-word here is a fitting measure of his anger, but earlier in the story, even before the quarrel, he uses it frequently. Why? What does it tell us about him? In what sense is it **appropriate** in the context of the story?

A word of warning finally: however friendly you feel – or want them to think you feel! – towards the examiners, avoid too chatty and personal an approach Here are three essay openings that make this mistake, and would earn poorer marks as a result:

The funfair
Ever been on the Big Wheel? No? You don't know what you're missing!...

Childhood fears
I was a bit of a coward as a child really. I don't usually like admitting it but you won't tell anyone, will you?...

The waxworks
You go in through this doorway that looks real spooky...

Compress — squeeze together, bring into smaller space

5.4   USING A DICTIONARY

Anyone who is serious about improving his or her English should own a dictionary. Many good ones are available, and most bookshops stock a selection of them. Here are just three:

The Concise Oxford Dictionary   (Oxford University Press)
Chambers Twentieth Century Dictionary   (W & R Chambers)
The Penguin English Dictionary   (Penguin Books)

A dictionary has to compress information of many different kinds into as small a space as possible. To do this efficiently the compiler (or *lexicographer*—look it up!) has four particular methods:

1 Abbreviations (i.e. shortened forms – there is usually a list of them at the beginning of the book.
2 Ways of avoiding having to print the same words over and over again.
3 Different type faces.
4 Signs and symbols (these are also usually explained at the beginning).

This entry in *The Concise Oxford Dictionary* shows how they are used:

> **parti'cūlar** *a.* & *n.* **1.** *a.* Relating to one as distinguished from others, special; ‖P~ **Baptists,** (Hist.) body holding doctrines of *particular election* and *particular redemption* (i.e. of only some of the human race); *particular* INTENTION. **2.** (Logic). (Of proposition) in which something is predicated of some, not all, of a class (opp. *universal*). **3.** One considered apart from others, individual, (*this particular tax is no worse than others*; *particular* AVERAGE[1]). **4.** Worth notice, special, (*took particular trouble*; *for no particular reason*). **5.** Minute (*full and particular account*); scrupulously exact, fastidious (*about, what* or *as to what* one eats etc.). **6.** Hence or cogn. ~ITY (-ă′r-) *n.,* ~LY[2] *adv.* **7.** *n.* Detail. item; **in ~,** especially (*mentioned one case in particular*), specifically (*did nothing in particular*); (in *pl.*) detailed account or information. [ME f. OF *particuler* f. L *particularis* (as PARTICLE; see -AR[1])]

You do not need to 'de-code' everything you see in a dictionary, but it is useful to get to know the particular methods used in your own dictionary so that you can make the best use of it in English work. Here are some general hints.

TO FIND THE WORD YOU WANT

To use a dictionary well you first need to **find** the word you want. Once you can do this quickly and accurately you will be able to find out how to **use** words, how to **spell** them, how to **say** them.

All dictionaries have words arranged in strict alphabetical order, so that, for example:

bit   comes before   bite
fascinate   comes before   fascism

A quick eye is needed to find the letter, perhaps in the middle of the word, which determines where the word is placed in proper alphabetical order.

For practice, set out the following words in the order they would appear in a dictionary (see also Self-test unit 6):

impediment	impassive	impetuous	impenetrable
impasse	impeach	impartial	imperial
impetigo	impel	impedance	impetus

Check your final list against your own dictionary. All the words appeared in two successive pages of a dictionary. If you find you are slow at this, work with a friend, and test each other with similar lists of your own.

Almost all dictionaries, even small ones, help your eye to find words quickly by printing words in heavy type at the top of each page, e.g.

> **plant**   **plaster**   **plastic**   **platinum**

These are the *first* and *last* words on each page. If you are looking for planetarium' you know you have gone too far without having to check every word, because –e– comes before –t–. You are in the right place for 'pla*te*au' (–te– before –ti–); but if you want 'pla*ty*pus' turn over. If it is the spelling you are checking, remember it is more likely to be in the dictionary than not; you may be looking in the wrong place. (A telephone directory is set out on the same alphabetical principle. Use it for practice in speed reading.)

Combined words will be found by looking under the main part. In the following list the part in italics shows you where to find them in *Chambers Twentieth Century Dictionary* (other dictionaries may list them differently):

*bar*maid	invisible *imports*	*parallel* bars
Cheshire *cat*	*level*-crossing	special *pleading*
faith-healer	old *maid*	*rear*guard

Sometimes, when both parts of a word are prominent, it will appear under each part. If in doubt it is safer to look up both; for instance, the term *universal joint* appears in *Chambers* under both parts, but is more fully explained under *joint*.

For practice, look up these words in your dictionary:

> bookworm   cheese-mite   song-thrush

How to use words

Some words are very *versatile*. For instance, the simple word 'plant' can have at least five meanings as a noun, and six meanings as a verb. A dictionary will sort all these out for you, usually numbering the different meanings 1, 2, 3 etc. This makes cross-referencing easier if the word is referred to elsewhere in the dictionary.

ver'satile *a.* Turning easily or readily from one subject or occupation to another, capable of dealing with many subjects, (*versatile author, genius, disposition, mind*); (Bot. & Zool.) moving freely about or up and down on a support (*versatile anther, head, antennae*); changeable, inconstant; hence or cogn. ~LY² (-l-lĭ) *adv.*, **vĕrsati'lity** *n.* [F, or f. L *versatilis* (as prec.; see -IL)]

Most dictionaries will tell you, by means of an abbreviation, what part of speech (see p. 131) the word is; or, if it can be used in several ways, will indicate the different parts of speech together with the meanings. Here are common abbreviations for the eight parts of speech. Can you complete the words?

a.	int.	pron.
adv.	n.	v.
conj.	prep.	

Verbs are often listed as *transitive* (v.t. *or* tr.) or *intransitive* (v.i. *or* intr.). These terms are explained on p. 132.

Dictionaries can also help you to use linked words accurately. Many words are normally related to others by means of particular *prepositions*, e.g.

> worthy *of* reward (not *to* or *with* or *at*)
> eligible *for* promotion (not *of* or *to* or *in*)

Sometimes words can be used with more than one preposition, the one to be used perhaps being determined by the context and the exact meaning required. Again a dictionary will help you here.

For practice, decide which prepositions you would use with these words, then check them in your dictionary. (Answers on p. 200)

complimented..........	different...............	immune...............
contrary.................	exempt	liable ....
deficient................	identical...............	persevere ....

How to spell (See also *Spelling*, p. 121)

Now that most spellings are standardised, dictionaries perform the useful task of listing the accepted spellings, together with any correct alternatives, e.g.

> recognize, –ise　　　judgement, –gment

When you use a dictionary to check spelling, make sure you have looked in all possible places. Letters that are not pronounced may mislead you, so don't waste time looking for 'rhododendron' after 'rodeo' or for 'knead' amongst the words beginning with n–.

If you do not find the word where you expect it to be, you are probably looking in the wrong place. Keep trying!

How to say words

Before spellings were standardised by the development of mass printing techniques they were more dependent on the actual sounds of the words. These sounds varied —as they still do—from one part of the country to another, according to local speech habits and dialects.

Easy means of communication, e.g. radio and television, have brought about a degree of standardisation in the way we *say* words as well as the way we *write* them. Now that English crosses so many national boundaries it is helpful to have recognisable 'received pronunciations'; dictionaries will record them. Any good dictionary will show how words are normally spoken, using a simple system of signs.

There are three important points to do with the way words sound when we say them:

(a) the vowel sounds (particularly whether *long* (–) or *short* (ᵕ), see p. 122;

(b) the consonants (whether singly, or in clusters of two or more);

(c) the placing of accent or stress.

(a) Vowels

Most dictionaries give a key to standard vowel sounds either at the beginning of the book or at the foot of each page. Here is one such key:

> māte, mēte, mīte, mōte, mūte, mo͞ot; răck, rĕck, rĭck, rŏck, rŭck, ro͝ok; caw, cow; bah, boil

Look for the key in your own dictionary. It will establish the way all vowel pronunciations are shown in the rest of the dictionary.

Practice Find out from your dictionary whether the vowel sounds indicated by italics are long or short:

c*a*nine	*e*difice	l*i*thograph	dr*o*ll	j*u*gular
b*a*rony	plenary	sp*i*ral	R*o*many	al*u*minium

Not all vowel sounds are so simple. Where more guidance is needed a dictionary will often give a phonetic spelling of the whole word, or the difficult bit, in brackets after the word:

> none (nŭn)   rucksack (ro͝o–)   jaunty (jaw–, jah–)   rough (rŭf)

(b) Consonants

All except four of our consonants have only one accepted pronunciation each when used singly. The four exceptions are c, f, g, and s, which each have two:

> *c*astle, *c*entre   *g*rand, *g*iant
> *f*ox, o*f*   *s*ample, a*s*

The dictionary will always indicate which of these is needed if there is likely to be any doubt. It will also help with variable-sounding consonant pairs or groups, like –gh:

> laugh (lahf)   bough (bow)

and with difficulties deriving from the phonetic inconsistencies of English spelling, like these:

> orchard (–tsh)   rouse (rowz)
> orchestra (–k–)   route (ro͞ot)

(c) Accent/stress

English is a strongly stressed language, and it is often important to know where the stress is placed in normal usage. Here are some easy examples:

> traditional   umbrella   murderous

It is not difficult to recognise that the stress falls on the second, the second and the first syllables respectively. But which syllables would you stress in these words?

> controversy   foreboding   bamboo   rosemary

Find out how your dictionary marks accented syllables; it is often by a raised comma ('), an acute sign (´) or a raised stop (˙) after the stressed syllable.

Remember that no dictionary claims to be infallible. Its job is to record *normal* usage, and this varies from year to year. If you enter into controversy over the way 'controversy' should be stressed, don't expect the dictionary to settle the argument. It may well record two pronunciations.

5.5   STYLE

We talk of a friend's *style* in clothes. More generally, we may say 'I like her style', meaning her way of carrying herself, choosing what clothes suit her best, how she will face the world each day. 'Now, that boy (or girl) has real style!' Here we are concerned as much with *personality* as with clothes or appearance. These days we often hear the expression 'life-style'. In this term the ideas we have already noticed are drawn together, so that we see a person's whole way of life as an expression of his or her individual personality.

Style is a useful term to describe writing, and the idea of style can, once we have fully grasped it, help with our own writing. Here too it starts with personality— the writer's personality, his individual outlook and his particular reasons for writing. The style of a piece of writing is *the way* in which a writer gives written expression to what he has to say. But it goes further than this; because *how* he writes depends on two other factors: *content* (i.e. what is to be said) and *audience* (i.e. who the writing is for).

Example A report written for a scientific journal on rainfall and flooding in a particular area will be written in a different style from a journalist's eye-witness account of the same floods in the local paper. A flood victim's letter to his relatives abroad would be in a different style again.

Only *practice* will allow you to develop your own style. But we can give you some helpful hints to follow, and show you how others succeed or fail in finding good writing style.

The distinctive style of John Travolta

Do's AND DON'Ts

Do's	*Don'ts*
(i) Try to be brief, simple, and sincere.	Avoid longwindedness and affectation.
(ii) Take trouble always to choose the right word.	Steer clear of commonplace words and phrases, and of clichés.
(iii) Keep your sentences clear in construction, and use active verbs where there is a choice.	Avoid clumsy or confused sentence structure; avoid excessive use of passive verbal constructions.
(iv) Aim for variety of construction between one sentence and the next.	Avoid making your writing monotonous; beware of repeated sentence patterns.

All the following examples were written by 15-/16-year-olds, in answers to examination questions.

Confused sentence structure (iii)

I was to be one of the noisy gossips in the opera, a character that did not cause me great difficulty in putting forward, according to my father!

Commonplace words and phrases (ii)

June 4th *dawned bright* with *not a cloud in the sky*, but just after midday, when preparations were *in full swing*, dark clouds *raced across the sky* and the wind picked up tremendously.

(The only memorable, because individually selected, group of words in this example is 'the wind picked up tremendously.')

Monotonous sentence patterns (iv)

Local factories usually prepare floats on which their employees can enter the Carnival, schools prepare floats, Brownies prepare floats, Guides prepare floats, and so the list goes on . . .

Affectation (i)

A fleecy cloud, a rich ploughed field . . . We have been moved by the beauty of spinning, dancing toes, we have touched St. Paul's with reverence, and laughed at the audacity of the wind.

(In spite of the writer's grasp of *vocabulary* this is affected, insincere writing. It does not ring true; the writer is trying to make us have feelings that are faked.)

Longwindedness (i)

The stately home was much more restricted; the course for you to take was plotted out, there were people watching you continuously, although I realise that this was to make sure nothing was stolen. Only certain areas were open to the public, and these were specially picked, decorated and furnished in a way to make people interested. Nothing there was really surprising and if I went again it would probably be almost exactly the same.

Brevity (i)

> The pit is a way of life ... hot, dry, dusty summers and dreary winters.

(These two examples of brevity are taken from an essay about a coal-mine. They are dramatically economical compared with the previous example. Not a word is wasted.)

Simplicity (i)

> Coal has been tipped in the gutter and left so you can't get in the gate until Joe comes to shift it.

(From the same essay. Look how much we are told in these 20 words: that coal has been tipped in the gutter; that it shouldn't have been left there because it obstructs the gate; that people using the gate will have to wait for a man to shift it; that the man is called Joe, and it is his job to shift the coal.)

The right word (ii)

> The air was damp with spray from the firemen's hoses, which lay across the road *like spaghetti*.

Passive verbal constructions (iii)

> Saturday is when most people do things they would be too idle to do on a Sunday. Lawns are mowed and gardens are dug; most of the shopping is normally done on a Saturday.

(The passive verbs '*are mowed*', '*are dug*', '*is done*' take away from the purposefulness and continuity of the Saturday activities.)

Active verbs, varied sentence structure (iii)

> 'That'll make you my boss then, won't it?' said David, and he walked over to the big red fire-engine, leaving Daniel alone with his thoughts.

(Here the writer wants to keep the initiative with David. The active verbs help him to do so. It is David who spoke, walked, left Daniel.)

BEGINNING AND ENDINGS

The opening sentence of a piece of writing has to attract the reader's attention, interest and curiosity. Here are four good examples:
- A crowd of people had turned out to watch the blazing building.
- The pit is a way of life.
- The whole trouble began when the masters started getting a £3 bonus for each boy who passed the GCE.
- As I look back on that night I still shudder with fear.

Each of these clearly refers to the main subject of the essay. Each leaves the writer free to develop this primary idea, without confusing it with others less important. Now look at this opening sentence to an essay entitled *A day to remember*:

> We had all been looking forward to this day for a long time, not only the young ones, but also the older ones who may have taken part in similar occasions before.

'We', 'this day', 'young ones', 'older ones', 'similar occasions'—there are too many loose ends here. Only the first two were in fact developed in the essay that followed.

A better opening might have been:

> We had all been looking forward to this day for a long time.

The reader thinks 'what day?' The writer has left himself free to develop the subject as it suits him; he may answer the reader's question, or leave it and first describe his anticipation of the day, or the preparation, keeping the reader guessing for a while.

● Keep your opening sentence simple and clear. *Don't* introduce ideas that you cannot, or don't want to follow up.

Your closing sentence needs to round off the piece of writing. It must not start any new ideas. It is often possible to draw together the main ideas in the essay. The closing sentence can refer back to the opening, or to the title of the essay. The writer of *A day to remember* ended better than he began, like this:

> The dancing continued until twelve o'clock, when everyone returned home happy and contented that we had all made this a day that we would remember.

Section III Self-test units

The tests in this Section highlight difficulties and common errors and are designed to help you to test yourself on the material in Section II. Answers (where provided) appear in red on pages 202-206 and a check-list of these tests appears on page 158.

Answers (where provided) appear in red on pages 202-206 and a check-list of these tests appears on page 158.

TEST 1   *20 minutes*

Accuracy

See how many marks you can score in this self-measurement test. Write your answers on a separate piece of paper and time yourself carefully. Marks to be scored are given with the answers on p. 202.

1 Here is a statement:
In a mixed class the girls who are cleverer soon get bored.
This means that those girls in the class who are cleverer than the others soon get bored. By adding *two* marks of punctuation you can make it mean that *all* the girls are cleverer. (Don't worry if you think this is untrue!) What are the marks and where do they go?

2 Here are two phrases: (a) *John and I*   (b) *John and me*
Decide which of them, (a) or (b), would fit better in each blank space:
When_____ come to your party we shall bring our presents with us. Mum and Dad gave_____ a bike each, so we can ride to your house._____ ride everywhere these days.

3 Punctuation again! comma (,) semi-colon (;) colon (:) dash (—)
Decide which of these four marks of punctuation fits best where the box is:
For this job you need the following □ drawing-pins, paste, brown paper.

4   *lay   laid   lain*
These words are often confused. Which of them belongs in the space?
Do you know how long you have_____ there snoring?

5 Match the five abbreviations below to their meanings:

n.b.	compare
etc.	note well
cf.	that is
e.g.	and other things
i.e.	for example

6 There are standard ways of ending letters. Decide which of the endings here you would use in a letter to the head of your primary school on his or her retirement. (Be careful! Some are wrong for any letter.)

(a) yours truely	(b) Yours Sincerly
(c) Your sincere ex-pupil	(d) Yours faithfully
(e) Yours sincerely	(f) your's Faithfully
(g) yours Sincerely	(h) Yours truly

7 Here is a longer test of your skill in punctuation. To set out the passage below you will need to use the following kinds of marks: two full stops (.) an exclamation mark (!) a question mark (?) three sets of inverted commas (". . .") an apostrophe (') and three capital letters.

you know i cant do I of course you do she said scornfully.

8 Now set out the piece given for question 7 correctly, deciding where to place the words in *three* different lines (or paragraphs).

9 Decide which of the two forms of words given you would use in the blank space in this sentence:

The safety kit _____ six different parts.

comprises *or* is comprised of

10 Each of the three sentences below contains one faulty word.

Decide on one of them, and put it right. (If you can find the other two as well, award yourself two bonus marks.)

(a) Without his having to say so openly his tone of voice inferred that he was bored.

(b) They told me I had past with a few marks to spare.

(c) In the excavations the strata they had reached was rich in Roman remains.

When you have done your best, turn to page 202 and find out how many you have scored. Don't worry if you got some of the questions wrong, or even if they were all wrong. This book will help you put right your mistakes.

TEST 2   *15 minutes*

Spelling (See unit 5.1)

1 These words are correctly spelt:
reign niece receipt piece siege
What is the rule that assures you of their accuracy?

2 The word *incarnate* has three syllables (in-carn-ate). How many syllables are there in these words?
   contemporary originally responsibility criticism occasionally similar
(When you are spelling unfamiliar words it is a good idea to split them up into their syllables.)

3 Fill in the blanks in:
If you are ill you may have a d – – – – – –.
Two people not in the same room are se– – – – – –.
Two people arguing are having an a – – – – – – –.
If you keep a shop you are running a b – – – – – –s.
If you have a job for four weeks you are a t– – – – – – y employee.
If you fail when you expect to succeed you are d – – – – – – – –d.

4 These words are correctly spelt:
   achievement believe chief deceit height
What would you say to people who argue that they are wrongly spelt?

5 What has the spelling of these words in common? When you have decided, write down four more in the same family.
   guarantee guess guide guitar brogue guy

6 The past of *kill* is *killed*; the past of *eat* is *ate*. Write down the past of:

> *choose submit prefer remember dispel occur*

7 These words are correctly spelt. How does the rule work that gets them right?

> *conceit feign relieve foreign ceiling*

8 What has the spelling of these words in common? Write down four more in the same family.

> *jealous treasure pleasant health*

9 What is noticeable about the spelling of this group of words?

> *resign gnaw design consignment*

(Answers on p. 201)

TEST 3   *20 minutes*

Spelling and usage (See units 5.1 and 5.3)

Many of the points tested here are discussed elsewhere in the book. If you get a low score the book will help you to improve.

1 *Road* is singular; the word *roads* is plural. Give the plural of:

> *recess spoonful tomato*

2 We make *helpful* negative by adding *un*—*unhelpful*. What are the negative forms of:

> *definite legal satisfied*

3 In the sentence *He's finishing the work* we say the verb is in the present tense. In *He finished the work yesterday* the verb is in the past tense. Now put the verbs in these examples into the past:

> *He is beginning.*
> *She is doing very well.*
> *I always choose nylon bearings.*

4 In *Sue performs that work on the guitar* we say the verb is active. In *That work is often performed on the guitar* the verb is passive. Put the verbs in these sentences into the passive:

> *He transmits the message.*
> *She speaks the words clearly.*
> *She lays her bag on the counter.*

Your answers should begin with *The message ...*, *The words ...*, *The bag ....*

5 In the group of words *knew, knotted, knife, khan* the first three have a *k* which is not sounded. *Khan* is the odd one out because the *k* is sounded. Say the following groups of words aloud, and in each pick out the word which sounds different in the part it shares with the other three.

> *average wastage engage courage*
> (Listen to the final syllable in each case.)
> *access occur excess succeed*
> (Listen to the c's.)
> *reason jealous health weather*
> (Listen to the first syllable in each case.)

6 Correct the italicised word in each of these sentences:

He never did *nothing* of the kind.

I *can't* hardly stand on this surface.

She hadn't *never* seen a squirrel.

7 An extra letter has crept into these misspelt words. Rewrite them correctly.

arguement   familly   ommit

atheletic   mischievious   similiar

8 A letter has been omitted in each of these words. Rewrite them correctly.

accomodate   Febuary   imediately

exept   goverment   suprise

9 Correct the letter that is wrong in each of the following:

mathamatics   definately   repitition

10 Each of these three misspellings is caused by bad pronunciation. Say and write the words correctly.

buisness   interduce   feul

(Answers on p. 203)

TEST **4**   *10 minutes*

Vocabulary

1 Think of a word or phrase meaning the same as:

lenient   incentive   redundant

relinquish   grotesque   synthetic

2 Think of a word or phrase meaning the opposite of:

impudent   opaque   tranquil

destitute   deciduous   acquiesce

(Answers on p. 203)

TEST **5**   *30 minutes*

Vocabulary

1 Does *spurious* mean fast, false or sharp?

2 Think of a seven-letter word beginning with *l* meaning handwriting that is easy to read.

3 From the ten words below choose five which best fit these meanings:

(a) notched like the cutting edge of a saw;

(b) (mark) that cannot be blotted out or erased;

(c) at the point of death;

(d) proud, overbearing, haughty;

(e) capable of more than one meaning.

moribund corrugated ambiguous biennial arrogant

innate indelible morbid serrated prodigious

4 What is the meaning of the prefixes *im–*, *il–*, *in–*, in the words *impossible, illegal, inessential?*

5 *Into* or *in to*

    (a) There's the bell; we must hurry_____ school.

    (b) John dived_____ the water.

6 *Upon* or *up on*

    (a) The ornament was high _____ the shelf.

    (b) She lay_____ the sofa pretending to read.

7 Which is more likely: *crossroads* or *cross roads?*

8 Would you sooner learn dancing from: a *dancing teacher* or a *dancing-teacher?*

9 If you are *cadaverous*, are you like a cad, a corpse or a caveman?

10 Which words are not needed in the following sentences?

    (a) From whom can I borrow a pencil from please?

    (b) I can't tell the difference between the dark-haired pair of twins.

    (c) My collection of glass animals is absolutely unique.

    (d) They returned back home tired and hungry.

    (e) John met up with his friend after work.

11 What is the singular of *media?*

12 What is the plural of *neurosis?*

13 Which of the words in brackets makes sense in the following sentences?

    (a) The best writers are (imaginary/imaginative).

    (b) Cartoons are not trying to give the (allusion/illusion/delusion) of reality.

    (c) 'I must (have/of) put my keys somewhere,' said Jane.

    (d) The (effect/affect) of the drug (effected/affected) the athletes' performance.

    (e) 'It's the (principle/principal) of the thing,' said the teacher.

14 Which study is to do with words: *entomology* or *etymology?*

15 If you are *ingenuous* are you more likely to be innocent or guilty?

16 Is *sporadic* very fast, very slow or occasional?

17 Sort the following 20 words into two groups of ten, one with the heading 'True', the other 'False'.

    frank perjury candour forgery fallacious verity paragon fraud duplicity sincere deceive guileless spurious honest lie distortion unfeigned fidelity irreproachable sham

18 Sort the following 20 words into two groups of ten, one with the heading 'Speaking', the other 'Writing'.

    signature drawl mute stationery shorthand discourse manuscript raucous intonation hieroglyphic inscribe eloquence utter brochure audible index orator essay journal recite

(Answers on pp. 203-204)

TEST **6**   *10 minutes*

Dictionary work (See unit 5.4)

1 Decide which part of each of the following words is the right one to locate the word in a good dictionary.

    bookworm newsprint floating rib floating kidney bench-mark goodwill good taste polar bear

2 The following words appear on two successive pages of *Chambers Twentieth Century Dictionary*. List them in the order they would be placed in the dictionary.

> cognition cocky coelacanth coffin codicil cognoscente
> cocoa cogent co-exist cocoon coerce coherence

(Answers on p. 204)

TEST 7   *10 minutes*

Style (See unit 5.5)

Make a list of all clichés, slang expressions and colloquialisms in the following piece. Then re-write the piece without using any of them, in your own clear words.

If I am for the high jump I'd rather the headmaster got straight down to the nitty-gritty and didn't beat about the bush. If I've been in the wrong and I know I've got it coming to me I'd rather just be given a thrashing and no messing about. That way it's all over and done with and no hard feelings.

(Answers on p. 204)

TEST 8   *5 minutes*

Composition (See unit 1)

Choose *one* of these essay subjects, and write *three* different opening sentences for it.
'*I have never felt so cheap.*' Write about an occasion when you might have thought this.
My visit to the hairdresser.
(There is no 'right' answer to this test. Ask a friend to choose the sentence he thinks would interest him enough to want to read on.)

TEST 9   *5 minutes*

Composition (See unit 1)

Some of the tools a carpenter uses are for *knocking* one thing into another, or for *cutting* and *biting*, or for *smoothing* rough timber. Words can be used in the same way, e.g.

'Say it, go on, say it – you're thick!
Dumb, ignorant, stupid – plain thick!'
The speaker here is trying to *hammer* home the message by using words in a plain, rough, disjointed manner – like a hammer.

Write two sentences
(i) to smooth over somebody's bad temper, by using calming, soothing words;
(ii) to make a person feel uncomfortable for having made a mistake, by using biting, unkind, sarcastic words.

(We cannot provide answers to this test; there are too many ways in which it could be answered. Test the effectiveness of your sentences by reading them to someone else and seeing what impressions they give.)

TEST **10** *5 minutes*

Composition (See unit 1)

A paragraph is a piece of writing containing one or more sentences (rarely more than five) dealing with one aspect of the topic under discussion or one stage of the story being told. It will start on a fresh line, the opening word usually set in from the margin.

Find two, or if possible three, successive paragraphs in whatever reading matter is handy — book, newspaper, magazine — and decide whether the writer uses any particular words to link one paragraph to another. If so, underline them or write them down. If not, re-write one of the sentences in each paragraph so as to make a natural link with the following or preceding paragraph.

(No answer can be provided for this test. Ask a friend, teacher, or parent to read and comment on your work.)

TEST **11** *20 minutes*

Comprehension (See unit 2)

You are trainee-manager in the disc department of a big department store. The general manager of the store sends for the head of your section and says, 'What's all this about sales rigging? – Let me have a report.' The section head is going to be away for the day so he asks you to prepare notes based on the following six questions. Answer them with the aid of the press cuttings below.

1 What influences the sale of pop music? (two words)
2 What is 'rigging'? (10 words maximum)
3 How is this rigging carried on? (about 30 words)
4 What organisations want to stop it?
5 What action are they starting to take?
6 What action can they take?

> **Record firm backs move to end chart 'rigging'**
>
> Britain's largest record company, EMI, promised yesterday to support moves to end 'rigging' of pop music popularity charts. Housewives and students have been paid to pose as genuine buyers at 375 record shops whose sales returns are used to work out the 'Top 50' chart published in *Music Week* and broadcast by the BBC.
>
> The chart, organised by the British Market Research Bureau, is the key to Britain's 'top ten' records. For £3,000 a record manager or company can buy a record into the charts.
>
> Unscrupulous record company executives buy back their own records from the key shops, using their network of housewives and students and a once-secret list of the shops.

This month, in an attempt to combat the rigging, the British Phonographic Industry, the record trade's watchdog, launched an investigation, using private detectives.

An EMI spokesman said last night: 'We are all obviously concerned that this sort of thing goes on and we fully support the efforts of the BPI to get to the bottom of it.'

Reproduced from *The Times* of 20th February 1978 by permission.

Urgent meeting on 'pop' charts

The British Phonographic Industry, the record trade's watchdog organisation, is to hold an urgent meeting this week to discuss alleged rigging of 'pop' charts.

Mr Geoffrey Bridge, its director-general, said yesterday that the possibility of the involvement of the police or the Director of Public Prosecutions would be discussed. But he believed chart-rigging had declined dramatically.

Reproduced from *The Times* of 21st February 1978 by permission.

New record chart aims to end rigging

A new popular music chart is to be set up at a cost of £110,000 to prevent the possibility of rigging. The weekly Gallup Independent Record Chart will begin in 10 days' time and be used by music newspapers and local commercial radio stations, it was disclosed last night.

It will provide an alternative to the BBC charts, which are co-sponsored by the British Phonographic Industry, the record trade watchdog, and are based on a sample of 350 of Britain's 7,000 record shops.

The names of the shops became known in the trade and there were suggestions that a list was circulated. To get a record into the charts an unscrupulous operator would hire people to buy copies from the listed shops.

To beat rigging, the Gallup Poll organisation is to prepare a national top 100 singles chart based on a mixture of record sales and radio time. There will also be a chart for the top 60 albums.

As well as the national chart, seven regional charts of the top 40 singles and top 20 albums will be launched. The new charts will be taken from 1,000 retailers contracted to fill a weekly diary of sales. From that, a random sample of 500 shops will be used to compile the final chart.

Gallup was commissioned to provide the charts by a consortium of interested parties headed by Mr Gregory Thain, aged 26, a company secretary.

He said it would still be possible to rig the placing of a record, but it would cost about £15,000 for two weeks compared with £5,000 under the present system.

Reproduced from *The Times* of 4th March 1978 by permission.

(Answers on p. 205)

Test 12   *15 minutes*

Comprehension (See unit 2)

Read the following advertisement and answer the questions.

Santex—*germicide for modern living*—*plus the little something extra which the others haven't got.*

Even in the cleanest home dangerous germs can multiply at an alarming rate—but only if you let them!

Why expose those you love to unnecessary risks, when a dusting of *Santex* will swiftly and scientifically destroy the bacteria and the smells they can produce.

New formula *Santex*—the *safe*, the *fragrant*, the *easy* way to protect the whole family.

Act now—delay could be dangerous.

Popular pack, 30p. Giant size (with new economical sprinklet control), 50p.

1 Why is the phrase 'even in the cleanest home' inserted?

2 Why is science brought in?

3 On what feelings is the writer hoping to work in the sentence beginning 'Why expose those you love...'?

4 Does the advertisement use any other methods you have already come across?

5 Is the advertisement aimed at the type of person who already wishes to buy a disinfectant?

6 What information would such a person need, and would he or she get it from the advertisement?

(Answers on p. 205)

For instructions about the next three tests (13-15) turn to Section II, Unit 2.4 (p. 56). Make an intelligent guess at finding an appropriate word for the spaces in each of the following passages.

Test 13   *15 minutes*

Comprehension

During the day — which is rainy, so the children are inside most of the time — there are a number of small bickerings between Joe and Mary, which arise either when Mary says the children can do something which Joe has already refused, or when Joe refuses them something which Mary has said they could do or have. Generally arguments about the children take place in their _____; but today the bickering went on whether the children _____ there or not.

Both Mary and Joe tend to _____ in to the children when they cry; so all _____ children cry very quickly when what they want is _____ them, and sob loudly until one or other parent _____ in. For instance: Joe says Elizabeth cannot have a _____ that Chris is looking at. Elizabeth starts to cry. _____ insists that Chris gives her the book. Or: Chris _____ an ice-cream, and is told by Joe that he _____ have one in this weather. Chris starts to cry. _____ comes back into the room and shouts at him, _____ that if he doesn't stop he'll have to go _____ bed. Chris's crying increases in volume. Mary dare not _____ directly against Joe's directions in a matter as major _____ ice-cream but she finds Chris some sweets, and a _____ to play with, to console him in his loss.

During the morning I produced a simple reading book, and asked Chris how much of it he could read.

Margaret Lassell, from *Wellington Road*, reprinted by permission of Routledge & Kegan Paul Ltd.

(Answers on p. 205)

TEST **14**   *15 minutes*

Comprehension

There were no more speeches. Rabbits have their own conventions and formalities, but these _____ few and short by human standards. If Hazel had _____ a human being he would have been expected to _____ his companions one by one and no doubt each _____ have been taken in charge as a guest by _____ of their hosts. In the great burrow, however, things _____ differently. The rabbits mingled naturally. They did not talk _____ talking's sake, in the artificial manner that human beings _____ sometimes even their dogs and cats—do. But this _____ not mean that they were not communicating; merely that _____ were not communicating by talking. All over the burrow, _____ the newcomers and those who were at home were _____ themselves to each other in their own way and _____ own time; getting to know what the strangers smelt _____, how they moved, how they breathed, how they scratched, _____ feel of their rhythms and pulses. These were their topics and subjects of discussion, carried on without the need of speech.

Richard Adams, from *Watership Down*, reprinted by permission of Rex Collings Ltd.

(Answers on p. 205)

TEST **15**

Comprehension

Sadie and Kevin sat on the top of Cave Hill with the city spread out below them. They looked down at the great sprawl of factories, _____ and houses that were gradually eating further and further _____ the green countryside beyond. Into the midst of the _____ came Belfast Lough. It was blue this evening, under _____ blue, nearly cloudless sky, speckled with ships and spiked _____ the shipyard gantries.

'I like looking down on the _____,' said Kevin.
'Me to,' said Sadie. 'It looks so _____. I wish it were!'

It was peaceful up there _____ the hill with the wind playing round their faces _____ tousling their hair. Sadie sat with her knees up _____ her chin, hugging her legs. She felt at ease _____ Kevin, though of course it was seldom she felt _____ with anybody, but she also felt a sort of _____ that she was unused to.

'It's funny,' she began.

'_____?' He turned on one elbow to look at her.

'_____ was just thinking a place looks better if you've _____ somebody with you.'

'Two pairs of eyeballs are better than one. As long as they're the right two pairs of course.'

Joan Lingard, from *Across the Barricades*, reprinted by permission of Hamish Hamilton Ltd.

(Answers on p. 206)

TEST **16**   *10 minutes*

Summary (See unit 3)

This is an engineer's log-book entry. In not more than 50 words of continuous English state, *without using technical language*, what was wrong with the motor and what the engineer did to put it right.

Fault & Repair a 2 HP 3 Phase Induction Motor which is overheating on Normal Load

Main tools, materials etc.
Low resistance ohmeter, replacement length of three-core cable

The following operations were carried out:

1 Cooling system examined to free air duct from blockage.

2 Rotating parts examined to check that rotor is not rubbing against stator and that bearings are free and undamaged.

3 Resistance of each phase winding checked to detect disconnections or possible short-circuited turns.

4 Rotor examined for high resistance joints between rotor bars and end rings.

Tests indicated that all these items are O.K., but motor was still overheating on load when supply was reconnected.

5 External leads were carefully checked and intermittent disconnection found in one phase lead. Connection was O.K. when motor was stationary (which ensured normal starting) but disconnection took place when motor was running and cable vibrating.

6 Cable renewed and motor then ran normally without overheating.

Time taken: 3 hours

From *Log Book for Engineering Craftsmen*, reprinted by permission of the Engineering Industry Training Board.

(Answers on p. 206)

Summary (See unit 3)

The passage below includes descriptions of the ways in which the activities of earthworms are useful to two groups of people. Write summaries (of not more than 50 words each) of their value to each group.

Archaeologists ought to be grateful to worms, as they protect and preserve, for an indefinitely long period, every object not liable to decay, which is dropped on the surface of the land, by burying it beneath their castings. Thus, many elegant and curious tesselated pavements and other ancient remains have been preserved; though no doubt the worms have in these cases been largely aided by earth washed and blown from the adjoining land, especially when this is cultivated. The old tesselated pavements have, however, often suffered unequal subsidence as a result of being unequally undermined by the worms. Even old massive walls may be undermined and subside; and no building is safe in this respect, unless the foundations lie six or seven feet beneath the surface, at a depth at which worms cannot work. It is probable that many monoliths and some old walls have fallen down from having been undermined by worms.

Worms prepare the ground in an excellent manner for the growth of fibrous-rooted plants, and for seedlings of all kinds. They periodically expose the mould in the air, and sift it so that no stones larger than the particles which they can swallow are left in it. They mingle the whole intimately together, like a gardener who prepares fine soil for his choicest plants. In this state the soil is well fitted to retain moisture and to absorb all soluble substances, as well as for the process of nitrification. The bones of dead animals, the harder parts of insects, the shells of land-molluscs, leaves, twigs, etc., are before long all buried beneath the accumulated castings of worms and thus are brought, in a more or less decayed state, within reach of the roots of plants. Worms likewise drag an infinite number of dead leaves and other parts of plants into their burrows, partly for the sake of plugging these up and partly as food.

(Answers on p. 206)

Summary (See unit 3)

This article appeared in *The Observer* on 19th February 1978. Use it to prepare a short piece of writing (100-150 words) about Muhammad Ali after his defeat.

Muhammad Ali after his defeat by Leon Spinks

No fighter in history ever stood up better to a punch on the jaw, and over the last decade and a half we have learned that blows to his spirit are no more likely to break him. The face that looked out at us from behind dark glasses in Harry Carpenter's interview the morning after the loss of the world championship was strangely diminished (the swellings seemed to have altered its planes to make it look smaller, and the effect was emphasised by the weary quietness of the words that came through the bruised lips) but his expression was serene. He was almost content to have lost to a man whose superiority on the night owed everything to youth.

Of course, there were moments of the old assertiveness, as when he laid a schoolmasterly 'Shhh' on others in the room who were threatening to submerge his monologue, and at the end when he said he would regain the title, declaring his intent in a style that was by Douglas MacArthur out of Hammer Films. But in the main he was so remote from the clamorous animation of earlier performances that it was natural to wonder if he will ever fully inhabit that area of his personality again.

It is true that he is often muted after hard fights. He drains every compartment in his nature of aggression when he is under severe pressure in the ring, and next day there may be little left but a reflective gentleness. So the mood of Thursday recalled another morning-after in New York seven years ago, when one or two of us made it into a crammed and rather tatty suite on the twenty-first floor of the New Yorker Hotel to hear how he felt after taking the first defeat of his career at the hands of Joe Frazier. Yet for all the identifiable echoes the two scenes were as different as the time-lapse had a right to make them. It is conceivable that Ali will come back to beat Spinks as he came back to beat Frazier but whereas one achievement represented a genuine return to the heights the other could only mean an ungainly clamber up a hillock for a last stolen look over the territory he has been ruling mainly by reputation for some time.

The last glimpse we had of Ali's true worth as champion was in the third Frazier fight in Manilla in October of 1975 and even by then he had declined slightly from the peak of inspired brilliance that utterly unmanned George Foreman in Zaire one year before. All the courage, resourcefulness, psychological force and dazzling technique that have helped to make Muhammad the most extraordinary pugilist of any generation were fused irresistibly in the middle of that tropical night to provide the climax of climaxes.

Everything he had done since returning to the ring after being banned for more than three years by the U.S. Government as a draft dodger seemed to have led inevitably to that unbearably dramatic recapturing of the championship. And, it would now appear, everything he has been doing since his victory in Kinshasa has led inevitably to last Wednesday in Las Vegas, to a night when the judges might have dispensed with score-cards and made their calculations on a calendar.

Ali won the Olympic Gold Medal in the light heavyweight division at Rome in 1960, Spinks did the same at Montreal in 1976; Ali has had 50 professional fights more than Spinks, who won the title in his eighth, but it is more relevant that he has lived 12 years longer than the new champion.

Hugh McIlvanney, 'Muhammad Ali after his defeat by Leon Spinks', reproduced from *The Observer* by permission.

(Answers on p. 206)

TEST **19**   *5 minutes*

Summary (See unit 3)

Below is part of a letter from two psychologists written to *The Times* after some people had been heavily sentenced for making and selling the drug LSD. (A fictional name replaces one offender's real name.) State the main point of the letter in one sentence (not more than twelve words).

Consider the size of the raid which would be necessary to catch those involved in our greatest drug problem. Hundreds of respectable business-men would have to be apprehended, their well worn importing routes blocked, their numerous factories closed and a massive and efficient sales organisation destroyed. They make millions of pounds each year and the evidence shows that more than a thousand people die *each week* from the drug. There is even evidence that the tax authorities are colluding in the traffic, and pocketing in excess of £1,000m per year.

This raid, however, would not need to be at dawn because the drug, tobacco, is legal. The tobacco trade makes Smith and co. look like enthusiastic amateurs. It may not be Smith's fault, but the severe jail sentences highlight a problem. Obviously the issue is not simple, but many of these inconsistencies in our attitudes towards drugs, which arose from historical accidents, are maintained by prejudice, hysteria and baser motives. Sooner or later it must be faced.

(Answers on p. 206)
(See also Test 20)

TEST **20**   *10 minutes*

Summary (See unit 3)

Read the letter quoted in Test 19. In about fifty words of your own summarise the writers' criticisms of the way our society deals with the drug problem.
(Answers on p. 206)

TESTS CHECK-LIST

Test No.	Subject-matter	Pages where located
1	Accuracy	145
2	Spelling	146
3	Spelling and usage	147
4-5	Vocabulary	148
6	Dictionary work	149
7	Style	150
8-10	Composition	150-151
11-15	Comprehension	151-155
16-20	Summary	155-158

Section IV General advice for candidates taking English examinations

BEFORE THE EXAMINATION

Some people can work right up to the last moment, but for most it is better to take a day off and start the examination completely fresh. This is especially so in English, where not so much depends on things learned by heart, but what matters is freshness, and the skill gained by practice. After a day off you should be both relaxed and energetic; it does not help to be tensed up and worried. If you have used this book well you should be confident that you will succeed. You will be familiar with all the types of question you are likely to meet, and be well equipped to cope with them.

An examination has something in common with other contests – swimming, orienteering, badminton. In these contests people pit themselves against the elements, or their environment, or other human beings. In an examination you face questions set by examiners. All of the examiners have been, and most still are, teachers. They do not like to fail candidates and often do all they can to find the extra marks that mean a pass. Examinations share with other strenuous contests the possibility that you will actually enjoy the battle. If you can manage to face it with zest this will show in the improved quality of your answers.

Unlike subjects such as Mathematics and Biology, where you simply have to show your grasp of facts, English gives you a chance to express *yourself*. This is why your physical well-being is as important in English as your mental alertness. Go to bed early the night before. Make sure you know the correct titles of your papers, the name of the centre and your own examination number. (It has been known for the wrong papers to be distributed!) Collect anything you will need in the examination room on the evening before: pens, pencils, ruler, etc. Smoking is not allowed in the examination room, and eating is discouraged. A few boiled sweets are the most you will want in any case.

IN THE EXAMINATION ROOM

Allow some minutes for reading and thoroughly understanding the instructions at the beginning of the paper. These will tell you such things as:
1 How many questions to do, and whether you have any choice;
2 how to present your answers on the paper or in the answer-book provided; and
3 the time allowed, sometimes with suggestions about how long you should spend on particular questions or sections.
Here are three typical examples:

(University of London GCE)

Instructions
One and three quarter hours.
Answer both questions. You should spend about one hour on the composition (Question 1), and three quarters of an hour on the summary (Question 2).

Candidates are reminded of the necessity for good English and orderly presentation in their answers.

1 **Composition** (50 marks). Write a composition on *one* of the following subjects. Choose a subject about which you can write interestingly; plan your composition accordingly to the nature of the material and the form (narrative, descriptive, discursive, etc.); write in an appropriate style and take care with grammar, spelling and punctuation. Your composition should be 450 words or more in length, but, apart from that, will be assessed on the quality, not the quantity, of what you have written.

(Joint Matriculation Board GCE Alt. E)

Careless work and untidy work will be penalised.

Answer all three questions.

Answers to all three questions must be written in the same answer book.

Pages 6, 7 and 8 of this question paper may be used for rough work.

The mark allocations for questions and sections of questions are shown in the right-hand margin.

(West Midlands Examinations Board CSE)

Write a composition based on ONE of the subjects listed over the page. You are advised to spend some time thinking about what you are going to write, and you may wish to make a plan. If you do so, please use the answer book and rule a line through the plan when you have finished.

If your handwriting is of average size, your composition should cover between three and four sides of the answer book.

Marks will be given for interesting ideas, sensibly arranged and expressed in clear and careful English; careless spelling and punctuation will lose marks, as will handwriting which is difficult to read. You may use a dictionary.

Two further pieces of advice from the Examination Boards:

1 'Own words' – When a question instructs you to write 'in your own words' you must *not* include in your answer key words and phrases from the passage. Obviously unimportant words like 'and', 'if', 'the', etc. do not matter, nor do common words like 'space' for which there are no satisfactory substitutes. But no credit will be given to an answer which merely repeats phrases and important words from the passage.

(University of Cambridge Local Examinations Syndicate)

2 The examination will be designed to test the ability
   (a) to write with facility, clarity and accuracy,
   (b) to understand what is read,
   (c) to use a vocabulary appropriate to an Ordinary level candidate's age, experience and needs,
   (d) to construct and join sentences and paragraphs,
   (e) to avoid mistakes of punctuation, grammar, spelling and idiom.

(Joint Matriculation Board)

Unless you are instructed differently, write on both sides of the answer paper, leaving a margin each side (narrower on the right). Start each question on a fresh page.

When you have fully taken in the instructions, read through the whole paper quickly. Tick the compulsory questions, and if there is a choice in the others, any that attract you. Make sure you are not preparing to answer more than you need; you may waste valuable time and effort. When candidates do this, examiners will mark only the number of questions required and rule out the rest. Be decisive. Don't waste too much time in making choices; you need all the time you can get for thinking about the content of the questions and writing your answers.

TIMING

This book has given you plenty of opportunities for you to time yourself in answering examination-type questions. If you have worked through them, it will stand you in good stead now. Reserve ten minutes for reading through and revision at the end; then divide your time according to the mark scheme, or any special instructions there may be. It is not sensible to spend an hour on a question which carries only 10% of the marks, and then have to race through another which carries 30%.

INDIVIDUAL QUESTIONS

Plan your answer to essay questions by jotting down ideas and important details. You will not have time to write out a full rough version, even though you may have been doing this in your preparation for the examination.

Answer the question actually set and not the one you hoped for or (worse still!) prepared a set answer for. Do not try to twist the wording. Keep to the number of words or length you are asked for. In particular, do not write too much; this is guaranteed to annoy the marker, who may have 50 or a 100 scripts to mark after yours. The marking of your paper will be fair and possibly generous, so do not spoil things by verbosity or irrelevance, or by failing to take notice of the exact wording of a question.

STYLE

Write simply and to the point. Punctuate as the sense requires; the habit of re-reading your work as if aloud should help you to get this right. Mouth the words silently if it helps; examination supervisors are used to all kinds of facial distortions and won't be surprised. A few spelling mistakes will not usually lose you many marks, but be as careful as you can. Watch especially the spelling of any words that appear on the question paper; these wrongly spelt make a candidate look slack and careless.

NUMBERING ANSWERS

Help the examiner by making it absolutely clear which question or part of a question you are answering. Here is a typical part of a comprehension test:

(Joint Matriculation Board GCE Alt. E 1979. Part I, qu. 2)
(h) Explain the meaning of three of the following words as used in the passage:
    (i)   irrespective (line 2),
    (ii)   equitable (line 23),
    (iii) complement (line 25),
    (iv)   lucrative (line 30).

One of these four words can be ignored. Decide which one you understand least well, then set out your answer, lettering and numbering exactly as in the question. Don't use a different form of the letter or number (e.g. H instead of (h), or 2 instead of (ii)). Here is our attempt:
(h) (ii)   fair
    (iii) add to
    (i)   without regard

Notice that because we have set out the answers clearly it does not matter that we changed our mind over which question to answer, and therefore put (i) at the end instead of the beginning. Obviously it is better to give your answers in the right order if you can, because the examiner will have this order in mind as he marks; but clear numbering and layout means you can, if necessary, change your mind without having to re-write a whole answer.

Leave a gap of at least a line between different parts of multiple answers like those to comprehension tests. The answer to a new question should start on a fresh page. If your answers cover several pages or answer books, arrange them in numerical order. In the examination office a candidate's paper may be divided between several markers.

WRITING AND PRESENTATION

If your writing is poor you should by now have done something about it. If you haven't, at least take pains to space your words evenly (fairly widely if your writing is small) and neatly on the lines, starting right next to the left-hand margin. Try to form each individual letter fully; finish off 'o's and 'a's. Some Examination Boards deduct marks for bad writing; all English examiners welcome good clear handwriting, because so much of the paper involves continuous writing. In particular, writing that is difficult or slow to read makes it hard to follow a story or an argument in an essay; and the essay questions nearly always carry most marks.

Normally start on the second line of each fresh page. Start fresh paragraphs about one inch in from the margin (this is called 'indenting'). Fill each line, so that when the page is full your work is surrounded by a white space. Good spacing and presentation can do much to make up for not-so-good writing. Mistakes are bound to occur when one is writing under pressure, or against a clock. When you need to cross out, do it with a single line, and preferably with a ruler.

READING THROUGH, REVISION, FINAL CHECK

You have kept ten minutes for this valuable part of the examination – remember? If you use the time well it may earn you more than ten extra marks.

First, sort out your answer sheets and get them into the right order for handing in. As you do so, re-check the numbering and lettering of each question, especially those in several parts. Enter your name and examination number where necessary – possibly on each page or on the front of each answer book.

Next, start your final read-through. It is often a good idea to lay a blank sheet of paper across the page, moving it down line by line so that you can give all your attention to each line of writing in turn. Look for the mistakes you *know* you make (e.g. double letters in spelling, *to* for *too* or *two*, *the* for *they*, small letters where capitals are needed, punctuation left out, or written indistinctly). If in this re-reading you come across a word you are not sure about, replace it by one you know you understand.

Finally, skim through each page with your eye on the whole page. Does it look clear, or messy? Is there anything on it that could confuse or irritate another reader? Are the crossings-out clear and neat? It is surprising how this final check at-a-glance can sometimes pick up a misspelling that a closer look has missed. As each page is checked, lay it with the others in the right order for handing in. If you need to do so, tie or clip all pages together.

Heave a sigh of relief; you have done your best.

Summary of advice

1 Get into the right frame of mind — keen but not tense; refreshed; hopefully determined.
2 Think of the convenience of your examiner: write legibly; make clear alterations; number your answers carefully. Come to the examination room with the proper equipment.
3 Read and follow the instructions on the paper. Answer the right number of questions. Never leave a blank.
4 If there is a choice, decide which are the best questions for you.
5 Apportion your time so that most is given to the questions carrying the most marks.
6 The examiner does not demand miracles. He does demand a reasonable competence. Rely on yourself to get rid of all the unnecessary mistakes which may squander your marks; for this purpose leave yourself time for a close, critical reading of your script before handing it in.

Section V Practice in answering examination questions

The questions that follow have been selected from GCE, SCE and CSE English papers of a range of Examination Boards. For hints on how to answer these questions, see Section VI (pp. 207-216).

GCE QUESTIONS

Composition/essays/letters

1 Using the special answer book provided, write two to two and a quarter pages on one of the following subjects. If, however, your handwriting is unusually large or unusually small, you should make some adjustment in the amount you write. It is assumed that average handwriting produces about eight words per line.

Either (a) This country is notorious for its weather. Sometimes there seems to be little difference between a poor summer and a mild winter, yet in very recent years we have suffered extremes of prolonged drought and severe blizzards. Either (i) describe an incident in your life when the weather played an important part, or (ii) imagine you are undertaking a journey when you are caught in a blizzard. Describe your experiences and your reaction to your plight. You may be alone or with a party.

Or (b) Ruin.

(Joint Matriculation Board)

2 Write on one of the following topics. Your work should cover about three sides of the pages in your answer book, i.e. it should consist of about 500-600 words. Take time to think before you begin.

Either (a) For one day in your life you have the power to read other people's minds. Describe what happens.

Or (b) Your family has been nominated for 'The Happiest Family in Britain' contest run by a popular newspaper. Describe what happens when one of the judges unexpectedly calls with the intention of spending the day at your house.

(Welsh Joint Education Committee)

3 Write on one of the following subjects. You must cover at least two sides of average handwriting. There is no need to write out the title.

Either (a) Write about the interest of any collecting *you* have done.

Or (b) Write a descriptive composition or a story suggested by the following lines. Some degree of relevance to the lines is expected.

> The yard is littered with scrap, with axles
> And tyres, buckled hoops and springs, all rotting.
> The wreckage of cars that have been dumped.
>
> The hut is still there. In the doorway
> Two men talk horses – but not as he did
> In the days when the Clydesdales came
> To be shod, the milk wagons for repair...

(Southern Universities' Joint Board for School Examinations)

4 Write from 350-500 words on the following:
You have inherited 1000 acres of barren, uninhabited, mountainous countryside. What do you propose to do with it?
(Oxford and Cambridge Schools Examination Board)

5 (FACTUAL) Explain one of the following games to a non-player: netball, five-a-side football, whist, badminton.
(Associated Examining Board)

6 (LETTER) In some areas people have open access to reservoirs and the land surrounding them for walks, picnics, sailing, canoeing and similar activities. In other areas all access is forbidden, in order to avoid the expense of special treatment to purify the water. Write a letter to the chairman of a Water Authority, requesting open access to all the reservoirs for which he is responsible. Explain fully the reasons for your request, and justify any costs involved.
(Joint Matriculation Board)

7 (LETTER) You are on a camping or caravan holiday with friends when an accidental fire destroys some of your equipment as well as most of your money. Write a letter home explaining the situation and asking for help.
(Welsh Joint Education Committee)

8 (LETTER) You have written to the secretary of a local charity, offering an idea to raise money. He replies, inviting you to develop this idea in detail. Write the secretary's reply.
(Associated Examining Board)

Comprehension

9 *Read the two poems carefully and answer the questions which follow them.* [50]

The Pylons

The secret of these hills was stone, and cottages
Of that stone made,
And crumbling roads
That turned on sudden hidden villages.

Now over these small hills, they have built the concrete*   5
That trails black wire;
Pylons, those pillars
Bare like nude giant girls that have no secret.

The valley with its gilt and evening look
And the green chestnut   10
Of customary root,
Are mocked dry like the parched bed of a brook.

But far above and far as sight endures
Like whips of anger
With lightning's danger   15
There runs the quick perspective of the future.

This dwarfs our emerald country by its trek
So tall with prophecy:
Dreaming of cities
Where often clouds shall lean their swan-white neck.   20

Stephen Spender

*Candidates should note that these pylons are made of concrete.

The Planster's Vision

Cut down that timber! Bells, too many and strong,
  Pouring their music through the branches bare,
  From moon-white church towers down the windy air
Have pealed the centuries out with Evensong.

Remove those cottages, a huddled throng!   5
  Too many babies have been born in there,
  Too many coffins, bumping down the stair,
Carried the old their garden paths along.

I have a Vision of the Future, chum,
  The workers' flats in fields of soya beans   10
  Tower up like silver pencils, score on score:
And Surging Millions hear the Challenge come
  From microphones in communal canteens
  'No Right! No Wrong! All's perfect, evermore.'

John Betjeman

Questions on *The Pylons*:

1. Describe briefly the scene depicted in lines 1–4.   [4]
2. Show how in lines 5–8 the pylons
  (a) in their construction and materials, and
  (b) in their appearance
are out of keeping with their setting.   [6]
3. Bearing in mind that poets choose words carefully, explain under (*a*) and (*b*) the use of 'customary' in line 11, and 'runs' in line 16.   [6]
4. Express clearly in your own words the meaning of:
  'This dwarfs our emerald country by its trek' (line 17).   [4]
5. The poet uses the word 'like' to introduce a special effect.
  (*a*) What is being referred to in the phrase 'Like whips of anger' (line 14)?
  (*b*) What does the phrase suggest?   [4]

Questions on *The Planster's Vision*:

6. The poet does not share the planster's vision.
  (*a*) Pick out from lines 1–4 **two** phrases which suggest this.
  (*b*) Explain briefly your reason for selecting **one** of them.   [6]
7. There is an obvious contrast between the bells which the planster wishes to destroy and the microphones with which he wishes to replace them. Write down under (*a*), (*b*), and (*c*) three other such contrasts made in the poem.   [6]

Question on both poems:

8. Use comment, reference and quotation to compare the attitudes of the two poets. Pay particular attention to the last verse of each poem.   [14]

(Oxford and Cambridge Schools Examination Board)

10 *The following passage describes the first visit of a young British actor to America. He is to play the part of the composer Liszt in a film. Read the passage carefully, and then answer the questions that follow.*

My room was disturbingly dark and smelled of conditioned air. Ominous glitters of light slitted through the shutters. I groped my way across the room, hit a table, and pushed open the windows. Hot smoggy air came up from the studio yard. Six men pushing half a snow-capped mountain trundled up the yard. A woman came running down, a bundle of
5 sequined dresses over her arm, a paper cup of coffee in her hand. To my far left, by the carpenter's shop, planks and sawdust and gilded doors were leaning against the concrete walls. To my right, high up, were the misty smog-smudged ridge of the hills and the great wooden sign striding the skyline, one letter missing, long since fallen: 'Hol-ywood'.

I had arrived at last. I was there where it all started: the most chaotic city on earth west of
10 Calcutta. My heart fell with despair: six months to go.

I examined the room. It was pine-panelled — fake plaster pine-panelled. The tweed carpet looked like old porridge and the chairs and settees were covered in violent tartan. There were hunting prints on the walls, a sword, a galleon in full sail, two refrigerators disguised as oak chests, lamp-shades with maps of the world on them, a small table with a flat bowl of
15 plastic sweet peas and dahlias. The bathroom, entered between the 'oak chests', was plain, clinically white, very masculine. A note told me to report to Room 2456 for a 'Music Conference'.

When I arrived, Victor Aller, small, benign, with glittering rimless glasses and beautiful hands, was sitting at the Broadwood piano playing something sad. I didn't interrupt him but
20 sat quietly in the chair beside him. He switched music and went into something extremely fast, short and vaguely familiar. He placed his hands on his knees and smiled at me.

'That's Chopsticks.'

'Oh.'

'You know it?'
25 'I think so . . . somewhere.'

'*Everyone* knows it. It's a child's exercise. Play it.'

'I have never played a piano in my life. I couldn't.'

A pause like a century.

'You gotta be Liszt.'
30 'I know that.'

'Liszt played piano.'

'Yes.'

'You don't dispute that?'

'No.'
35 'He played piano like no-one else played piano.'

'I believe . . . .'

'And you don't?'

'No. Never.'

'Well, we gotta start then. That's what I'm here for. To teach you to play the piano and
40 fast. And like Liszt.'

'Thank you.'

'Don't thank me till I have.' He played some scales rapidly. Dull with fear, I watched his hands. 'These are just scales . . . we'll have to do a lot of this, just to exercise your fingers . . . show me your span.'
45 'What's that?'

'Hell! Put your hands out in front of you and spread your fingers . . . that's a span.'

I did as he asked. My hands looked supplicating. They were.

'Nice span you got. You play tennis?'

'No.'
50 'Football?'

'No.'

'Ping pong...table tennis?'

'No, neither.'

Another long stupefied pause. The air-conditioner hissed and throbbed.

55   'You play that game you have in England...with a bat and a ball...like rounders?'

'Cricket?'

'That's it. Cricket. You play that?'

'No.'

'Hell.' He played another set of scales. 'And you gotta be Liszt?'

60   'They tell me so.'

'In five weeks we start shooting in Vienna. You going to be ready?'

'What do *you* think?'

'Not in a million years, let alone five weeks. You got 85 minutes of flaming
music in this production. Eighty-five minutes, not including the conducting.'

65   'Well, I'd better start. I mean, perhaps you could show me, very slowly, a bit of
something I have to play...not Chopsticks. It's too fast.'

'So is the First flaming Concerto....'He started, very gently and softly, to play. It
was good. He played with deep feeling and tenderness. I listened and watched, horrified.
How could I ever remember where the fingers went, which keys to use, the black or the

70   white?

(a) In what way do the things seen by the author from his window (in the first
paragraph) confirm the fact that he is in the centre of the American film
industry?   **8**

(b) The author clearly dislikes his room. From lines 1 to 16, write down **six**
of the phrases which show his dislike of the room's appearance or furnishings
and in each case state briefly the reason for his dislike. Begin a new line for
each phrase.   **12**

(c) What can be learned from the passage about the abilities, attitudes and
personality of Victor Aller?

Justify each point you make by a brief reference to the passage.   **12**

(d) What does the encounter with Victor Aller (line 18 to the end of the
passage) tell us about the author?

Justify each point you make by a brief reference to the passage.   **9**

(e)   (i) Suggest a reason for the author's writing: 'My heart fell with
            despair' (line 10).   **2**

        (ii) Explain carefully:
            the reason for the pause mentioned in line 28;

        and the reason for the pause mentioned in line 54.   **4**

        (iii) Victor Aller is an American. Quote **one** of the sentences he speaks
            (not including the expression 'gotta') which shows his American
            style of speech, and after it write what a British musician would
            have said (in standard English).   **2**

(f) Explain **briefly** the meaning of each of the following words as used in
the passage:

        (i) trundled (line 4); (ii) chaotic (line 9); (iii) supplicating (line 47).   **3**

Total 52

(Joint Matriculation Board)

11 *Read the following passage carefully and then answer the questions set on it.*

Everyone injured in a road accident will get compensation from an official fund,
irrespective of who was to blame, if the Government adopts a recommendation in a Royal
Commission report due this week.

The basis of the scheme is that, by amending the law to introduce 'no fault liability',
5 someone injured in a road accident need no longer go to court to prove negligence in order
to get compensation.

Under the present, much-criticised system, there are countless instances of cases that
have taken years to come to court and of awards considered either ridiculously low or
ridiculously high. The Loach case, reported in 1976, is one not unusual example. It followed
10 a car crash on the M1 in May 1971, which killed Ken Loach's five-year-old son, seriously
injured his wife and killed her 84-year-old grandmother, broke Loach's jaw, and
emotionally injured his other small son. Everyone agreed that the accident was caused
by a wheel falling off another car and that the Loaches were blameless. But, after five
years of litigation, the family was left not only without any hope of compensation, but
15 with a bill of nearly £1,000 for legal costs.

Under the Pearson scheme, compensation in all accident cases would be automatic,
prompt and paid at regular intervals, as long as the victim needed it. Payments could be
adjusted as the victim improved or deteriorated and also to take account of inflation.

The Commission's view is that the cost of the scheme should be borne by the motorist;
20 there are two main ways the Government could collect the money. It could set up its own
third party insurance office and make it compulsory for motorists to insure with it; or it
could simply add a new tax to the price of petrol, on the ground that this would be the most
equitable way of sharing the cost — because the more miles a motorist covers, the greater
the risk of an accident.

25 The Government is expected to favour the second course because it would complement
the energy conservation policy both by discouraging unessential motoring and making it
more attractive for motorists to use smaller and more economical cars.

Opposition to the scheme will be led by organisations representing motorists and lawyers.
Since it will no longer be necessary to sue for compensation, lawyers will lose a large and
30 lucrative part of their business. It has been estimated that from one fifth to one third of all
the money involved in the present accident compensation system goes in lawyers' fees.

Motorists' organisations will see the Pearson recommendation as yet another blow to
an already over-taxed section of the community. But the Government will view this
protest against the fact that the cost to the country of caring for road accident victims is
35 more than £400 million a year. Transferring some of that cost directly to the motorist
would greatly relieve this burden on the National Health Service.

(a) What, according to the writer, is the present procedure if one wishes to
claim damages for injuries received in a road accident? **Use your own words.**   2

(b) What changes are envisaged in the new recommendation?   6

(c) From a consideration of the Loach case what appear to be faults in the
present system?   3

(d) Explain the two possible ways of financing this scheme.   2

(e) Why does the Government prefer the second of these?   3

(f) Who will oppose the proposal and why?   4

(g) How will the Government answer one of these protests?   2

(h) Explain the meaning of **three** of the following words as used in the passage:
  (i) irrespective (line 2),
  (ii) equitable (line 23),
  (iii) complement (line 25),
  (iv) lucrative (line 30).   3

(Joint Matriculation Board)

Summary

12 *Read the following passage carefully and answer the questions which follow it.*

It took hundreds of millions of years to produce the life that now inhabits the earth – aeons of time in which that developing and evolving and-diversifying life reached a state of adjustment and balance with its surroundings. The environment, rigorously shaping and directing the life it supported, contained elements that were hostile as well as supporting. Certain rocks gave out

5 dangerous radiation; even within the light of the sun, from which all life draws its energy, there were short-wave radiations with power to injure. Given time – time not in years but in millennia – life adjusts, and a balance has been reached. For time is the essential ingredient; but in the modern world there is no time.

The rapidity of change and the speed with which new situations are created follow the

10 impetuous and heedless pace of man rather than the deliberate pace of nature. Radiation is no longer merely the background radiation of rocks, the bombardment of cosmic rays, the ultra-violet of the sun that have existed before there was any life on earth; radiation is now the unnatural creation of man's tampering with the atom. The chemicals to which life is asked to make its adjustments are no longer merely the calcium and silica and copper and all the rest of the minerals

15 washed out of the rocks and carried in rivers to the sea; they are the synthetic creations of man's inventive mind, brewed in his laboratories, and having no counterparts in nature.

To adjust to these chemicals would require time on the scale that is nature's; it would require not merely the years of a man's life but the life of generations. And even this, were it by some miracle possible, would be futile, for the new chemicals come from our laboratories in an endless

20 stream; almost five hundred annually find their way into actual use in the United States alone. The figure is staggering and its implications are not easily grasped – five hundred chemicals to which the bodies of men and animals are required somehow to adapt each year, chemicals totally outside the limits of biological experience.

Among them are many that are used in man's war against nature. Since the mid-1940s over two

25 hundred basic chemicals have been created for use in killing insects, weeds, rodents, and other organisms described in the modern vernacular as 'pests', and they are sold under several thousand different brand names.

These sprays, and aerosols are now applied almost universally to farms, gardens, forests, and homes – non-selective chemicals that have the power to kill every insect, the 'good' and the 'bad',

30 to still the song of birds and the leaping of fish in the stream, to coat the leaves with a deadly film, and to linger on in soil – all this though the intended target may be only a few weeds or insects. Can anyone believe it is possible to lay down such a barrage of poisons on the surface of the earth without making it unfit for all life? They should not be called 'insecticides', but 'biocides'.

(From *Silent Spring* by Rachel Carson)

(a) Rachel Carson states that 'in the modern world there is no time' (line 8). In not more than 80 of your own words summarise what she says in support of this statement in the next two paragraphs (lines 9–23).

(b) In the last two paragraphs of the passage, what information is given which supports the description of man's activities as a 'war against nature' (line 24)? Answer in continuous prose, using not more than 60 of your own words.

(Oxford and Cambridge Schools Examination Board)

13 The following passage is taken from an article on the packaging of goods. *Using only the information given in the passage,* write a summary consisting of **two** paragraphs on:

(*a*) the advantages of modern packaging; *and*
(*b*) the problems caused by modern packaging.

You should not attempt to summarise everything there is in the passage, but should select from it only the material you need for your two paragraphs.

Write in clear, concise English and *use your own words as far as possible,* although you may retain words and brief expressions which cannot be accurately or economically replaced.

Your summary should not exceed 140 words altogether; at the end you must state accurately the number of words you have used.

Almost everything bought nowadays has to be broken out of its box, packet, tube, carton or tin before it can be used. Non-returnable wrappings impose serious strains on local authorities, whose responsibility it is to collect and dispose of our rubbish.
5 Ratepayers have to find the 50 million pounds annually required to deal with the processing of 14 million tons of refuse. The destruction of waste is also difficult, as much of the packaging we use consists of materials which stubbornly refuse to be broken down naturally by decomposition. Expensive incinerators have
10 to be installed and the smoke they produce causes some pollution of the atmosphere. Packaging, too, in the form of litter spoils the environment we all share, whether it is in the town, in the countryside, or on the beach.

Industry and selling agencies, however, continue to introduce
15 more and more packaging every week. One large agency argues its views without the trace of an apology: cigarettes, wrapped in tinfoil and placed in a box, which is then wrapped in cellophane, retain their flavour better and have a longer shelf-life than products less carefully packaged; products sold in jars are
20 protected from the contamination which would be bound to occur if they were handled continually by shop assistants or, in self-service stores, by intending purchasers. The higher cost of wrapping goods carefully is reflected in their higher prices, but money spent on ensuring greater freshness and the higher
25 standard of hygiene achieved by good wrapping is money well spent.

The housewife, surrounded by clamouring young children, needs to be able to make her purchases both quickly and economically. Packing goods in such a way that their price and
30 weight are seen at a glance will help her to make her choice. Some unscrupulous manufacturers may try to deceive her by increasing the size of a carton whilst reducing the quantity of its contents, or by changing the shape of a bottle in order to conceal the fact that it contains fewer fluid ounces or cubic
35 centimetres; but recent attempts to standardise packet-sizes by introducing 'Eurosizes' help to make the housewife's task easier. Uniformity in the size of packets also leads to quicker transportation and more efficient display and storage of goods. If marketing costs are held down, some of the savings can be
40 passed on to the consumer in the form of stabilised prices. Not everyone approves of standardisation, however. Colourful

wrappings do make goods look attractive and provide variety; they can stimulate a healthy demand, which leads to increased competition between manufacturers and the maintenance of
45 employment for the workers in the companies.

Those who watch over the interests of the consumer sometimes argue that wrappings are unnecessarily complicated and merely serve to confuse the shopper; it is difficult to compare accurately in the bustle of a supermarket the value of a pear-shaped bottle
50 of shampoo containing 1300 ccs. and sold for 35p. with that of a round-shaped bottle containing 1650 ccs. and sold for 42p. To make the necessary comparisons a housewife needs a pocket calculator and an escape from her clamouring children. In the end the article will sell on the strength of its attractive packaging.
55 Only when she reaches the check-out will she realise just how bulky the cartons, bottles, and tins have made her shopping; two journeys to the shops will be necessary instead of the one she made in the days when packaging was less elaborate.

Nevertheless, anything which helps to brighten our lives is
60 worthwhile. The merest suggestion on a packet that we shall be fitter, more loved, richer, or happier if we buy the product will lure us to spend more than we can afford and ignore the blatant waste of the earth's resources in the making of unnecessary boxes, packets, tubes, cartons and tins.

(University of London)

14 *Read the following passage carefully and then answer the questions that follow.*

Even in fresh water sharks hunt and kill. The Thresher shark, capable of lifting a small boat out of the water, has been sighted a mile inland on the Fowey River in Cornwall. Killer sharks swim rivers to reach Lake Nicaragua in Central America; they average one human victim each year.

Sewage and garbage attract sharks inland. When floods carry garbage to the rivers they provide a rich diet which sometimes stimulates an epidemic of shark attacks. Warm water generally provides shark food, and a rich diet inflames the shark's aggression.

In British waters sharks usually swim peacefully between ten and twenty miles offshore where warm water currents fatten mackerel and pilchards for their food. But the shark is terrifyingly unpredictable. One seaman was severely mauled as far north as Wick in Scotland. Small boats have been attacked in the English Channel, Irish Sea and North Sea.

Most of the legends about sharks are founded in ugly fact. Even a relatively small shark — a 200 lb. Zambesi — can sever a man's leg with one bite. Sharks have up to seven rows of teeth and as one front tooth is damaged or lost another moves forward to take its place.

The shark never sleeps. Unlike most fish, it has no air bladder, and it must move constantly to avoid sinking. It is a primitive creature, unchanged for 60 million years of evolution. Its skin is without the specialised scales of a fish. Fully grown, it still has five pairs of separate gills like a three-week human embryo.

But it is a brilliantly efficient machine. Its skin carries nerve endings which can detect vibrations from fish moving several miles away. Its sense of smell, the function of most of its brain, can detect one part in 600,000 of tuna fish juice in water, or the blood of a fish or animal from a quarter of a mile away. It is colour blind, and sees best in deep water, but it can distinguish shapes and patterns of light and shade easily. Once vibrations and smell have placed its prey the shark sees well enough to home in by vision for the last fifty feet.

The shark eats almost anything. It will gobble old tin cans and broken bottles as well as fish, animals and humans. Beer bottles, shoes, wrist watches, car number plates, overcoats and other sharks have been found in dead sharks. Medieval records tell of entire human corpses still encased in armour.

The United States military advice on repelling sharks is to stay clothed — sharks go for exposed flesh, especially the feet. Smooth swimming at the surface is essential. Frantic splashing will simply attract sharks, and dropping below the surface makes the swimmer an easy target. If the shark gets close then is the time to kick, thrash and hit out. A direct hit on the snout, gills or eyes will drive away most sharks. The exception is the Great White shark. It simply kills you.

In answering the following questions you are asked to **use your own words** as far as possible, to keep within the required number of words, and *to use only information that is contained in the passage.*

(*a*) What does the passage tell you about how a shark behaves? (Answer in about **90** words.)

(*b*) What evidence is supplied to show that sharks have been, and still are, a great danger to man? (Use about **60** words.)

(*c*) Give **four** courses of action a man should follow if menaced by sharks. (**30** words should be sufficient.)

(Welsh Joint Education Committee)

Sce (ordinary grade) questions (For notes see Section VI, pp. 207-216.)

Composition

1 Write a short story suggested by one of the following statements.
    (i) 'That's my last word,' he said.
    (ii) It seemed a great chance, but I had learned my lesson.
    (iii) 'Absolutely terrified!' was the answer.
    (iv) Sometimes it doesn't pay to get too involved.

2 Has your education prepared you well for life? (You could write about how relevant the subjects you studied were; about how you were treated by your teachers; about how they influenced you and about the qualities and attitudes your school or college tried to develop in you.)

3 Write in any way you please about one of the following extracts. Although the extract need not appear in your composition, there must be a clear link between it and what you write. You should respond to the mood of the extract and not just to the ideas expressed in it.

(i) '... let us be men,
   Not monkeys minding machines.'

(ii) A ragged urchin, aimless and alone,
   Loitered about that vacancy, a bird
   Flew up to safety from his well-aimed stone.

Interpretation and language

Note: This part of the examination involves the skills we have described under the general headings of 'comprehension' and 'summary'. Two passages are set, questions on the first placing considerable emphasis on *drawing inferences* (   ), those on the second (a more factual topic as a rule) usually including *summary*. Each of the passages is normally about 30–35 lines in length. Below (questions 4 and 5) you will find two brief extracts from the 1980 Paper 2 along with some typical questions. (For guidance on how to go about answering them, see Section VI, pp. 207-216.)

4 *Passage 1*

When I ran on to the field, it was almost dark. A heavy mist hung over the valley and enclosed the ground in a tight grey wall of drizzle. It was bitterly cold. The players ran around in groups, small and unreal beneath the half-empty flanks of the terraces—insects released in space. Everything outside the dark wreath of the crowd was hidden. We were isolated; all that was familiar and encouraging had vanished, leaving us in the shell of the stands.

Johnson, who had arranged the trial, had been at the tunnel mouth as I ran on to the field. This was supposed to be his hour of triumph, yet he stood there sullen and dejected as I passed him. I could still see him, as we waited for the other team to emerge, climbing slowly up the centre steps of the stand.

1 (a) The terraces were 'half-empty' (line 3). Suggest two reasons for this, one from each of the paragraphs.   (*2 marks*)
  (b) Give one example of the 'familiar and encouraging' things that had vanished   *(1)*
2 Find two words in the first paragraph which suggest the gloominess of the occasion.   *(2)*
3 What other evidence can you find to support the idea that Johnson was 'sullen and dejected' (line 9)?

5 *Passage 2*

Every week most of us face stress in our daily lives. We run for and miss that bus or train that will take us to work. We face worrying tax demands and bills: the mortgage, the bank overdraft, the rent or some other ∧ anxiety nags at us. We have the occasional quarrel with the husband, wife, boss or colleague. All these experiences, which are the normal wear and tear of living, are stressful.

Then there are the more serious stresses. If a parent, a partner or a close friend dies, the bereavement takes its toll of our mental and physical health. Divorces, court cases, accidents or an illness in the family are all major strains. Oddly enough, success can be stressful, too. Promotion, starting a new job, more responsibility—all take their toll.

1 (a) The first passage deals with the same single general topic – stress. Why do you think the writer decided to use two paragraphs instead of one? *(2)*

  (b) 'Oddly enough, success can be stressful too.' (line 10)   *(1)*
  Explain (i) how success can be a cause of stress;
              (ii) why the writer says 'oddly enough'.   *(1)*

2 A word has been deliberately omitted from line 3. Suggest one word which would make most sense in the context.   *(1)*

3 Explain the function of the colon (:) in line 3.   *(1)*

For further practice, we recommend you to attempt the following questions already given elsewhere in this Section:
first type – GCE Q.10, CSE Q. 9;
second type – GCE Q. 11, CSE Q. 13, GCE Q. 14.

Reading

6 Sometimes a person in a book (fiction or non-fiction) is faced with a difficult decision or a crisis of some kind. Select one such book, give a brief account of the problem involved, state what decision the person makes and explain how he or she comes to this particular decision. You must not use a play or drama script for this question.

7 (a) Name a theme you have been studying this year, e.g. love, loyalty, poverty, prejudice, relationships.

  (b) Show how your understanding of this theme has been made wider and deeper by the ways it has been dealt with by *any two* writers of prose, poetry or drama. (You could, for example, choose writers who hold different, even opposing views; or writers who give a fuller picture, the one by writing the facts, the other by writing novels about the facts; or writers from other times or places who show you how attitudes towards your chosen theme vary.)

8 Give the name of any magazine or periodical which you read regularly and which fits into the category of light reading. Give an account of those things which you find particularly interesting and enjoyable in the publication you have chosen. Deal with at least three qualities in some detail.

Cse questions (For notes or answers, see Section VI, pp. 207-216.)

Compositions/essays/letters

1 What in your life so far would you wish to see repeated in the upbringing of any children you might have, and what changes would you hope to make for them? (You may use a dictionary if you wish. You should write about 400 words, but the exact number is not important.)

(East Midland Regional Examinations Board)

2 Do you think it is a good idea or a bad one to have a part-time job while you are still at school? Try to present your point of view convincingly and to support it, if possible, from your own experience. Remember to take into account any objections or disadvantages.

(East Anglian Examinations Board)

3 More and more people are going abroad for their holidays; some return with complaints about foreign people, food, etc., whilst others return delighted with their experiences. Write as fully as you can about what you liked or disliked about a foreign visit.

(Met. Regional Examinations Board)

4 Describe, as fully as you can, the scene in one of the following. (Try to capture not only the sights, but also the sounds, the smells and feelings which the scene arouses):
   (a) A small local shop.
   (b) A Youth Club in two contrasting moods.
   (c) The evening atmosphere of an outdoor spot in your area, where young people like to gather.
   (d) A camp scene.
   (e) A sports meeting.
   (f) A local carnival or event.
   (g) A place with character and atmosphere.

(Southern Regional Examinations Board)

5 Read the following extract and then answer ONE of the questions which follow.

Charles and Enid, his girl friend, are walking up the road one evening from the bus. You are with them.
Charles: Can I have the book back which I loaned to you last week?
Enid: Which book was that?
Charles: My copy of the 'AA Book of the Road'.
Enid: Oh, that. Sorry. I loaned it to Roy. He's going on holiday.
Charles: But I need it myself.
Enid: I'm sure he won't keep it long. You did say that I could return it at any time.
Charles: Yes, but that was a week ago.
Enid: Well, I'm sorry. I assumed that when you said you were not in a hurry for it you meant just that.
Charles: I hadn't decided then to go on holiday in the Lake District.
Enid: Well, then...
Charles: Can you ask him for it tonight?
Enid: Yes, of course. PAUSE. Wait a minute, though. He's not at the club tonight.
Charles: When will you see him next?
Enid: I don't know. Possibly next Saturday.
Charles: But I need it for Saturday morning. I'm setting off after breakfast.
Enid: You could try phoning him.
Charles: Why me? You phone him—you loaned him my book.
Enid: Yes, I know. But it is YOUR book.
Charles: That's not the point. Please phone him and ask him to bring it round.
Enid: I'm very busy tonight—it's the committee meeting. I'll phone tomorrow.
Charles: You'll forget. Phone tonight.
Enid: Are you trying to tell me what to do? I'll do it tomorrow.
Charles: Look, I need that book. You borrowed it so you get it back. You had no right to loan it to Roy, anyway.
Enid: There's no need for you to get angry. I'll get your wretched book for you... TOMORROW!

Charles: I like that! You borrow my book, loan it to somebody else, and when
   I want it back you can't be bothered to do anything.

Enid: You really are stuffy. I wish I'd never seen your silly book.

Charles: That's the last time I lend you anything.

(He turns into his own gateway angrily.)

Either (a) Write a letter to a friend in which you give an account of this conversation. Imagine that both you and your friend know Enid and
   Charles.

Or   (b) Imagine that at the end of the conversation one of the people taking
   part turned to you and asked for your opinion on who was at fault.
   Write your views about the quarrel.

(West Midlands Examinations Board)

6 (LETTER) An old lady who is a widow and friend of your parents has com-
plained that you were one of a group of teenagers who disturbed her sleep one
night as you came noisily out of a party. Your parents have asked you to send
a letter of apology to her and to offer to do something for her in some way.
Write the letter.

(North Regional Examinations Board)

7 (LETTER) Suppose that you are a wealthy person who has been approached for
a donation to an old people's home and to a dispensary for sick animals. You
have decided to favour only *one* of them. Write a letter to a friend explaining
your choice and urging him, if he is approached, to make the same choice.

(Associated Lancashire Schools Examining Board)

8 (LETTER) Recently in your local paper there have been a number of letters to
the Editor complaining about the behaviour of schoolchildren and young
people on the buses. Write *two* letters:

   (i) the sort of letter of complaint received by the Editor;

   (ii) your own reply, defending the pupils of your school.

In both cases set out the letter correctly and, where necessary, invent names and
addresses.

(Welsh Joint Education Committee)

Comprehension/Summary (often combined in CSE questions)

9 *Read the following passage and answer the questions on it:*

Journeying through Spain

A few days later, in a village south of Valdepeñas, I ran into Romero, a young tramp like myself, who
was carrying his goods wrapped in a bundle of sailcloth and explained that he was on the road for his
health. When he heard what I was doing he threw up his arms and said that was just the thing. He
would go with me anywhere, he said, collect the money when I played, scrounge me food, and show
5 me the country.

As I'd been alone for some time it seemed a good idea, so we left the village together — Romero
prancing beside me, talking of ways to make money, boasting of his spectacular skill as a cook, of the
various tricks he knew of enticing fowls from farmers and of begging from nuns in convents. He was a
handsome young man, witty and unscrupulous, and I felt he had some useful things to teach me. We
camped the first night on a threshing floor — a circle of flagstones in the middle of a field — and lay side
10 by side under a single blanket watching the red sun go down. I still remember the moment: the sun

huge on the horizon and the silhouette of a horseman passing slowly across it, with Romero whispering and rolling me cigarettes, and his warmth as the evening cooled.

My pleasure in his company lasted about three days, then soured and diminished quickly. No
15 longer could I imagine myself prince of the road. I'd developed a growing taste for solitude, and Romero's presence had cut into this sharply. Besides, he was sluggish and lazy, was always whining for drink and complaining about his feet. Certainly, he detested walking, and after a mile or so would throw himself down and kick like a baby; so after lunch one day, while he was sleeping by the roadside, I put some money in a shoe and left him.

20 It was an extraordinary relief to be on my own again, and I made for the hills as fast as I could. But he must have awoken soon after, for presently I heard a distant shout, and there he was, coming in furious pursuit. Throughout the rest of the day I caught glimpses of him, a small toiling figure, head down and determined, scurrying indignantly along in the dust. Feeling both guilty and hunted, I quickened my pace, and he gradually fell away. There was one last cry, as from an abandoned wife,
25 and I never saw him again.

Adapted from *'As I Walked Out One Midsummer Morning'* by Laurie Lee

(*a*) In paragraph one,
  (i) What word does the author use to describe himself?
  and
  (ii) How was the author managing to get money?
(*b*) Why was Romero on the road?
(*c*) How did Romero offer to help the author before the author agreed to take him along?
(*d*) Why else did the author take him along?
(*e*) 'scrounge', 'tricks', 'enticing', 'unscrupulous': what impression of Romero does the author give us from these words? (There is no need to define each word.)
(*f*) Choose **three** phrases which suggest the closeness of their relationship at first.
(*g*) List what it was about **Romero's** behaviour which made the author tire of him.
(*h*) What was the main reason why the **author's** pleasure in Romero's company 'diminished quickly' (*line 14*)? Answer in your own words as far as possible.
(*i*) Why do you think the author 'made for the hills' (*line 20*)?
(*j*) Why did the author feel 'guilty and hunted' (*line 23*)?
(*k*) In each of the pairs of words below, the word in the left-hand column means more than the word in the right-hand column—which is why the author preferred to use it. Give the meaning of **each** of the words in the left-hand column. Here is an example:
  (**Example:** whining (*line 16*): asking
  Answer: 'Whining' shows how he asked, that is, begging, weakly, like a dog.)
  (i) prancing (*line 7*):walking
  (ii) silhouette (*line 12*):shape
(*l*) Why did the author describe Romero as an 'abandoned wife' (*line 24*)?

(*36 marks*)

(*North Regional Examinations Board*)

10 Below is a table showing the numbers of books issued by a public library to men and women at different times of the year. Write a report, based on the table, showing:

   (i) how the tastes of men differed from those of women, and

   (ii) how change of season affected borrowing habits in both cases.

	Numbers of books issued			
Classes of books	Men readers		Women readers	
	April-Sept.	October-March	April-Sept.	October-March
Fiction	1000	1600	1200	2000
Biography	2000	2200	1000	1150
Do-it-yourself	450	700	200	500
Gardening	650	800	1250	900
Politics	520	560	900	1400
Sport	200	650	200	225
Outdoor pursuits	500	850	400	550
Travel	1000	1700	800	950

(Associated Lancashire Schools Examining Board)

11 *Read the passage below and then answer the questions which follow.*

The factory was on the industrial estate, built about 10 years ago when the collieries closed down. A white-coated young man met the girls—a dozen of them, all leavers—and myself, and we followed him into the factory.

   'This,' said the young man proudly, 'is one of the latest electronically controlled salt and
5 pepper pot top moulding machines.' We watched dutifully as the steel strip went in at one end, the lights lit, the presses pressed, and the salt and pepper pot tops rolled out at the other end. The girls were not particularly impressed by this technological marvel, and were relieved when we continued past the automatic tea-vending machine (which did interest them) and into the assembly section. Two long tables faced each other. At one of them eight girls were
10 putting powder compacts into boxes. They speeded up when they became aware of us watching them, but otherwise gave no sign of greeting. Another eight girls sat putting hinges into the powder compacts.

   As we walked on past the presses, the chemical baths, the enamelling sprays, the polishing department, we saw about three dozen girls all told, mainly under 20,
15 and some barely out of school themselves. I shall always remember the polishing machines. They droned noisily behind their metallic casings and each one had a large hole with a stool in front of it.

   On each stool sat a girl with a box of unpolished compact lids by her left hand. The circular revolving table turned at a steady speed as each girl fed the rotating spindles with lids,
20 which then passed into the hole, emerged gleaming, and were deftly removed by the girl, who put them in a box by her right hand. Layer by layer, the one box emptied and the other filled.

   The noise seemed to grow louder as we stood there. Conversation was impossible. Afterwards, I asked the young man how long girls do this isolated and monotonous job. He seemed surprised: 'They do it all day—with two tea breaks.'

25   When we left, the girls seemed to be relieved to be outside even though it was drizzling. As we walked along, I remembered the past four years. The girls aren't angels, nor are they particularly bright. But at least they'd done something at school. We had tried to arouse their interests in life, open up their minds and expand their horizons a little.

Many of these girls have little option but to go to a factory like the one we visited. It
30 seems a criminal waste of ability on the part of industry that it makes such degrading
demands on girls in particular. Every day since that wet Tuesday I have felt uneasy when I see
those girls in school. 'What's it all for?' I ask myself.

From: John Carlin 'With two tea breaks and all' *The Times Educational Supplement.*

(a) What reason is suggested in the passage for the building of the industrial
estate?
(b) Why do you think the factory was being visited?
(c) Why do you think the young man was surprised by the question (line 24)?
(d) What *two* pieces of evidence can you find in the passage to show that the
writer is realistic about the schoolgirls?
(e) (i) What effect did the arrival of the visiting party have on the girls working
in the factory?
(ii) Why do you think they behaved in this way?
(f) Explain the meaning of the word 'isolated' (line 23). Give *two* reasons for
the use of this word to describe the job.
(g) Put into your own words the meaning of the expression 'open up their
minds and expand their horizons' (line 28).
(h) (i) Say fully what effect the visit has on the writer.
(ii) Explain what he questions in the final paragraph.

(South Western Examinations Board)

12 *Read the following extracts carefully. Answer the questions that follow.*
(a) Advertising has done much to raise the standards of physical well-being.
The catalogue of its benefits, real and claimed, is a long one. It has speeded
the introduction of useful inventions to a wide as distinct from a select
circle. It has brought prosperity to communities which did not know how
to sell their rotting crops. By widening markets it has enabled costs of raw
materials to be cut, accelerated turnover, lowered selling prices. It has
spread seasonal trade and kept people in employment. It has given a
guarantee of dependability — for who (as that advertisement used to ask)
would buy a nameless motor-car put together in a back-street workshop?
Its defenders claim that advertising has abolished heavy underwear, made
people clean their teeth (which was more than their dentists could persuade
them to do), and made them Nice to be Near. These gratifying results have
been achieved not only by informative, but by persuasive and indeed
intimidating advertisements. The prime object of the exercise was not, of
course, to benefit humanity, but to sell more fabrics, more toothpaste,
more disinfectant.

'The Shocking History of Advertising'
E. S. Turner

(b) Sir,
What is responsible for the decline in values in Britain today? Seldom is
one of the chief culprits mentioned – I refer to advertising.

The way people are persuaded to live beyond their means, spending on
frivolous things that fulfil no real need, is nothing short of scandalous. To
sell these fringe products advertisers resort to tricks. The English language

is misused to deceive us. Our fears, hopes and weaknesses are exploited. Exaggerated and misleading claims are employed to make us buy things, including those that do us harm, such as drugs and tobacco.

Contrary to all we once believed we have learnt to accept the philosophy of advertising – that happiness can be measured by what we possess. At all costs we must keep up with the Joneses.

Much space is devoted to 'brand' advertising which is an expensive waste of time. All this does is to push up prices. Does it really matter which soap, toothpaste or petrol we use? There's not a hap'orth of difference.

It's about time large-scale advertising was banned. Then we'd all *really* be better off.

Robert Blunt

(c) (i) *Everyone* is changing into Levi's.
 (ii) Slimfit fashions for *the fuller figure*.
 (iii) Cinzano Bianco – the *bright lights* taste.
 (iv) Try Wall's *Country-Style* Pork Sausages.
 (v) *Invest* in Littlewood's Pools.

Answer *all* the questions. *Brief answers only are required to the questions on extracts (a), (b) and (c).*

Extract (a)
 (i) What does the writer mean by referring to some benefits as 'claimed'?
 (ii) The writer has used a short phrase to say that advertising has increased sales. Give the phrase.
 (iii) Why does the writer believe advertised goods are more dependable?
 (iv) What is meant by making people 'Nice to be Near'?
 (v) Give the three words which Turner uses to describe the three types of advertising.
 (vi) Which type of advertising is likely to cause most concern, and why?

(7 marks)

Extract (b)
 (i) The writer starts by speaking of the 'decline in values'. Later in his letter he gives an example of what he considers to be such a decline. What is it?
 (ii) The expression 'fringe products' is explained in a short phrase. Give the phrase.
 (iii) Give two 'tricks' of the advertisers' trade of which the writer complains.
 (iv) What is meant by 'keeping up with the Joneses'?
 (v) Why is 'brand' advertising said to be a waste of time and money?
 (vi) In his last sentence, Blunt refers to a point made early in his letter. What is it?

(7 marks)

Extract (c)
The writer in extract (b) complains of the language in advertising being used to deceive us. Study the five slogans printed. Comment *briefly* on the words italicised in each, explaining in each case how they seek to persuade the reader. Number your answers (i) to (v).

(5 marks)

(d) General Question
The writers of extracts (a) and (b) appear to hold very different opinions.
Write a paragraph (not more than 100 words) to support *ONE* of the writers.
Do not copy his words. Try to introduce one or two ideas of your own.

(6 marks)
(Yorkshire Regional Examinations Board)

13 *The following passage is an extract from 'Roadcraft'– the police drivers' manual.
Read it carefully and answer the questions which are printed after it, using your
own words as far as possible. Note that the numbering of the paragraphs is that
used in the manual.*

How vision is affected by speed

6   Crowds of pedestrians can move about on the pavements of a busy shopping
thoroughfare without colliding with one another, not so much because they
are all the time looking out for obstructions, but mainly because their
speed of movement is so slow that they can change their pace and direction
in time to avoid collision. The length and breadth of their view may be short
when they move slowly. If, however, one of them wishes to get along quickly
he begins to look further ahead, to pick out the places where the crowd is
thinnest and to direct his course and increase his speed accordingly. He then
finds that his view of other pedestrians at close quarters deteriorates, so that
quite often, if one of them comes into his path suddenly, he narrowly avoids
collision.

7   The driver of a motor vehicle adjusts the length and breadth of his view in a
similar way, but of course, over greater distances, because his speed is a good
deal more than that of the pedestrian. When driving at 60 mph the focal
point is a considerable distance ahead and stationary objects there appear
clear and well defined, whereas the foreground becomes blurred. At this
speed a distinct effort is required to pick out foreground details, and if more
than occasional glances are directed at them there will be a natural tendency
for the driver to reduce his road speed.

8   When road speed must be kept low owing to traffic conditions, the focal
point naturally shortens and the driver observes details. These often indicate
that a danger situation is developing and he then has time, owing to his slow
speed, to take the precautions which will prevent him from becoming
involved.

9   From this natural tendency of the eyes to focus according to speed, it is
clearly dangerous to drive fast in the wrong places. If traffic is medium to
heavy, foreground details must be seen, and to enable the eyes to do this and
the brain to function as a result of the stimulus received, speed must be kept
within reasonable limits.

10   Fatigue brought about by continuous driving over long periods is first felt
as eye strain and lack of concentration, and although special efforts may be
made by the driver to maintain his normal standard of observation, he will
find the task becomes increasingly difficult, his speed will slacken and his
recognition and assessment of danger situations become late and inaccurate.

Answer *all* the following questions. Remember to *use your own words as far as possible*.

(a) Why is there little danger of people colliding when a crowd of pedestrians is walking slowly? [*3 marks*]

(b) Why does the danger of collision increase if people increase their speed? [*3 marks*]

(c) What are the 'vision' problems for a driver travelling at 60 mph? [*3 marks*]

(d) Why, according to paragraph 8, does a driver travelling slowly have more chance of avoiding an accident than one travelling at speed? [*3 marks*]

(e) What is meant by the following phrases: 'natural tendency' 'foreground details' 'the stimulus received'? [*1 mark each*]

(f) What are the effects of tiredness on a driver? [*3 marks*]

(West Midlands Examinations Board)

Reading

14 Choose a difficult or unsatisfactory relationship that is important in a book you have studied.

(a) Describe briefly that relationship and the people involved.

(b) Suggest why the relationship does not work and what might have made it work.

(c) Say how typical of real life you found this relationship to be.

Always mention the title and author of the book you are writing about. The word 'book' may be taken to include 'short story'. Credit will be given for a detailed knowledge of books and you should give suitable quotations and make frequent references to incidents and characters.

(West Midlands Examinations Board)

Literature

Many CSE Boards include in their English syllabuses lists of books for recommended reading or prescribed particular books or anthologies for closer reading. (See syllabus requirements, pp. 6-17, for details of your Board's requirements.)

Examination questions on Literature may therefore be set on one particular type of book, such as an anthology of poems or short stories, or a play. Questions tend to be phrased in general terms, e.g.:

(i) 'Choose any two poems from the anthology which are character sketches. Give details of each character and the feelings expressed in the poem, commenting on the effectiveness of the writing.'

(ii) 'A successful play should make us feel involved in what is taking place and concerned about what will happen to the characters. Describe briefly any play you have read or seen performed which involved you in this way and explain in what way you felt concerned.'

Section VI Answers
Answers to Core unit exercises

This Section is divided into three parts: (1) answers to practice exercises given in the core units of Section II, (2) answers to the Self-test units of Section III, and (3) hints on answering the examination questions given in Section V.

COMPOSITION (see Unit 1)

'Personal slant' question (p. 29):
Three sentences are used for only one idea. The second and third sentences add nothing new.

In the Amazon Hotel (questions 1-5 on p. 40)
1   The colour of the make-up kit.
2   The reason for their stay in New York.
3   The hotel was for women only.
4   She refers to 'being all right again'.
5   She gave the sun-glasses case to the baby to play with.

COMPREHENSION (see Unit 2)

Passage A Imitative music (pp. 50-52)

Q.3   The second opening is obviously more precise. Instead of the vague 'many' the writer immediately refers to one of the three examples to be chosen.

Q.4   (a) a murmuring brook; (b) thunder.

Q.5   The second opening promises to lead to a better answer. Instead of a general comment on how the writer feels about pop music we have accurate references to the passage ('three simple types'), as well as an indication that the writer has some knowledge of pop groups.

Passage B Something gets to them (questions on pp. 53-54)

Q.2   The girl feels antagonistic to Peter, and therefore sides with the fish. She tries to shame him into throwing the little fish back, first by implying he is not a proper fisherman, secondly by promising to respect his skill in spite of 'hating' it.

Q.4   The first opening is the better one, because it pays attention to the context of the paragraph. This is asked for in the question in the words '... at this point in the story'.

Q.5   The two phrases which add nothing to the changed atmosphere are 'lain so still' and 'began to reel in'. All the others help to express the excitement both children are feeling.

Q.6   Their ages must be between 10 and 13. The boy seems a little older than the girl. Neither wants to be thought 'a kid' or 'a baby', but both behave child-ishly in some ways – the boy teasing the girl by holding on to the fish, the girl 'sobbing', then quickly forgetting all about her distress.

   They have obviously known one another well for some time; they could be related – cousins perhaps. (They are not likely to be brother and sister, because she refers to 'your father'.) They are good friends, but take their closeness for granted. Each depends on the other, the girl looking to the boy for leadership, he to her for support and encouragement.

Passage C Statistics—newspaper readers (p. 57)

1 2,904,000.
2 Daily Mirror.
3 Daily Telegraph.
4 Managerial, administrative and professional.
5 News of The World, Sunday Mirror, Sunday People, Sunday Express, Sunday Times, Sunday Telegraph, Observer.
6 Sun (age 15–24).
7 Daily Express.
8 By observing that the percentages either do not reach 100 or exceed that figure.
9 5,081,000.
10 508,100.

Passage D Advertisement—'Coolstream' (p. 59)

Q.1 Because people like being one of a crowd.
Q.2 The freshness of the countryside in spring—'country-fresh', 'sparkle of spring', 'flowers'.
Q.3 Because it cleans and is supposed to invigorate. It removes fears of BO and the user can face the world without risk of being criticised.
Q.4 Any one of: 'sensitive skins', 'sparkle of spring', 'fragrance as fresh as the flowers of the field', 'lavish lather'. Alliteration helps to imprint words and the ideas behind them in the mind of the reader or hearer.
Q.5 It is scented and produces lather.
Q.6 Soap is an everyday thing found in kitchens as well as bathrooms. So the advertisement wants to stress that *Coolstream* is out of the ordinary, something superior to common soap; it wants the reader to use the brand-name next time he or she needs to buy soap.

Passage E Heavy traffic (p. 60)

Q.1 C	Q.2 B	Q.3 A	Q.4 D
Q.5 D	Q.6 B	Q.7 B	Q.8 C
Q.9 A	Q.10 C	Q.11 B	Q.12 D
Q.13 C	Q.14 D	Q.15 A	Q.16 B
Q.17 C	Q.18 D	Q.19 A	Q.20 B

Passage 1 Television as a source of information (p. 63)

Q.1   surfeited — overfilled (overloaded)
(The second of these is used a little later in the passage, so the other is preferable.)

         regime — routine
        context — framework
       chronic — recurrent, permanent
       allusion — reference

General comment: as no numbers or letters were given, we quoted each word before giving its equivalent.

Q.2 scanning, skimming.

Q.3 They come within our range of vision, but we do not consciously see them.

Q.4 Our ability to ignore information that does not affect us is like an electric switch designed to operate when a circuit is overloaded. This is a vivid comparison: an electrical installation could be damaged by too big a current; our brains can be damaged by having to respond to too many stimuli.
(It is worth spending more time and words on this answer because it earns several marks. The two sentences answer the two parts of the question.)

Q.5 They explain how home television viewers fail to take in all the information presented, because most homes are full of distractions (like the loud bangs outside the classroom).

Q.6 centre — used with reference to the family, because members of a family focus on home, as well as using it as a base of operations.
arena — term normally used for main performance area in circus, sports stadium or theatre—thus appropriate for 'emotional tension'. The home is an arena where emotional conflict is acted out.
(This question also earns several marks, so deserves a fuller answer.)

Q.7 Television programmes.

Q.8 Whatever item of current affairs is being dealt with, the producer must assume in his viewers some basic understanding, and some background knowledge of the subject. Yet there are bound to be wide variations of both amongst the vast TV audience. Allusions that are clear to some with specialist knowledge may be incomprehensible to the general public. Another problem is that any programme has to compete with other home activities and distractions.
(This answer earns most marks, so requires time and care. It is in effect a *summary* question (see p. 77), referring mainly to the last paragraph. We added the final sentence to include some references to the rest of the passage.)

Passage 2 'Roots' (pp. 65-67)

Q.1 By switching off the radio her mother shows she has made up her mind about the music without listening to it.

Q.2 She thinks Ronnie would be critical of her family's dullness and lack of culture.

Q.3 She hesitates before choosing 'majesty', an unusual and effective word.

Q.4 Dignity and poise matching the beauty of the countryside.

Q.5 'I never...' repeated three times has the effect of showing how strongly Beatie feels about having been denied opportunities to broaden her cultural interests.

Q.6 Your own personal opinion is sought here, but it needs to be backed by evidence; e.g. if you decide Beatie is *not* fair to her mother you might say she undervalues Mrs Bryant's natural dignity and her care for Beatie when she was smaller—'I fed you. I clothed you. I took you out to the sea.'

Q.7 They were similarly unable to find words for their new experiences.

Q.8 No. She cares about her mother enough to want her to share her own enjoyment of classical music.

Q.9 Mrs Bryant listens quietly to the record, and admits that not all classical music is 'squit'.

Q.10 Again this demands a personal choice, but it is clear that (iii) and (iv) are more important than (i), and that (ii) is not supported by what happens in the passage.

Passage 3 Natural enemies (pp. 67-68)

Q.1 Two of the following:
> The garden was large.
> The box hedges harboured pests.
> The flower-beds were numerous and neglected.
> The fruit-bushes were diseased.

Q.2 (a) By buying the property the owner had, of his own free will, accepted the hard labour involved in looking after the garden.
(b) The garden of Eden was given to Adam before he sinned. The writer compares the re-planned garden to Eden because it is so much more pleasant to live and work in.
(c) Enemies working secretly within the frontier—in this case in the garden.

Q.3 Because he liked the colour of beech leaves, whether alive (green) or dead (gold).

Q.4 'liberation'. The implied comparison is between someone imprisoned in a forced labour camp and a free person. Re-planning the garden has 'freed' the owner from his obligation to work in the badly planned garden.

Q.5
ill-tended	neglected, badly kept
alacrity	keen readiness, willing speed
drastic	violently effective, radical
ensconced	sheltered and protected
umbrageous	shady
segregated	separated, marked off
configuration	shape
insidious	secretly destructive, stealthy

Passage 4 Dating pottery by thermoluminescence (pp. 68-69)

Q.1   emitted — given out, produced or appearing
('Given out' is best; test this by replacing *emitted* with each of the possible answers.)
     incandescence — glow, or light
('Glow' is the better word. 'Light' will just do, but it does not give the idea of slowly appearing and slowly fading that is conveyed by *incandescence*.)
     deposited — laid down, put there, or accumulated
('Laid down' is much the best, because it gives the required idea of the layered formation in which limestone is found.)
     rigours — severity, harsh conditions, or difficulties
(Which do you think is the best word here? 'Rigours' are hardships endured

by people, though in this passage the word refers to the intense heat in which pots sometimes break up.)

    survive — last, endure, persist, or exist

('Survive' has no exact one-word equivalent; it conveys more information than the words we have given, i.e. about what happens in the earth.)

    decade — ten years

    related — connected with

Q.2 Because it has not been so long exposed to radiation *or* (a less good answer) Because it has not been in the earth so long.

Q.3 Its useful life as a utensil.

(The 'archaeological life-time' dates from the time the pottery was made to when it is re-discovered by archaeologists.)

Q.4 It destroys the ability to give out light.

(The answer is found in the middle of the third paragraph.)

Q.5 Thermoluminescence occurs when certain crystalline materials in pottery are heated to 500°C. At this temperature the stored energy in the materials is released in the form of light.

Q.6 It enables archaeologists to date fairly precisely any layer containing pottery fragments. This helps historians to build up an accurate picture of the people that used the pottery and the society they lived in.

Passage 5 The new castle (pp. 69-71)

Q.1 Welcome to New Castle; Colonel Campbell At Home; The Perfect Soldier.

Q.2 The butler's words were inaudible because of the bagpipe music.

Q.3 (a) The brass of the candelabrum was tarnished.

    (b) Only a few of the electric light bulbs lit up.

Q.4 The smoke, the cold and the dogs contributed most to Guy's discomfort.

Q.5 The author's description of Mrs Campbell makes her seem insignificant and therefore has the effect of making her husband's appearance even more startling.

Q.6 The smallest dogs make the most noise—'...dogs, ranging in size from... deerhounds to a...pomeranian, gave tongue in inverse proportion to their size'.

Q.7 Tommy puts his hand round the dog's closed jaws and swivels its head round and round. The dog seems to like this treatment and begins to wag its tail.

Q.8 The castle was not very big but extremely strongly built; the outside suggested a German building. Inside the castle all the woodwork was pitch-pine, and there were stuffed animals everywhere. The castle had double doors and the great hall was up a flight of steps. From the roof timbers of the hall hung a light fitting, originally for candles, but now the discoloured, circular, brass candle-holders held electric light bulbs. Only a few of them were lit. There was a large round dining table. The austerity of much of the furniture was offset by some chairs covered in old patterned cotton. The heraldic shields round the fireplace were blackened by smoke. There were also many objects of stone, wood and plaid, and furniture made out of deer's antlers.

Passage 6 Engineering training (p. 71)

Q.1 Module

Q.2 He will work at production items within a range determined by what the firm needs, together with what the trainee is best at. He will be supervised and tested, and will need to be accurate, and to work according to safety standards and within time schedules.

(Note that we have paraphrased the word 'aptitude' as 'what the trainee is best at', in order to show the examiner that we understand it.)

Q.3 (a) trainee's aptitude (b) firm's requirements

Q.4 (a) accuracy (b) finish

(Others that could have been chosen are 'safety' and 'time-limits'.)

Q.5 A trainee must have a supervisor to certify all the work done.

Q.6 A second-year trainee will have to choose what to specialise in, his choice being limited to what the firms needs. He must then have all his work supervised and assessed. Any work he does will have been chosen to include all appropriate production items. He will have to keep a log book which is checked by his supervisor. He will learn to work accurately, to pay attention to finish, and to work within accepted time and safety limits. (79 words)

(Although some of this material has already been used in previous answers, the question enables the candidate to answer more fully. As with many so-called 'comprehension' questions this is in effect asking for the ability to *summarise*.)

Passage 7 The football game (pp. 72-74)

When you begin to look at the passage to find material for Q.1, train your eye to look for capital S's. Not all will be 'Sugden' (there are some 'Sir' and 'Spurs'), but intelligent scanning saves time.

'Mr Sugden' appears in the first line and 'Sugden (teacher)' a few lines further down. The next time 'Sugden' appears, it is preceded by 'Mr' and followed by '(referee)' so your brain registers that you have now found two of Mr Sugden's parts; simultaneously your eye drops down a few lines to the next 'Sugden' and there's the third part: '(player)'.

It is not obligatory to describe the parts in the order in which they are mentioned provided that you make clear which one you are describing. After reading the extract, you probably remember most about Mr Sugden (player) so start with that, beginning your answer:

Q.1   Mr Sugden plays three parts: teacher, referee, player.
        As *player*, Mr Sugden is not very good . . .

  Keeping your eyes open for capital S's, collect information from the passage, e.g.
        fails to stop ball—'rolled under studs'
        couldn't dribble—'too far ahead each time'
        his pass to wing 'shot out of play a good ten yards in front of him'
        Tibbut can outjump S
        gets out of breath—'S started to chase . . . ball crossed line before he could reach it'

Such notes can quickly be written into a good paragraph to show Sugden's standard of play.

As *teacher* ...

too keen on his appearance and on winning himself—childish
(Do you think this is the main point against Sugden as teacher?)
blames others for his own faults—winger didn't run fast enough
stands on his dignity—'Don't argue with me, lad!'
expects the impossible—Billy to save a goal headed into the top right-hand corner of the net
no sympathy for the mud-covered Billy—S largely responsible for this
Do you think Sugden's criticism of Sparrow, the right back, is justified? If you answer no, you could add it to these points, all of which add up to a pretty poor report on Sugden as a teacher.

As *referee* ...

Information on this role is given only at the beginning of the game and the end of the extract. Sugden starts the game efficiently, perhaps too efficiently, waiting for the exact second? At the end, his team, Manchester United, is one goal down. The referee (Sugden) awards a penalty. A player (Sugden) scores. The author makes no comment but leaves the reader to draw his own conclusions. What are yours? Does Sugden take unfair advantage of his position?

Q.2 The snatches of the boys' conversation are the best places to look for this answer. They are prepared to defend themselves (give examples) but are remarkably polite in the circumstances. Private mutterings though are more outspoken—'chuffing carthorse', 'hopeless'.

Have the boys got Sugden weighed up? Do they humour him out of habit? Look at Tibbut's wink and his readiness to go along with Sugden's refusal to allow him to choose Liverpool as his team.

If you know a teacher like Sugden, do resist the temptation to get carried away and write pages of criticism! Keep to Sugden and the information about him in the passage; that will be enough to give you full marks for Q.2.

Passage 8 The zoo (pp. 74-75)

Q.1 50 words are not very many when the author likes so much about the zoo. Our first attempt was too long:

The author likes the extraordinary variety and surprising contrasts to be found in the animals and also in the buildings which house them and which serve the public. He enjoys the possibility of seeing and hearing the zoo animals from outside in Regent's Park, and of imagining other purposes for the zoo beyond its being a place for children to visit. Finally, he relishes the zoo as a place which takes nothing too seriously. (74 words)

After pruning we came up with this:

The author likes the surprising variety of animals and buildings, and the odd effect of seeing and hearing zoo animals from outside. He likes the idea of the zoo as a place for adults as well as children, a place which takes nothing too seriously. (45 words)

Now it's a little on the short side; do you want to add anything?

Q.2   utilitarian — functional, useful
       diverse — varied, various
       robust — strong, sturdy
       uniform — standardised, regular

Having a good vocabulary gets you three quarters of the way to full marks for this kind of question, but there are two other points to bear in mind.

(a) 'as . . . used in the passage'. Always test your word to see if it fits the passage; e.g. 'robust' can mean 'strong' and 'healthy', but 'a healthy aviary' is not right so choose 'strong'.

(b) Keep the same part of speech, i.e. choose a word that does exactly the same job as the original word; e.g. 'diverse' is an adjective describing 'new shapes' so try 'varied' or 'various' but not 'variety'. With verbs, keep the same tense; e.g. at the end of the passage, 'takes the micky . . .' is the present tense so whatever you choose must be the same — 'mocks', 'deflates'.

Q.3 First find the quotation and identify the three examples:
       'to get to know someone'
       'to talk over all but the most hard-headed business'
       'to drown one's indignation . . . Nature's jokers'

Answering 'in your own words' (and it is essential to do so and not to quote) is a way of proving that you have understood the original. Sometimes it is difficult to find alternatives, not because the original is obscure but because it is so obvious. No GCE or CSE candidate will be in doubt as to what 'to get to know someone' means, so it becomes a test of ingenuity and good vocabulary to find an alternative. 'To become more closely acquainted' is perhaps closer to the original than 'to make friends'.

The crux of the second example is 'hard-headed business' and not to miss the 'all but', i.e. all kinds of business *except* the hard-headed. How about: 'to discuss any work problems except the toughest/most demanding'?

The third may look difficult but take it slowly and you'll find a connection between humans and animals — 'indignation at human imbecility' and 'the antics of . . . Nature's jokers'. If you don't recognise 'Nature's jokers' as animals at first, read on until you come to the 'baboons and sea-lions'. The connection between humans and animals is that when people's stupidity ('human imbecility') becomes too much to bear, you can forget about it by watching the antics (find another word) of the animals in the zoo. So the version might read: 'to forget one's fury at other people's stupidity by watching the funny animals'.

POETRY

Passage 9 Moorings (pp. 75-76)

Q.1 Reptile – the dinghy's mooring chain, half overgrown, looks like a snake in the grass.
     Filched – the dew on the oars ('sweet' water in contrast to the sea water all

around) is fancied to have been stolen or filched from the air. This is an apt way of suggesting the silent formation of dew.

Breathes in – the rhythmical ebb and flow of the tide are compared to a living creature breathing.

Q.2 The third stanza describes the rapid noise and movement of the only two living things in the scene. This activity contrasts with the quieter, more static description of the sea and the boat.

Q.3 We cannot give answers to this question. Possible choices for comment might be: a *salt* ring; *nods* at nothing; a false *net* of light; *cork* that can't be; *harsh* seaweed *uncrackles;* to its *kissing;* the *skin* of the water.

Q.4 The main image concerns the moored dinghy, which is seen as a tethered horse. This idea is established in the opening stanza, the dinghy's movement on the water being described as 'pawing' and 'nodding'. The next three stanzas fill in details of the boat's surroundings; then in the final verse the poet returns to the image, referring to 'his stable', and to the pawing of a 'restless steeplechaser'. The poem ends with the boat's imagined voyage, in which its movements over the waves become the leaps of a steeplechaser over hurdles.

Cathedral builders (questions, p. 117; poem, p. 114)

1 (a) The structure and syntax of the first three stanzas emphasise the repetitiveness of the work: 'They climbed ...', 'And came down ...', 'Every night slept ...', 'And every day ...'. Stanza two in particular, with its list of hum-drum activities—'quarrelled', 'lied', 'spat', 'sang'—separated by commas, portrays their lives as routine and ordinary.

(b) Their home circumstances are just like those of people living today or in any age, e.g. (1) after work they 'came down to their suppers and small beer'; (2) when they grew older they 'became less inclined to fix a neighbour's roof' (an authentic touch, because neighbours would naturally rely on them to do such jobs).

(c) 'Heaven' is a more appropriate word than 'sky', for instance, because it reminds us of the building's purpose, reinforcing the idea of 'towards God' in line 1. Also the *h* follows the alliterative pattern: *h*oisted, *h*ewn, in*h*abited, *h*ammers, which suggests hard breathing from sustained physical effort.

(d) Migrating birds have habitual and instinctive flight paths. The official sounding phrase 'impeded the rights of way' suggests, ironically, that the swallows have established a legal right to that part of the sky. The idea helps us to imagine the great bulk of the cathedral as it must have seemed when first completed, and at the same time places it in a natural environment.

2 On the day the bishop came to consecrate our cathedral a little gang of us builders stood in the crowd. Most people shoved to get near the front to see his lordship in his fine robes, but we didn't. We stopped near the back to get the best view of the building. My mate who I've worked with all my life stood by me. He nudged me and pointed to the arch above the west door.

'Remember that day up there when I was crawling about and you were on the ladder end? Remember the wind?'

I surely did. I've been up in some weathers but that day was the roughest. All weathers, all seasons—icy winter dawns, blazing summer noondays; our whole lives were spent in raising the stones of that massive building they were all staring at now. I could hear the bishop's voice:

'...this wonderful work of God given its form through the hand of man—'
My mate nudged me again.

'Never been up a ladder in his life, doesn't know sandstone from granite!'

I felt sorry for the bishop. He could only ever walk on the floor of our building, in the shadow cast by it, inside or out; he could never feel the satisfaction we had known in our lifelong work.

'I'd rather my lad grew up to be a builder than a bishop,' I said to my mate.

SUMMARIES AND NOTES

Passage on domestic water supply (p. 80)

Mains water is under the householder's control as soon as it crosses the boundary of his property. There may be a stop-cock here; there will certainly be one just inside the house, probably near the kitchen sink.

The rising main, controlled by this stop-cock, normally supplies two outlets: the kitchen sink cold water tap (used for drinking and cooking); and a storage tank in the loft. This tank then supplies the hot water system, and other cold taps. In older water systems the kitchen tap may be fed from the loft tank.

To be prepared for an emergency, the householder should find out where the stop-cock is situated, and which tap can empty the rising main once the stop-cock is closed. This 'draw-off' tap is usually the kitchen sink cold tap. If the stop-cock fails to cut off the supply, the householder should consult the water company. (147 words)

Notes

1 We found that the passage had two elements: (a) advice on what to do and how to find stop-cocks, etc. (b) plain description. The writer moves casually from one to the other, but it proved better in the summary to deal with each in turn.

2 This summary demonstrates that it is not necessary to stick to the order of the points in the original passage.

3 Examiners expect candidates to present the summary in their own words. This does not mean, of course, that you need to contrive artificial alternatives for technical terms like 'stop-cock', or for other exact uses of language.

4 You will notice that the friendly, informal tone of the original has been lost in the summary. In general, summaries of this kind aim at extracting information, the factual basis of the subject, rather than the author's attitude to it or to his readers, however important these may be in the original.

Passages on pollution in the Mediterranean (pp. 84-87)

This is an exercise in extracting information from a group of reports and then arranging it. Our method was to skim through; to re-read, noting items under 'the need...' and 'the difficulties...'; and finally to write up the sorted-out facts. These are the points we noted:

The need

I paras. 4, 5, 6   untreated sewage; tankers
                      factory poisons; polluted rivers
                      no cleansing tide
                      infections; poisoned fish

   last para.   threat to tourism

II   smaller fish
                      extension of pollution

III para. 5   polluting matter straight into sea
    para. 6   atmospheric pollution etc.

The difficulties

I paras. 10, 11   enormous cost — feelings of poorer countries

III para. 2   difficulty in covering all forms of pollution;
                     immense cost and impact on poorer countries
    para. 4   previous proposals too ambitious
    para. 6   research delays
    para. 7   differing organisation of countries concerned

Before we produced our answer we noted that some of the facts were repeated and that the material we collected would have to be re-arranged. The following is what we finally produced, in only 173 words. Have we left out anything of importance, or are there any places where expansion is needed?

The sea and air of the Mediterranean are being heavily polluted by the discharge of sewage from many cities, by poisonous industrial wastes, by tankers, by already polluted rivers, and by factory chimneys. The problem is worsened by the lack of a tide to change the water. The results of the pollution are: poisoned fish, smaller fish, the spread of infections to bathers, and, finally, the threat to tourism — the Mediterranean is the world's main holiday resort — which is the livelihood of several countries.

The main difficulty in agreeing on the measures to check pollution is the enormous cost — up to £2,800m, or £4 a head for every person in the countries concerned. This has made the smaller countries very anxious to identify the sources of the troubles. Further difficulties have been experienced in reaching an agreement that would cover all forms of pollution; in research delays; and in the ambitious nature of earlier plans. Finally, the difficulties have been increased by the different laws and industrial systems of the numerous countries involved.

Passage 1 Renaissance Italian frescoes (pp. 93-94)

The first step in making a fresco was to prepare a layer of rough plaster (arriccio) on the wall. The centre of this layer — or with larger pictures a grid — was marked by means of a taut, paint-soaked cord; then the design was drawn free-hand with charcoal. After corrections the final drawing was 'inked in' in red (sinopia). The painting was now created by spreading smooth plaster (intonaco) over the surface and painting on it. This was done a section at a time, the drawing being rapidly sketched on the new plaster as the original disappeared beneath it. (98 words)

Now that it is possible to remove frescoes intact, the original drawings can be seen. These 'sinopie' are often the only examples of the artist's unrestricted skill, because drawings on paper or parchment were rare. They were always done by the master, not by apprentices, and were often extremely beautiful. Sometimes they incorporated changes insisted upon by the patron. Thus the technique that has led to their discovery is valuable. (70 words)

Passage 2 Children and stability (pp. 94-95)

We found this a difficult passage to summarise, and if your version is different it may well be better.

A young child needs stability because of his nature. Normally this is unruly and destructive at first, as he tests his strength on his home. If the home can stand it, and show that a firm framework is there, the child, reassured, will settle down to his own activities. He behaves like this because his character is not yet formed, and because he does not yet understand his environment. If there are loving adults around, his development will continue. But if the home fails him, he will become anxious; if he cannot find security somewhere, he may even go mad. (100 words)

Notes
1 'Nature' in our first sentence sums up the four or five opening sentences of the passage.
2 Will our phrase 'because he does not yet understand his environment' do for 'the relation to external reality'? What do you think?
3 Most of the last paragraph describes what happens when the home fails, and does not concern our question except for the points we have picked out.

Passage 3 Writing detective stories (pp. 95-98)

The writer's aim is to baffle the reader; almost any method may be adopted to achieve this end. Important clues must not be concealed, but otherwise the writer is not obliged to reveal everything that goes on in the characters' minds. The good writer will try to bluff and double bluff the reader, but misleading trails should not be introduced simply to deceive the reader. They should have some relation to the natural development of the story and the characters.

If this advice is followed the reader will not feel cheated at the end of the story, but will be surprised when the identity of the murderer is revealed. If the reader is past caring who 'did it', the writer has failed to provide enough suspense.

Sometimes every character is a suspect, so that the reader is constantly guessing while the choice is narrowed down. The reader should have enough information to enable him to eliminate suspects on both psychological and factual grounds.

Real life is not a good basis for detective stories. The writer must accept the necessity for fantasy but try to work out the development of the story in logical steps. (194 words)

How writers work

The answer above contains much of the material needed for this question. The main difference is that here the emphasis is on *method*, *(How ...)* rather than *advice*, and, of course, the presentation must be in note form.

You could start this question by fixing the word 'method' or 'how' firmly in your mind, and then running your eye over the passage to find the relevant points, e.g.:

para. 1 don't conceal material clues
           avoid red herrings
para. 2 how to place clues — genuine or false
           how to be too clever for readers but not for characters
para. 3 presentation of murderer
para. 4 maintaining suspense

These notes will be too brief for a final intelligible version but they help to extract the relevant points quickly and can easily be expanded.

Passage 4 The use of chemicals in agriculture (pp. 98-99)

Our method was first to skim through the passage for the general ideas, which are not difficult, and then to make a list of points for each of the two questions. Here is our list, which we then used to write our answers.

1 Belief that plants need nothing but chemicals
Results:
big industry to discover and sell chemicals
money before food
factory farming
pollution
destruction of fertility
farmer obliged to use poisons, possibly dangerous
waste of energy in producing chemicals
quantity not quality — mistaken research

2 *Alternative:*
let soil itself grow things instead of acting as a medium for chemicals
do this by returning organic waste to soil and building up its fertility
organic farming produces yields as high as those of factory farming and sometimes greater profits
possibilities if organic farming backed by research

This is how we wrote up the points in our summary:

1 The belief that plants need nothing but chemicals and that the soil can be neglected has had undesirable results. Agriculture became a big industry, concerned with inventing and selling artificial products. The farm itself became a factory, manufacturing plants and animals to make money rather than produce food.

Further results were pollution and the destruction of the soil's fertility, as farmers were obliged to use more pesticides. Moreover there is a waste of energy in making these chemicals; and what counts is quantity not quality. (85 words. Are any savings possible?)

2 The soil itself should be allowed to grow things, instead of acting as a medium for chemicals. This is achieved by returning all organic waste to the soil, thus building up its fertility. The method is productive, profitable and has great possibilities. (42 words)

(Note that the important parts of the original for this answer are found in para. 4, second half, and para. 5.)

Passage 5 Vole plagues (pp. 99-101)

The causes of vole plagues are not fully established. Newly planted forests, where sheep and cattle no longer graze, and therefore where the grass grows longer, are thought to encourage an increase in the vole population. The long grass provides not only food but also protection from the normal predators. Another theory is that the slaughter of predators to preserve game birds allowed voles to increase.

The effect of vole plagues is clearly visible in the widespread damage to grass and young trees. The vole population can run into millions and, as a vole can eat its body-weight in ten days, the destruction of the countryside is inevitable. Farmers have suffered losses in ewes and lambs because there was not enough grass, and in Scotland in the latter part of the nineteenth century, food had to be imported. When the voles have eaten all the grass they begin on young trees, nibbling through the bark, killing many trees and stunting the growth of others.

The cure for the plague is even more difficult to identify than its cause, and varies from the sprinkling of holy water in Turkey to a biological theory of 'shock disease', triggered off by increased competition for food. Setting traps and protecting trees with fine-meshed netting is ineffective and impracticable in the face of such enormous numbers of voles, and not even a Government Commission could suggest any solution. (235 words)

Passage 6 The art of the cave-dwellers (pp. 101-103)

At first it is not easy to connect the two quoted statements; yet until we understand them we can't start the summary. The best way to deal with something apparently obscure like this is to tackle it bit by bit. 'Art and science...' What examples have we been given? 'Art' is easy—the cave-paintings; but 'science'? The nearest we can get to this seems to be the tool-making skill of early man.

Now, if we start thinking about it, these *do* both show man 'visualising the future'—preparing for the hunt the next day, or month. Once this is clear to us we can soon see what is meant by the other quotation: a telescope is an instrument for looking into the distance. The cave-paintings and the tools and weapons were ways of 'looking' into the future.

After this preliminary thinking we are in a position to set to work on the summary. We are not allowed many words, but not many are needed. Here is our version:

When a cave-man painted hunting scenes on cave walls he was imagining the dangers of hunting. By making pictures of these dangers he could prepare himself to face them, just as he could make tools and weapons for future hunting. He also used his imagination—as we do—to convert the two-dimensional pictures into three-dimensional reality. By making paintings he used his imagination to anticipate dangers; we use ours, when *we* see the paintings, to re-create the culture of the cave-dwellers. (83 words)

WRITING LETTERS

Here is our answer to the practice question on p. 107.

> 'Walcot Dene',
> Shooter's Lane,
> Kempton,
> BROWSHILL,
> Herefordshire BL4 5SL.
>
> 14th May 1980.

Miss Pamela Johnson, M.B.E.,
Shotton Park,
Kempton,
BROWSHILL,
Herefordshire.

Dear Miss Johnson,

As secretary of the Kempton Over-60s Club I have been responsible for organising a very successful sponsored 'slim' in aid of the Kempton Home for the Disabled. As you know, the Home has recently moved into larger premises at Kempton Hurst, and is in need of funds to develop and extend its facilities there. Our Club has raised £550 towards this valuable work.

Knowing your concern for disabled people, I am writing to ask whether you would be prepared to be Guest of Honour at a tree-planting ceremony in the grounds of Kempton Hurst on the afternoon of Thursday 22nd May, when we shall formally hand over the cheque to Lord Mount, patron of the Home. We hope this will be an important occasion, that will attract publicity to the work of Kempton Hurst in particular, and to the need for further support for the disabled in this area. Your name, and your fame as an international ballet star, would ensure the success of the occasion.

The actual planting ceremony will be quite short. You will be asked to use a specially inscribed silver trowel, and to make a short speech. Proceedings will begin at about 2 p.m., and should be over by 4.15 p.m., when tea will be served in the Hurst to all invited guests. These will include the Lord President of the County and local dignitaries and officials, probably about forty in all.

Our Club, and the staff at Kempton Hurst, would greatly appreciate it if you could help us in this worthy cause. Please let me know if you need any further information. I look forward to hearing from you.

> Yours sincerely,
>
> *Eva Blöm*
>
> (Mrs) Eva Blöm,
> Hon. Secretary, Kempton Over-60s Club,
> Organising Secretary, The Friends of Kempton Home.

Three letters to a sprocket manufacturer (pp. 107-108)

I The engineer concerned found this letter adequate for its purpose, and enjoyed the wit of the conclusion. We agree, but would prefer:
(a) a date (useful in a business letter for filing purposes);
(b) accurate punctuation and spelling (two question marks, two full stops, and at least three commas missing; *original* misspelt);
(c) more courtesy — 'How much' seems curt as a request for price;
(d) less clumsy sentence construction; it should be easy to avoid the 'but'... 'but' and repetition of 'as'.

An examiner would also object to the unconventional way of signing off.

II This was less satisfactory to the manufacturer, because the machine is a rare model and the information is incomplete (no bore dimension, not known whether flat or dished sprocket required). We note also:
(a) no year given in date;
(b) no punctuation in address, no question mark for first sentence;
(c) sloppy use of *etc.* (and full stop omitted after the abbreviation); what does he want besides the price?
(d) 'forward...on' ('on' is superfluous);
(e) rather sprawling final sentence (containing another question) 'If you... would you... so I... to you... as I'm... as I...';
(f) irrelevant information (the reference to college);
(g) misspelling of *college*.

III The engineer found this letter the least satisfactory of the three. The information about the chain 'slightly larger' is hopelessly vague; it is not even clear whether the Suzuki mentioned is the motorcycle in question. The engineer had to ask, among other things, for the ratio (gearbox: rear sprocket).

We find the layout and phrasing adequate, apart from the confusion of meaning referred to. The final sentence is particularly muddled — 'either sprocket ...*it*...' (which sprocket?). This sentence in fact adds no useful information and could be omitted. Note also:
(a) comma missing at end of first line of address;
(b) 'Bank' and 'Yours' should have capital letters;
(c) At the end 'Hope...' should read either 'Hoping...' or 'I hope...'.

Reports, practical writing

1 **HOME SAFETY GUIDE**

READ THIS SHEET! IT MAY SAVE YOUR CHILD'S LIFE –

OR YOUR OWN

Most accidents happen at home – more than on roads or railways, at sea or in the air.
Please use the hints in this *Guide* to make *your* home a safer place.

DANGER POINTS
- Electric plugs and appliances
- Gas appliances
- Open fires and flames
- Floor surfaces
- Staircases and windows

Electric Loose fittings or connections can cause electric shocks. They can also spark or overheat and cause fires. *Regularly check* all plugs, wires, connections and insulation.

Gas If escaping gas collects it can cause an explosion. It can also poison. *Regularly check* all pilot lights, on/off controls, valves and fittings, especially before leaving a room or the house empty.

Open fires *Never* leave an open fire without a spark-proof fireguard. Position paraffin stoves where they cannot be accidentally knocked over. Keep matches away from small children, and children away from fires.

Floors Use non-slip polish for tiles, parquet, linoleum and other smooth surfaces. Attach non-slip or rubber backing to mats on polished floors. Repair frayed carpets.

Stairs *Regularly check* that stair-carpets are firmly fastened, and are not frayed or worn into holes. *Regularly check* banisters and hand-rails for damage or wear. Fix guards for small children at top and bottom of stairs.

Windows Never leave windows flapping or unsecured. Close them when the room or the house is empty. Keep an eye on children near open windows.

PRACTISE ALERTNESS! **KEEP THIS SHEET HANDY!**

2 *Accident report*

The accident happened on Tuesday 22nd April at 1.10 p.m. I was walking back to school after lunch. As I turned down the road where the school entrance is about 200 metres away, I could see a bright green car parked nearly opposite the school gates. I noticed it because I particularly dislike that colour. As I got nearer, on the same side as the car, I could hear a small motor-bike behind me (125 cc). I turned round to see if I knew the driver and when I turned back again there was a bus coming up the slight hill. The next thing was a thud and a clatter as the motor-bike collided with the rear of the car. The rider fell behind the car, and the motor-bike beside it. The bus, which had been going fairly slowly, stopped further up the road and the driver came back to help. The rider got up unhurt and the bus driver helped him pick up his bike. There was no-one in the car and I couldn't see any damage to it. I think the man on the motor-bike must have lost his concentration because there was plenty of room for him to get between the car and the bus.

3 *Anti-litter speech*

We love litter when it is in the litter-bin.

This week the 5th Years begin their 'Clean up the school' campaign. 5A, B and C will be watching you in the corridors and classrooms, 5X, Y and Z in the grounds. We have plenty of plastic sacks and if anyone is seen to drop litter – even a sweet paper – the penalty is collecting litter from the grounds, after school, wet or fine.

The classrooms with least litter at the end of the day on three consecutive days will be awarded one of our Campaign Credit Posters, like this (Hold up).

This campaign has the backing of the Head and all the staff. It is not just a gimmick but a highly educational operation to improve the quality of school life. A suggestion box will be put in the entrance hall, and the best ideas for dealing with litter will be read out next week. Please make sure that your suggestion papers go right into the box and do not litter the entrance hall.

Next week Martin Milton of 5Y will give details of 'Litter Lines', a poetry and essay competition with startling prizes.

Thank you for your attention.

4 *Nuclear Tests*

Paragraph 1: The chart compares the number of nuclear weapons tests above and below the ground in the 18 years before the Limited Test Ban Treaty and the 17 years following it. The total number of tests is given for each of the nations possessing nuclear weapons, with a rough indication of how many tests were carried out above ground. The charts show that of the four main nuclear powers only one, France, continued with tests above ground after the treaty, but three new nuclear powers, China, India and an unidentified one, ignored the treaty. After the treaty the total number of tests went up for USA, USSR and France, but the UK reduced hers by a little over half.

Paragraph 2: The chart is concerned with three kinds of danger from nuclear weapons: atmospheric pollution from tests, increases in the numbers of weapons tested (and therefore made) by the main nuclear powers, and the development of new nuclear powers. The first of these dangers has been effectively reduced by the treaty; instead of almost 400 atmospheric tests before August 1963 there were only 50 or 60 in the seventeen years afterwards. However, the chart shows clearly that both the other dangers have increased substantially since the treaty. The total number of tests has almost doubled (from 27 per year to 46 per year), and three new nuclear powers have tested weapons. It is also significant that all the new nuclear powers ignored the treaty banning tests above ground.

PUNCTUATION

(Exercise on question marks, p. 128)

The three questions are:

 (i) . . . what to wear (indirect)

 (ii) Would I look out of place in a long dress?

(iii) . . . what would she be wearing (indirect)

(Q.2 on page 129)

The dash indicates surprise in (b) and (c). The exclamation mark adds to this in (b), indicating alarm as well.

(Paragraph 1 on page 129)

It's lost its bone. The first 'It's' is a short form of 'it has', therefore needs the inverted comma to replace the missing letters *ha*.

GRAMMAR AND USAGE

Indirect Speech (practice question, p. 135)

'You ought to hold it . . . Everyone knows that.'

She said that he ought to hold it still. He retorted that he knew what he was doing; that the fish were used to things moving; they were all fed already; they had had plenty. The girl said there were not many mayfly, to which he rejoined that that was the reason for their not jumping. She contradicted him by saying that fish did not jump for mayfly; they waited till they got waterlogged. He asked sharply why fish jumped in that case, and the girl's answer was that they jumped for joy. He accused her of talking nonsense, but she insisted, saying that she had read it. He angrily disagreed, reiterating that fish jumped for mayfly and that everyone knew that.

Using a dictionary

Prepositions (practice, p. 139)

complimented *on*	different *from**	immune *from, to, against*
contrary *to*	exempt *from*	liable *to (for)*
deficient *in*	identical *with*	persevere *in, at, with*

* Purists allow only *from* as correct, but *to* is so frequently used nowadays as to be acceptable. Some dictionaries also recognise *than*, but it is less confusing to use *than* only after a comparative, e.g. sooner than, more accurate than.

Answers to Self-test units

Test 1 Accuracy (p. 145)   *score*

1 Two commas: *In a mixed class the girls, who are cleverer, soon get bored.* This has the effect of making the meaning '... the girls, who anyway are cleverer than boys, soon get bored.'   2

2 (a), (b), (a)   4 if *all* correct, 1 each for 1 c 2 correct

3 colon, or colon and dash together (:—)   2

4 lain *(lay is the past tense—he lay there; laid is the past of to lay—she laid the table)*   1

5 etc.=and other things (Latin: *et cetera*)
   cf.=compare (Latin: *conferre*)
   e.g.=for example (Latin: *exempli gratia* ('for the sake of example'))
   i.e.=that is (Latin: *id est*)
   n.b.=note well (Latin: *nota bene*)   4 if *all* correct, 1 for each if less correct

6 Yours sincerely (e). (a), (b), (f), and (g) are incorrect. (d) and (h) are suitable for a business letter. (c) is less conventional, but acceptable.   2 or 1 for (c)

7 'You know I can't.' 'Do I?' 'Of course you do!' she said scornfully.   10

8 'You know I can't.'
   'Do I?'
   'Of course you do!' she said scornfully.   3

9 *comprises.* To comprise means to include within a whole, so there is no need for a preposition.   1

10 (a) implied (b) passed (c) stratum (or change *was* to *were*). *Strata* is a plural form in Latin.   1
                                                                                 ——
                                                                          total 30

Test 2 Spelling (pp. 146-147)

1 When the syllable is pronounced 'ee', place –i– before –e– except after –c–.
2 contemporary—5; responsibility—6; occasionally—5; originally—5; criticism—3; similar—3
3 disease separate argument business temporary disappointed
4 When the syllable is pronounced 'ee', place –i– before –e– except after –c–.
5 The *u* after the *g* indicates that the sound is hard (as in *got*). The *u* is silent. Other words: disguise, guilt, intrigue, rogue
6 chose *and* chosen, submitted, preferred, remembered, dispelled, occurred
7 When the syllable is pronounced 'ee', place –i– before –e– except after –c–.
8 The *ea* sounds like –e– (as in *pet*). Other words: feather, head, realm, wealth
9 The silent *g*

Test 3 Spelling and usage (pp. 147-148)
(Score: each answer earns three marks; total 30.)

1 recesses   spoonfuls   tomatoes
2 indefinite   illegal   dissatisfied
3 He began.   She did very well.   I always chose nylon bearings.
4 The message was transmitted. The words were spoken clearly. The bag was laid on the counter.
5 engage   occur   reason
6 anything   can   ever
7 argument   family   omit   athletic   mischievous   similar
8 accommodate   February   immediately   except   government   surprise
9 mathematics   definitely   repetition
10 business   introduce   fuel

Test 4 Vocabulary (p. 148)

1 *lenient*   tolerant
  incentive   motive/spur
  redundant   unnecessary/superfluous
  relinquish   give up
  grotesque   absurd/odd
  synthetic   man-made/artificial compound
2 *impudent*   respectful
  opaque   clear/transparent
  tranquil   lively
  destitute   well off
  deciduous   evergreen
  acquiesce   disagree

Test 5 Vocabulary (pp. 148-149)

1 false
2 legible
3 (a) serrated   (b) indelible   (c) moribund   (d) arrogant   (e) ambiguous
4 not
5 (a) in to   (b) into
6 (a) up on   (b) upon
7 crossroads
8 dancing-teacher
9 corpse
10 (a) the second 'from'   (b) pair of   (c) absolutely   (d) back   (e) up with
11 medium
12 neuroses
13 (a) imaginative   (b) illusion   (c) have   (d) effect/affected   (e) principle
14 etymology
15 innocent
16 occasional
17 *True*   *False*
  frank   perjury
  candour   forgery
  verity   fallacious

True	*False*
paragon	fraud
sincere	duplicity
guileless	deceive
honest	spurious
unfeigned	lie
fidelity	distortion
irreproachable	sham

18 | *Speaking* | *Writing* |
|---|---|
| drawl | signature |
| mute | stationery |
| discourse | shorthand |
| raucous | manuscript |
| intonation | hieroglyphic |
| eloquence | inscribe |
| utter | brochure |
| audible | index |
| orator | essay |
| recite | journal |

Test 6 Dictionary work (pp. 149-150)

1 BOOKworm   NEWSprint   floating RIB   FLOATING kidney
  BENCH-mark   GOODwill   good TASTE   POLAR bear

2 (a) cocky (b) cocoa (c) cocoon (d) codicil (e) coelacanth (f) coerce (g) co-exist (h) coffin (i) cogent (j) cognition (k) cognoscente (l) coherence

Test 7 Style (p. 150)

for the high jump	slang
got down to the nitty-gritty	cliché ⎱ the use of both these together in the same
beat about the bush	cliché ⎰ sentence is tautological
got it coming to me	colloquialism
no messing about	colloquialism
all over and done with	cliché
no hard feelings	cliché

If I am to be punished I prefer thè headmaster to come straight to the point. If I am in the wrong and know I must be punished, I prefer a caning, which is soon over; it would not be resented by me.

Tests 8, 9 and 10

No 'right' answers can be provided for these three tests. There are too many ways in which they could be answered. Compare your answers with those of someone else, or perhaps ask a friend, teacher or parent to read and comment on your work.

Test 11 Comprehension (p. 151)

1 The charts.
2 Getting a record into the charts by bogus purchases.
3 A record company discovers which shops are used to calculate the sales of records and falsifies these sales by hiring people to buy the records back on behalf of the company.
4 The British Phonographic Industry; EMI; 'a consortium of interested parties'.
5 Using private detectives to find out the facts; proposing to set up a new chart.
6 Enlist the help of the Director of Public Prosecutions; use an independent organisation to compile the new chart on fresh lines; set up regional charts.
(There is no firm dividing line between questions 5 and 6; no. 6 expects you to mention future action rather than that already started.)

Test 12 Comprehension (p. 153)

1 The advertisement is likely to be most effective with houseproud or anxious parents/housewives.
2 The general public has no detailed scientific knowledge, and is therefore ready to believe extravagant claims when backed by 'science'.
3 Parental feelings.
4 (a) repetition of brand name
　(b) spurious appeal for haste and urgency
　(c) size names ('popular', 'giant') chosen to encourage purchase
　These are all well-known sales techniques.
5 Yes. (Evidence: 'cleanest home', 'plus the little something extra which the others haven't got'.)

information desirable	given in advert?
What germs are destroyed?	no
How does the product compare with other disinfectants on the market?	no
What side-effects or possible dangers might there be (e.g. poisonous when taken internally)?	no

---

Test 13 Comprehension (pp. 153-154)

1	absence	2	were	3	give	4	the
5	refused	6	gives	7	book	8	Mary
9	wants	10	can't	11	Joe	12	saying
13	to	14	go	15	as	16	toy

Test 14 Comprehension (p. 154)

1	are	2	been	3	introduce	4	would
5	one	6	happened	7	for	8	and
9	did	10	they	11	both	12	accustoming
13	their	14	like	15	the		

Test 15 Comprehension (pp. 154-155)

1	offices	2	into	3	town	4	a
5	by	6	town	7	peaceful	8	on
9	and	10	to	11	with	12	ill-at-ease
13	contentment	14	What	15	I	16	got

Test 16 Summary (p. 155)

One of the cables leading to the motor had an intermittent fault, which resulted in the motor overheating. It showed only when vibrations from the motor were transmitted to the cable. After isolating the fault by a series of tests, the engineer renewed the faulty cable. (46 words)

Test 17 Summary (p. 156)

Archaeologists: Worms cast their cover and protect everything left on the surface of the land. Worms have therefore been instrumental in preserving valuable archaeological remains such as pavements, and even whole buildings. (32 words)

Gardeners: Worms help gardeners, first by moving, sifting and mixing the soil, leaving it in good condition for holding mineral-rich moisture. Secondly, by covering organic substances like bone they help these to rot so that plants can feed from them. Finally, they bury leaves and plant fragments which also rot and become humus. (53 words. Decide which three words should be omitted to bring this within the limit set.)

Test 18 Summary (pp. 156-157)

Muhammad Ali had lost the fight but he seemed to have won a new serenity and contentment. He has been quiet after a fight before, as if the effort had drained him of all his aggression, but this time it seemed that his old flamboyance might have gone for ever.

Even his face looked different—not just because of the bruises and swellings. It looked smaller and somehow diminished. There were touches of his old style, especially as he proclaimed his intent to regain the title. Ali will never again be the incomparable Ali who defeated George Foreman but his spirit will never be broken. (105 words)

Test 19 Summary (pp. 157-158)

Our society is inconsistent in its responses to drug-taking. (9 words)

Test 20 Summary (p. 158)

The authors point out that although the smoking of tobacco kills more than 1,000 people each week its sale remains legal. Both businessmen and tax authorities profit from it. The letter implies that the heavy sentences passed on LSD offenders reveal dangerously inconsistent attitudes towards different drugs. (47 words)

Hints on answering examination questions

The following hints on how to approach and answer the examination questions quoted in Section V (pp. 164-183) have been written by the authors and include skeleton answers only.

COMPOSITION

The GCE, SCE and CSE composition questions included in Section V represent a typical selection. As you can see, they all fall within one or more of the four types of composition described in Section II (Unit 1). You will also notice that there is no significant difference between subjects set for GCE or SCE and CSE. CSE papers tend to include a higher proportion of discussion-type essays (involving personal opinions and views), and this is reflected in the selection in Section V of this book. For practice you can usefully choose any of the essay questions for any of the three examinations.

Rubrics

These are the instructions you are given, either at the beginning of the whole paper or immediately before essay topics. We have included some typical ones (GCE questions 1, 2 and 3 on p. 164, and CSE question 1, on p. 175). It is always a good idea to read them with special attention; to ignore them will certainly lose you valuable marks, however good your essay may be.

Length of essay: You are nearly always given some guidance about this. For instance, the Joint Matriculation Board (JMB), in GCE question 1 (p. 167), require two to two and a quarter pages with an average of eight words to the line. Their answer books have 30 to 32 lines to the page, so they are asking for about 550 words. It is a good idea to know beforehand what 100 words of your normal handwriting looks like on an average examination page. There is no point in wasting valuable examination time counting words. Demands vary from 400 to 600 words for a main essay question. Some papers include shorter essay-type questions in addition to the main one (GCE question 5 on p. 165 is an example of one such question), or include them within comprehension or summary questions. You will be told how long these should be. The number of words is even more important in summary questions (see p. 212).

Other instructions or advice: If your essay is to be based on a picture, a poem (GCE 3 on p. 164) or some other piece of writing, the way you write it should indicate its source. Sometimes you are advised to make a plan before writing your essay in full (e.g., GCE 3b). In Section II (Unit 1) we have given you plenty of guidance on planning essays. The West Midlands Examination Board (WMEB) sets out its advice in a very clear rubric (see question p. 160); their suggestion that you should make the plan in your actual answer book is a good one because this will show the examiner how carefully you have thought out your subject. Do remember to rule a line through all rough work before handing in your paper.

Notes on individual questions

GCE 1 (a)   Although this is on a common topic, the weather, you are asked for two different types of composition. (i) is the descriptive type of essay while (ii) is the fictional type. For (i) to be a good choice your 'incident' will need to have been quite recent, or a very vivid one. You need accurate details to make your description ring true, and these fade from the memory quite quickly. Alternative (ii) gives you more of a lead with the story and offers you an additional choice ('alone or with a party'); its success will depend on the vividness of your imagination. Obviously it will help if you have ever been out in a heavy snowstorm.

GCE 1 (b)   Some examining boards make a point of setting very short subjects, even single-word ones. In some ways these give you considerable freedom of choice. On the other hand there is little guidance as to what type of essay is required. 'Ruin' could refer to a building or to a person, to the upsetting of a plan or the destruction of the environment. It could lead to a fictional, discussion or descriptive type of essay. Because one-word, or very short, essay subjects appear so often, we suggest here ways you could develop this one for essays of each type:

Fictional: A gas explosion in the house next door suddenly shatters the peace of your evening meal. What follows? You will need to describe the people involved, the damage to both people and property, and the sequence of events following the explosion.

Discussion: You believe that a large caravan-site on a particular stretch of coastline has ruined the natural environment. State your case as forcefully as you can, detailing every aspect of the change – visual pollution, undesirable increase of traffic, pressure on local services and amenities, etc.

Descriptive: Describe a ruined motte and bailey castle near your home, or wellknown to you, in two or three different seasons or weathers. The important thing with this kind of essay is to make sure that the subject remains in the centre. Don't use it merely as a jumping-off point for a composition on some other favourite or familiar topic.

GCE 2 (a)   *Fictional essay*. This is a straightforward topic if you are interested in people and their behaviour. It will help to make your essay lively and vivid if you apply your 'power' to people you know well.

GCE 2 (b)   *Fictional essay*. This would be effective only if the family described included considerable variety – of ages (perhaps three generations), temperaments, etc. It would not be easy to write well about a family of fewer than four people.

GCE 3 (a)   *Discussion essay*. Your task here is to persuade your reader that what you collect can be interesting, both in itself and in the search for new specimens. See Orwell's essay again (Unit 1) for a good example of stating personal views.

GCE 3 (b)   *Descriptive or fictional essay*. The second part of the question is a useful warning.

GCE 4   *Fictional essay*. This topic is difficult to classify positively. Don't be misled into telling the story of how the land came to be your property. You would have more chance of writing well on this subject if you were a country-dweller, perhaps with first-hand experience of a farming, forestry or other open-air pursuits.

GCE 5 *Descriptive essay*. This would not be a main essay question, so would not require more than 150-200 words. You need first-hand knowledge and a logical brain to do it well.

GCE 6, 7 See Letters below (pp. 209-210)

CSE 1 and 2 *Discussion essays*. You will need to make notes for both these topics. These will give your essay some focus. For CSE 1 a two-part structure is suggested; make use of the suggestion. In CSE 2 you are asked to make up your mind one way or the other, *then* to argue your case as strongly as you can. With this kind of subject you must always try to think of possible objections to your point of view, so as to present a really convincing case.

CSE 3 *Descriptive essay*. You can include both likes *and* dislikes here, in spite of the 'or' in the subject.

CSE 4 *Descriptive essay*.

CSE 5 (a) See Letters, below. (b) Your answer will be a discussion-type essay. The question does not require a full-length composition.

LETTERS (GCE 6, 7, 8, CSE 6, 7, 8)

See Section II (Unit 4) for guidance on lay-out and content of letters. The length will depend on the question's importance in the paper as a whole. GCE 6 and 7 require longer, fuller letters than the others. Decide what kind of person each letter-writer is – age, sex, job, home and work environment. This will help you to make the letters convincing.

The following indications of time, and marks to be gained, are given for these letter questions:

No.	Length of paper (mins.)	Time suggested for this question (mins.)	Marks allocated (%)
GCE 6	90	20	$28\frac{1}{2}$
GCE 7	180	not given	10
GCE 8	90	30	30
CSE 6	105	20	$16\frac{1}{2}$
CSE 7	90	30	not given
CSE 8	135	not given	not given

(one of three questions)

IMPORTANT: If you want to use any of these questions for actual examination practice, do the work, keeping as close as you can to the time-limit suggested, *before* consulting the following notes to these six questions. Get a friend or relative to read and comment on your letter.

GCE 6 Here you have quite a lot of information, which demands careful planning. Your letter aims to persuade the chairman to do something; he is not likely to act on it if it is muddled or confused, or if the tone is curt or off-hand.

Your preliminary notes may go something like this:
  (i) Introduce yourself – local resident, open-air enthusiast, sports organiser?
  (ii) Introduce subject. Compare area to one where open access permitted.
  (iii) Advantages of open access – walks, picnics . . . etc. (as in question).
  (iv) Points making above advantages specially desirable in this area (e.g. other recreational facilities limited, large or growing population).
  (v) Refer to problems involved in allowing open access – costs (suggest how they might be met, and if from public funds like rates, how justified).

Beginning and ending: Style 1 (see p. 105). You don't know the chairman, and to assume more familiarity, as style 2 would imply, may arouse his resentment. This would damage your chances of success.

GCE 7   This is to your family, so the tone can be informal, even light-hearted. They will want to know what happened in some detail. (You will need to use your imagination for this.) Invent friends' names if necessary, and a likely sounding name and address of the camp-site. Remember that the money or help needs to reach you without delay.
Beginning and ending: Style 3 (see p. 105)

GCE 8   The question needs careful reading; two letters are mentioned and a third suggested, and it would be possible to write the wrong one altogether in the stress of an examination. First, having grasped that you are writing as secretary of a local charity, jot down what the letter needs to contain. Your notes may look like this:
  (i) Thanks for letter.
  (ii) Refer to idea suggested. (N.B. what *was* idea? Sponsored walk? Some entertainment? Decide on this.)
  (iii) Who else involved? School? Club? Adult organisation?
  (iv) Invite correspondent to write again, or meet to discuss idea more fully.

Beginning and ending: Style 2 (see p. 105) would be appropriate here. It is a *local* charity. As secretary you are probably known to your correspondent. In any case, you want to sound courteous and encouraging. (This concerns the *tone* of your letter as well.)
Layout: As you are writing to a private individual you don't need to include his or her address at the top of your letter. A subject heading after the opening 'Dear . . .' would be helpful, e.g. *Your idea for a sponsored walk to . . .*

CSE 6   Much of the success of this letter will depend on *tone*. Decide first on your version of what happened. Were you in fact one of the culprits, or were they just one or two rowdy ones? Perhaps you were trying to make them keep quiet. A few notes will help you to get the story clear in your mind before you start writing. The letter must also contain your apology, and your offer of help. She is a widow. You could perhaps do something which she used to depend on her husband doing – household repairs, spring cleaning, taking her for a car ride?
Beginning and ending: Style 3 (see p. 105). Invent names and addresses if you need to.

CSE 7   Your friend must also be wealthy if he or she is likely to be approached by the charities. Decide on your own and your friend's name, age, situation (in employment? retired? unexpectedly wealthy – football pools win or Premium Bond draw?). This will make it easier for you to imagine the situation, and to decide which charity to support. Give a reason for your choice that will make sense to your friend.

Beginning and ending: Style 3 (see p. 105)

CSE 8   Both the letters asked for are planned for publication in the local newspaper. Think who reads it, and let that decide your tone and general style. Letters to the editor usually follow Style 1 (see p. 105), though newspaper editors often edit them in conformity with the paper's usual style. Letters often start simply: 'Sir, . . .'

COMPREHENSION

(GCE 9, 10, 11; CSE 9, 10, 11, 12, 13)

In Section II (Unit 2), which deals with comprehension, we showed you how this particular English skill involves five linked mental activities. Questions asked about passages set for comprehension usually concentrate on one or more of these activities, so in the notes that follow we shall refer you to whichever is being focused on. Sometimes, particularly in CSE papers, a *summary* question may be included as well.

Notes on individual questions

GCE 9   Although this is based on two poems all the questions about them are of standard comprehension type. You would do well, however, to read Section II (Unit 4.3), which deals with poetry, before tackling the question. Types of question are:

1, 5(a)	Type I (also a short *summary* in 1)	
2, 4, 5(b), 6(b)	Type III	(see pp. 48-50)
3, 4	Type II	
6(a), 7	Type IV	
8	Type V	

GCE 10   Notice that although this passage involves plenty of dialogue and describes an encounter between people rather than simply stating facts or opinions, we use just the same techniques in studying its meaning, i.e. in *comprehending* it.

(a), (e)(iii)	Type I
(b)	Types IV and III
(c), (d), (e)(iii)	Type V
(e)(i) and (ii)	Type III
(f)	Type II

GCE 11   The emphasis in this test is on accurate *observation* (see p. 49). We have helped you with the first two questions.

(a)	Type I You need to find six consecutive words in line 5 to answer this question exactly.
(b)	Types I and III combined (see lines 4-6)
(c)	Type III
(d), (e), (f), (g)	all Type I
(h)	Type II

CSE 9   This test from a CSE paper involves more independent thinking than GCE 11. Many of the answers involve *reflection*, drawing *inferences* and coming to your own *conclusions*.

(a)(*i*), (b), (c), (d)	Type I. The answer to (d) is in line 6.
(a)(*ii*), (e), (h), (i)	Type III

(f), (g)	Type IV
(j), (l)	Type V
(k)	Type II

CSE 10   This type of comprehension test is dealt with in Section II (Unit 2.5). As you can see, it also involves drawing inferences (Unit 2.3). Both questions are really variations of Type III.

CSE 11   The first part of the final question here ((h)(*i*)) is asking for a *summary*. The other questions are within our categories:

(a) (e)(i)	Type I
(b)	Type III or V
(c) (h)(ii)	Type V
(d)	Type IV
(e)(ii), (f)	Type III
(f) first part, (g)	Type II

CSE 12   This question concentrates on the language of advertising. See Section II (Unit 2.6, Persuasive writing). Because there is less substance to the three extracts than to some comprehension passages there are no questions asking simply for observation (Type I). Questions (b)(*v*) and (d) involve *summarising*. We have helped you with questions (a)(*v*) and (b)(*ii*).

(a)(*i*)	Types II and III
(a)(*ii*), (a)(*v*), (b)(*i*),	all Type IV. The answer to (a)(*v*) is on lines 11
(b)(*ii*), (b)(*iii*), (b)(*vi*)	and 12, and to (b)(*ii*) on lines 3 and 4.
(a)(*iii*), (d)	Type V
(a)(*iv*), (c)	Type III
(a)(*vi*), (b)(*iv*)	Types III and V.

CSE 13   This is much more straightforward than CSE 12, and the emphasis is on accurate reading and observation. The final question (f) involves a brief *summary* of the last paragraph.

(a), (b), (c)	Type I
(d)	Type III
(e)	Type II

SUMMARY
(GCE 9 (1), 12, 13, 14; CSE 11 (*h*), 12(*b*)(*d*), 13 (*f*))

The method for answering these questions on summarising is set out clearly in Section II (Unit 3). The tendency is for traditional summary questions, formerly known as *precis*, to occur more often in GCE and SCE than in CSE papers. GCE 13 is a typical traditional test of summarising ability. The *rubric* to this question contains good general advice on summarising, and you will do well to think carefully about it. Bear in mind also the need for skill in summarising when you are writing about books (see Unit 4.2).

Notes on individual questions

GCE 9(1)   The question asks you to 'describe briefly' the scene chosen by the poet. In a sense this is a summary, but you will find it impossible to use fewer words than the poet because he has already concentrated the language. Thus: the villages, with their stone-built cottages, are 'hidden' by the folds of the hills, amongst which the 'crumbling roads' twist and turn. Those 23 words do not yet provide an accurate description of the scene in the first stanza, which itself uses only 22 words.

GCE 12 The chief difficulty in this question is to avoid the emotive charge the writer gives to her statement. A summary should be as objective as possible. Words like 'impetuous', 'heedless', 'unnatural', 'tampering', 'futile' are concerned not so much with presenting facts as with persuading the reader to support the writer's interpretation of those facts. An examination candidate failing to notice this might produce summaries that are too derivative of the original. We have given you our answers to (a) and (b) below. We suggest you write your own version first, then check it against ours, which was based on a careful set of notes (see Unit 3.3).

(a) The speed of scientific discovery and consequent technological innovation is much greater than any previous natural changes on earth. Two good examples are nuclear science and the synthesising of new chemicals. These have both produced dangers – of radiation and chemical pollution – which living organisms cannot adjust to in the way they have done to natural hazards, because the changes happen so fast. The clearest example is the rate of production of new chemicals: 500 annually in the US alone. (79 words)

(b) The chemicals produced for killing unwanted animal and vegetable species – over 200 in the last 35 years, sold in thousands of brands – are non-selective. In addition to killing the particular weeds or insects regarded as pests they are lethal to many other species, and also pollute vegetation and soil. Thus they endanger all life. (54 words)

GCE 13 Although this passage presents plenty of straight information for you to select from, it is a trickier test than GCE 14 because the writer's method is less clear-cut. He moves back and forth from arguments in favour of packaging to its disadvantages, without committing himself to either. Another difficulty is that you are asked to produce a two-paragraph summary that is less than a quarter of the length of the original passage, and are given no guidance as to the number of words in each paragraph. A careful set of preliminary notes is essential here. You should head two columns 'advantages' and 'problems', then work through the passage, jotting down the points as they occur. We shall not do this for you, but the following key will help you to check your list for completeness before writing your summary:

> advantages – lines 16-26, 27-30, 35-40, 41-45, 59-60;
> problems   – lines 2-13, 31-5, 46-58, 60-4.

As you can see, more space is devoted to problems than to advantages, so this should be reflected in the respective length of your two paragraphs. Your paragraph (a) will need about 60 words, your paragraph (b) about 80 words.

GCE 14 This is a more straightforward test than GCE 12, because the intention of the passage is to inform rather than persuade. For (a) you need to draw information from the first, second and third paragraphs and the first part of the fifth. Question (b) can be answered from the second part of the sixth paragraph and from the seventh paragraph.

CSE 11(h)(*i*) For this question you need to select carefully only those parts that describe the writer's feelings. Lines 23-4 contain a good example. It should be possible to answer this question in about 40 words.

CSE 12(b)(*v*) The answer to this question can be drawn from the fourth paragraph of extract (b). You should not need more than about 20 words.

CSE 12(d)   You are asked here both to summarise and to add ideas of your own. A re-reading of the passage for GCE 11 may help to give you some ideas.

CSE 13(f)   This question concentrates on only one paragraph of the passage. Which?

READING/LITERATURE
(Questions CSE 14; and SCE 1, 2, 3, 4, 5, 6, 8)

We have given general guidance and help in dealing with this kind of question in the sections on *Writing about Books* (Section II, Unit 4.2) and *Poetry* (Unit 4.3).

Questions like these are not asking for close attention to any particular passage or poem, such as is expected in comprehension tests, or Literature papers based on closely studied set texts. Instead you can draw on what you know from your recent study of literature in school or from your favourite leisure reading. You are always given a wide choice, so can decide beforehand which form of literature – prose fiction or non-fiction, long or short; plays; poetry; magazines – you feel most confident about, and concentrate first on questions dealing with your chosen genre.

Important! Always name the book(s), play(s), poem(s) you are talking about, giving title(s), author(s) and any other necessary information (e.g. what kind of book – TV play, one of a series, travel book, etc.).

Notes on individual questions

CSE 14   You need to think carefully about the wording of this question. Relate it to a book recently read – either a fictional story, or one based on real life (biography or autobiography, travel, adventure etc.) The 'relationship' you choose, between two or more people – the interpretation might be stretched to include a relationship between a person and an animal – has to be (i) difficult or unsatisfactory, (ii) important in the book. The *rubric* is worth remembering and applying to any questions you have to answer on your reading.

SCE 1   *Fictional essay.* The statements are provided as a stimulus. You are not asked to include the one you choose in your essay, although if you feel it would help to focus your story to do so, nothing need prevent you. As you are offered four choices, and there are six other questions in the paper, each of them offering further choices, it is important to number your answer accurately. 'You may also provide an appropriate title for the guidance of the examiner.' (part of rubric)

SCE 2   Discussion essay.

SCE 3   The invitation to 'write in any way you please' leaves the decision on what type of essay you produce entirely in your hands. In the 1979 Composition section of the SCE examination candidates were told: 'you are free to use poetry or prose, or write a play-script, as you think suitable.'

SCE 4

1   (a) *First paragraph*: Clearly the weather is a major factor. *Second paragraph*: The match is only a trial (line 6). Even if your knowledge of rugby or other sports is only slight, this point becomes clearer in the rest of the passage.
    (b) You will not find the answer printed in the passage. You will have to think, and the following process of elimination helps.

(i) It cannot be the spectators because whatever it is is outside the 'dark wreath of the crowd.'

(ii) It cannot be the sun, which would not under any circumstances be concealed by the crowd.

(iii) It is, in fact, any ordinary, everyday thing beyond the stadium, e.g. streets, traffic, hills, trees, home.

2   If you are asked for two examples of something there are generally more than two in the part of the passage to which you are directed, e.g. heavy, grey, dark.

3   You need to think again here. It is a reasonable assumption that the slowness with which he walks up the steps (line 8) is due to his dejection.

SCE 5

1   (a) To answer this you need to understand the gist of the two paragraphs. Look for key phrases: *first paragraph*: 'normal wear and tear'; *second paragraph*: 'the more serious stresses'. What is looked for is an awareness of the different degrees of stress dealt with.

(b) *(i)* A simple extraction of information to be found on line 8 is required here.

(ii) You have to think for yourself here. 'Oddly enough' suggests that this is not what we would normally expect. Success is usually associated with happiness and contentment.

2   This is not as wide open as it might at first appear to be. The other words in the list relate to financial matters and so a word like 'financial', 'money' or even 'similar' is required.

3   Even if you have never heard of a colon (in which case, see Section II, Unit 5.2, Punctuation) you can attempt this question by examining how the part of the sentence following the colon relates to the preceding part. In this instance the colon is followed by an expansion or elaboration of the statement which precedes it.

SCE 6   The question gives you clear guidance about the way you must plan your answer, in three sections: (a) *brief* account (don't be tempted to spend all your time on this), (b) the person's decision – it should not take you many words to state this, and (c) how the decision was arrived at.

SCE 8   Lighter reading is not very often brought into English examinations. If you take a regular magazine (e.g. a weekly woman's journal, a teenage magazine, a 'digest') this question should be straightforward. Examples of the 'qualities' you choose to discuss might be: the balance of longer items (e.g. stories, serials) to shorter ones; human interest items such as letters or individual advice ('lonely-hearts') pages; layout, including style and proportion of illustrations; advertising material – variety, presentation, interest to you personally.

COMPLETE TRIAL ('MOCK') EXAMINATION PAPERS

Lengths of paper and syllabus requirements are so varied in detail, in spite of being so similar in content, that it is impossible to present a single complete set of questions as a general purpose trial examination. However, if you want to prepare yourself for the experience of the actual examination it is a simple matter for you to choose enough questions from those given in this section, which have all been selected so as to be fully representative.

How to compile your own GCE, SCE or CSE English (Language) paper

1   Check the syllabus requirements of your Examination Board from the list given on pp. 6-17. Take particular note of how many papers, what length, choice, etc.

2   Select from pages 164 to 183 questions (and rubrics) dealing with the topics required. If possible include one or more questions chosen from those actually set by your Board.

3   Write or type your selection as your own 'mock' GCE, SCE or CSE paper(s).

4   Set aside a suitable time or times, so that you can keep rigidly to the time limits required by your Board.

5   Marking: try your hand at marking your own trial examination. It is a good idea to do this several days after the papers have been completed.

Glossary

Abbreviation. A shortened form of a much-used word: e.g., Mr (for Mister); Co (for Company); etc (for et cetera = and other things.)

Accent(ed). The stress or emphasis put on part of a word in saying it, as in: *per*manent, pro*fess*or, *dis*cotheque. N.B. the difference in meaning in *per*mit and per*mit*.

Accusative. The name of something on which action is taken is called the *object*, which is then sometimes described as being in the *accusative* case.

Adaptation. The changing of something, usually a novel, to meet a special need: e.g., the film is an *adaptation* of a story by Conrad.

Adjective. A word that tells us more about a noun: *blue* sky, *fried* fish, the *National* Trust.

Adverb. A word that adds to the meaning of a verb or adjective: e.g., she writes *quickly*; you'll *soon* see; *slightly* lame; *extremely* cold; *well* done.

Agreement. In grammar, the rule by which a particular word form determines the form of certain words following: e.g., *That* child is running (*or* runs, *or* has run) across the road. *Those* children *are* running (*or* run, *or* have run) across the road.

Alliteration -ive. The repetition, usually of a consonant, at the beginning of words: cold comfort; feverish fits; Professor Pink prefers plums.

Anecdote. An amusing very short story about a person or event.

Appreciation. The full understanding of a piece of writing, usually of literary merit: e.g., a poem.

Appropriateness. The fitness of a style of expression to the circumstances in which it is being used.

Argument. The reasons given to support or prove a point; hence, more generally, the thread of thought holding a piece of writing together.

Articulate -ation. To pronounce words clearly. Distinct and clear pronunciation.

Assessment. Judgment, weighing up the value of something.

Association. The linking of ideas and meaning: e.g. spring is *associated* with joy and renewal.

Audible. Loud and clear enough to be heard easily.

Aural. Connected with hearing, intelligible to the ear.

Board. A number of people appointed to manage an examination or a business.

Brackets. The punctuation marks ( ) used to separate a group of words: e.g., Bill passed his examination in English (as his teacher forecast) but failed in French.

Brevity. A short way of expression: As a speaker she wasted no time, for she always concentrated on *brevity*.

Case. The change made in a word to indicate its relationship with another word: 'I saw *him* (not he)' is one of the rare examples in English.

Clarity. Clearness.

Cliché. An expression which has lost force through being over-used: He is *exploring every avenue* to find a solution.

Colloquialism. An expression used in everyday conversation.

Colon. A stop (:) used to introduce a list or quotation, or to divide a sentence into two parts.

Comma. A stop (,) used at points at which a very brief pause would be made in reading aloud.

Comparative. The form of an adjective usually made by adding -er: *quicker*. It is used to compare two things or people or their behaviour.

Composition. An essay or other piece of writing made up by the writer and not just copied.

Comprehension. The understanding of a piece of writing.

Conclusion. The last part of something, the final opinion or statement.

Conjunction. A linking word such as *and, but, because*.

Consonant. Any letter of the alphabet except *a, e, i, o, u* and sometimes *y*.

Context. The writing which surrounds a particular word or phrase.

Dash. A stop (—) used to indicate a break in thought; to act as a bracket; or to introduce a summary or explanation.

Deduce. To reach a conclusion by arguing from something known: e.g., She deduced from the slime that a snail had crossed the passage.

Dialogue. The use of direct speech to add life to narrative or description.

Direct speech. The actual words of a speaker, always shown by quotation marks.

Excerpt. An extract from a play or other piece of writing.

Exclamation mark. A stop (!) used to indicate surprise or strong emphasis: Get out!

Extract. A passage taken from a longer piece of writing.

Factual. Containing facts, based on facts.

Fiction. An imaginative piece of writing, such as a novel or short story.

Formula writing. Writing, without real freshness or originality, according to a set scheme.

Full-stop. Used at the end of sentences, and after abbreviations, this (.) is the most important of all stops.

Future tense. The part of a verb used to indicate time to come is said to be in the *future tense*: 'I *will* go; they *won't* stop me'.

Genitive. The form of a word used to express ownership, usually represented in English by '*s*, *s*' or *of*: A *girl's* watch; the *spectators'* cheers; the style *of* modern art.

Gist. The important part of a statement, book, etc.: The reporter took down the *gist* of the candidate's speech.

Grammar. The study of words and the ways in which they work.

Identify with. To regard as the same: Girls often *identify* themselves with the heroine of a film or novel.

Image -ery. The use of mental pictures in speech or writing: As strong as a horse; you're the cream in my coffee.

Imaginative writing. Creative writing that comes from the imagination.

Imply. To suggest in an indirect way: So you're *implying* that I took your umbrella?

Inappropriate. Unsuitable in style to the occasion: e.g., His 'cheerio' to the chairman of the interviewing panel was quite *inappropriate*.

Indirect speech. The style into which direct speech is turned when reported: e.g. ['I'm going', he said] becomes: I heard that *he was going*.

Infer. To reach a conclusion by reasoning from facts: Her mother *inferred* from Sheila's lack of enthusiasm that she didn't like the idea.

Inflexion. The change made in a word to show its relationship with other words: he, him; they, them; etc. See *Agreement*.

Interjection. A single word or phrase, such as 'Rubbish!', 'Hard luck', etc., interrupting someone speaking.

Intransitive. The term applied to verbs which have no object. They *were hurrying*; she *slept* well.

Inverted commas. Also known as quotation marks, their main use is to enclose words actually spoken 'Anyone in?' he shouted.

Italics-icised. Sloping letters used for titles of books, plays and films, and sometimes for emphasis. *This is italicised, that is, printed in italics*.

Journalism. The profession of a journalist; writing for newspapers and periodicals.

Journalese. The style of writing used in popular newspapers, intended to attract and hold the reader's attention by monosyllabic words, especially in headlines, and a special vocabulary: e.g., Show Biz Pay Slash Shock.

Key words, phrases. The important parts of a passage of writing which tell a hasty reader what is being said about the subject.

Layout. Arrangement of written material on the page; plan.

Lucid. Clear and readily intelligible.

Main verb. The essential part of a sentence, without which there can be no complete meaning: e.g., The train *arrives* at 2 p.m.

Metaphor. A device for concentrating and for adding vigour to an author's or speaker's meaning. One thing is identified with another: Sal Stokes was the *star* in the film; she *rocketed* to fame in a few days.

Moderator. A teacher appointed by an Examination Board to visit schools and ensure that school-based examinations like CSE Mode 3 and oral examinations are set and marked at the same level.

Narrative. The telling of a story, an experience or an event.

Nominative. The term used by grammarians for the subject of a verb, said to be in the nominative case: *Cars* menace our peace; *they* are a nuisance.

Noun. A grammatical term for words which name something: frog, Jean, caution, committee.

Object. In grammar, the word or words for the person or thing acted on by a verb: Jill wrote *pages*, but Jim could find *little* to say.

Objective (adj). Regarding things from a calm and detached point of view.

Omission. Something left out.

Omit. To leave out.

Open-ended. Planned or organised so as to allow for various different results or conclusions.

Oral. Spoken; an oral examination tests a candidate's ability to speak.

Pace. The rate or speed at which something moves or is carried on.

Paragraph. Part of a piece of writing, dealing with one aspect of the main subject.

Passive. The form of a verb changed to show that a person or thing is acted on: She *was chosen*, though her wrist *had been sprained* a week before.

Past tense. The form of a verb used to indicate that the action, etc, has already happened: I *went* early, because I *had done* all I could.

Phrase. A group of words without a main verb, acting as a noun, adjective or adverb, e.g. *Travelling light*, we reached the top *in five hours* – quite a *reasonable performance*.

Possessive. A noun in its possessive form tells us that the person or thing referred to owns or is connected with something: *Jane's* bike needs a new tyre.

Predicate. In grammar, a group of words that tells us something about the subject: The other passenger *was reading a paperback*.

Prefix-es. An addition at the beginning of a word to alter its meaning. *Pre* added to *arranged* gives us the meaning *arranged beforehand*.

Preposition. A word used to show the relationship of a noun or pronoun with another word: e.g., Nowadays one is usually free *from* pain *in* the dentist's chair.

Present tense. The form of a verb indicating that something is going on at the moment of utterance is said to be in the present tense: e.g., I read *or* I am reading.

Pronoun. A word used in place of a noun: e.g., *They* were waiting; *that* is right; *which* do you want? *I* can't tell *him* from *her*.

Prose. Continuous writing or speech without the patterns of rhyme and rhythm used in poetry.

Quote. To repeat part of a passage of writing. (The noun is *quotation*.)

Register. The choice of vocabulary and speech forms for particular circumstances. Children use different *registers* in playground and classroom.

Relevant. Connected with the matter being discussed.

Reported Speech. The style used for recording something said: e.g., 'Jill said, 'Are you coming, Sue?' becomes in *reported speech* 'Jill asked Sue if she was coming'.

Review. An account of a book, play or film written for the benefit of those who have not seen the original.

Root. The part of a word on which all variations of the word are based: e.g., *ject* is the root found in: abject, dejected, inject, interjection, object, project, reject.

Semicolon. The stop (;) placed between two sentences that are about the same subject, and are grammatically complete and able to stand on their own. Also to mark off each of two or more groups of items in a list.

Serialisation. The arrangement in a series of separate parts of a play or novel, often for broadcasting.

Slang. Words and expressions in popular use. Usually new and lively, they are not normally used in writing, except in letters to friends.

Standardised spelling. Before the age of print spelling was often a personal matter. There is now a generally accepted (i.e. standardised) form of spelling for most words.

Stanza. In poetry, a verse of two or more lines.

Stress. See *Accent*.

Subject. The word or words in a sentence indicating the topic about which something is said: e.g., The *castle* was built 800 years ago.

Subjective. Regarding things from a personal point of view.

Superlative. Words like: *best, tallest, most expensive* are the superlative forms of adjectives. See also *Comparison*.

Syllable. The smallest unit of speech. I, you, from, film are words of one *syllable*. *Begin* has two *syllables*; *dictionary* has four.

Syllabus. The ground to be covered in working for an examination.

Synonym. The term applied to two or more words with nearly the same meaning: odour, smell – fatigued, weary, tired – aged, old, elderly.

Syntax. The arrangement of words in constructing sentences and phrases.

Tense. The changes in a verb to express the time when an action takes place. English has three *tenses*: past, present, future.

Transcribe. To copy or make a record of, in writing.

Usage. The way in which words are actually used in a language; forms of language which have become accepted through long use. *It's me. . .* is now accepted as correct usage, though at one time grammarians might have disapproved.

Verb. A word expressing an action or a state: e.g., She *caught* a bus because she *was* in a hurry. All sentences must have a verb.

Verse. Poetry, in rhythmical and sometimes rhyming form; also, a division of a poem.

Visual. Seen with the eye, or in the imagination.

Visualise. To see in the mind: e.g., Try to *visualise* the scene.

Vocabulary. A range of words used by an individual or a group: e.g., He has a good *vocabulary*; most occupations have a *vocabulary* of their own.

Index

Accent/stress 140
Active and passive of verbs 132, 143
Addresses of Examination Boards 5
Adjectives and adverbs 133
Advertising, language of 59, 153, 180-181
Agreement 132
Answers
  Core units, composition 184, comprehension 184
    summaries and notes 193
    letters 198
    poetry 191, 192-3
  Self-test units 202ff.
Appropriateness in written English 135
Aural English 117, 120

Books
  choosing 3, 111-112
  writing about 112-113

Certificate of Secondary Education (CSE)
  examination requirements 9
  practice questions 175
  hints on answering 207ff.
Cloze procedure comprehension tests 57, 153
Colon 128
Comma 128
Composition 18ff.
  tests 150
Comprehension 47ff.
  types of question 48
  answering questions 51
  check-list of passages 76
  further tests 151
Consonants 122, 140
Conversation 119

Dash 129
Descriptive writing 19, 37ff., 40, 43
Dialogue 19, 129-30, 134-5
Dictionary, practice in using 33, 137ff., 149
Direct and indirect (reported) speech 134
Discussion 119

Essays
  fictional 18
  discussion 28
  descriptive 35
  picture-based 43
  plans for 29, 34, 35
  length 207
Examination Boards 5
Examinations
  advice for 159ff., 207ff.
  practice questions 164ff.
Exclamation mark 129

Full stop 127

General Certificate of Education (GCE)
  O-level requirements 6
  practice questions 164ff.
  hints on answering 207ff.
Glossary 217
Grammar 130ff.

Hand-writing 162, 207
Hyphen 129

Indirect (reported) speech 134
Inferences, drawing 54
Inglis, Fred 60
Intransitive verbs 132

Letters
  writing 104ff.
  business 104ff.
  business English in 106
  examination questions 165, 177
Lewis, John 45
Listening (aural English) 117, 120
Longwindedness 142

Multiple choice comprehension tests 60

Notes
  making 87
  layout of 88
  using abbreviations in 89

Objective tests 60
Oral English 117, 139

Parts of speech 131
Passive verbs 132, 143
Persuasive writing 58-59
Planning essays 29, 34, 35
Poetry 75, 114-117, 165-166
Prefixes 122
Pronunciation 139
Punctuation 126ff.

Question mark 128
Quotation marks 129

Reading 3
  aloud 118-119
Red deer 90
Register 135
Reported speech 134

Scottish Certificate of Education (SCE)
  examination requirements 9
  practice questions 173
  hints on answering 207ff.

Semi-colon 128
Speaking 117-120, 139
Speech
  parts of 131
  direct and reported 134
Spelling 121ff., 139
  tests 146, 147
Statistics, interpreting 58
Style 105, 141, 150, 161
Summarising 77ff.
  check-list of passages 103
  further tests 155
Syllables 122, 146
Syllabus requirements
  General Certificate of Education 6
  Scottish Certificate of Education 9
  Certificate of Secondary Education 9

Syntax 131

Tests check-list 158
Tone 105, 115
Transitive verbs 132

Usage 130ff., 147

Vocabulary 33
  tests 148, 149
Vowels 122, 140